Clifford Owusu-Gyamf

The Spirit With Us

Afrikanische Theologie
African Theology
Théologie Africaine

Band / Volume 11

LIT

Clifford Owusu-Gyamfi

The Spirit With Us

Towards A Contextual African Pneumatology and Theological Anthropology

LIT

Cover image: Sunsum symbol

Publication supported by the Theological Faculty of the
University of Geneva

This book is printed on acid-free paper.

Bibliographic information published by the Deutsche Nationalbibliothek
The Deutsche Nationalbibliothek lists this publication in the Deutsche Nationalbibliografie; detailed bibliographic data are available on the Internet at https://dnb.dnb.de.

ISBN 978-3-643-80335-1 (pb)
ISBN 978-3-643-85335-6 (PDF)

A catalogue record for this book is available from the British Library.

Flössergasse 10
CH-8001 Zürich
Tel. +41 (0) 78-307 91 24
E-Mail: zuerich@lit-verlag.ch https://www.lit-verlag.ch
Distribution:
In the UK: Global Book Marketing, e-mail: mo@centralbooks.com
In Germany: LIT Verlag Fresnostr. 2, D-48159 Münster
Tel. +49 (0) 2 51-620 32 22, Fax +49 (0) 2 51-922 60 99, e-mail: vertrieb@lit-verlag.de

Table of Contents

SUNSUM
(The Akan adinkra symbol signifying personality, energy, power, spirit, and purity)

DEDICATION

To my cherished siblings: Amponsaa, Adwoa Amanfo, Yaa Serwaa, Akwasi Asumadu, Abenaa Konadu, Akwasi Agyei, Adwoa Sarpong, Michael (deceased), Kwabena Akomea, and Yaa Akyaa.

Your constant support, encouragement, and love have served as the pillars upon which I have constructed not only this work, but my entire life as well.

Our ancestors taught us the spiritual interconnectedness of life through the concept of *sunsum*, which I have diligently explored in this book. I see this concept reflected in the bond we share as siblings. Just as God's *Sunsum* unites the universe in harmony, so too do the ties of kinship that we have experienced throughout our lives and growth.

It is with immense gratitude and love that I dedicate this book to you, for without your support, this journey of African spirituality would not have been possible.

May the wisdom and insights contained within these pages stand as a testament to the unbreakable bonds we share, and may our lives continue to be enriched by the love, support, and unity that have brought us this far.

With love and appreciation from me to you all.

Acknowledgement

There are individuals and institutions that I want to acknowledge for their invaluable support to my work and my training as a scholar.

First and foremost, I want to express my deepest gratitude to Professor Robert Owusu Agyarko, the pioneer scholar in the field of contextual Akan pneumatology. His groundbreaking work has not only paved the way for my own research but has also inspired others to explore this important area of study. His continuous encouragement for me to excel in this field of research cannot go unmentioned.

I am very grateful to the Faculty of Theology at the University of Geneva, where I had the privilege of obtaining my doctorate. Their dedication to academic excellence and intellectual rigor has undoubtedly shaped my scholarship. But more importantly, I want to acknowledge their generous sponsorship of the publication of my dissertation in a two-volume book series.

I would be remiss if I do not express my deepest appreciation and admiration for my doctoral supervisor, Professor Christophe Chalamet. He has been much more than a supervisor; he has been a friend, mentor, and advisor throughout my academic journey, from my master's degree to my doctoral research. The interest he has expressed in this field of study, combined with his kind support and guidance, has had an indelible impact on my growth as a scholar. Professor Chalamet's keen insights, thoughtful critiques, and genuine interest in my work have been instrumental in shaping my research and pushing me to strive for excellence. I am truly grateful for the opportunity to have worked under his tutelage, and I am proud to count him not only as a mentor but also as a friend. His influence will continue to resonate in my future academic pursuits and throughout my life.

I also acknowledge the incredible work of various scholars who have contributed to Akan scholarship and knowledge production. Their tireless efforts to demonstrate the richness and spiritual depths of African traditional cultures have been instrumental in challenging many wrong notions about African socio-religious traditions. I am particularly grateful to those who are actively working to shed light on the contributions that African traditional cultures have made to our collective quest for knowledge and a better future.

To my colleagues and friends who have encouraged me on this journey, I offer my heartfelt thanks. Your unwavering support, constructive criticisms, and intellectual camaraderie have been invaluable to me.

Lastly, I want to express my appreciation to all the researchers, academicians, and scholars whose work has informed and enriched my own. Your dedication to knowledge and understanding has made this book possible.

With gratitude and respect.

FOREWORD

In this thought-provoking exploration, Clifford Owusu-Gyamfi delves deep into the heart of Akan pneumatology, unraveling its profound implications for Christian theology. As we immerse ourselves in the pages of *The Spirit with Us*, we are not only challenged to question the established notion of *Sunsum* as the Akan equivalent of the biblical concept of the Holy Spirit. But to embark on an intellectual voyage, delving into the concept of *honhom* as a more fitting and nuanced alternative.

With meticulous research and thoughtful analysis, the author questions the foundations of the traditional understanding of *sunsum* as a distinct spiritual entity within Akan culture. He presents a case for embracing *honhom* as the central pillar of contextual Akan Christian pneumatology. This shift in perspective not only unveils a rich tapestry of theological insights but also sparks a fresh and vital debate on this critical subject.

However, the author acknowledges the significance of *sunsum* in Akan spiritual development, underlining its role in bridging the connection between God, humanity, and all living beings. *Sunsum* is described as a dual force, both immanent and transcendent, shaping the ethical and moral aspects of life in relation to God and creation. Agyarko's contributions to Akan pneumatology are highlighted, particularly his contextualization of the Holy Spirit as Onyame *Sunsum*, emphasizing the Spirit's transformative role in renewing human hearts and the entirety of creation.

But the author puts forth a novel perspective by proposing *honhom* as a more suitable concept for contextual Akan pneumatology. He argues that, *Honhom* carries multiple meanings, including breath, wind, air, soul, and spirit, aligning harmoniously with both biblical and Akan conceptions of life. It is envisioned as the animating principle that unites all living things through the divine presence of God. The author's study challenges the conventional notion of *sunsum* as an exclusive representation of the Holy Spirit within Akan culture and argues for the suitability of *honhom* as a foundational concept for contextual Akan Christian pneumatology.

Throughout the book, the author skillfully navigates the intricate theological landscape, elucidating the reasoning behind adopting *honhom* as the foundational concept. It is revealed how *sunsum*, despite its significance in Akan spiritual discourse, may fall short in capturing the true essence of the Spirit, as delineated in the Bible. Instead, *honhom*, with its ethereal attributes signifying air, wind, and the principle of life, emerges as a more comprehensive and resonant alternative.

The author delves into an exploration of the nature of the Spirit as portrayed in the Bible and its influence on the translation and comprehension of the Holy Spirit in Akan languages. The argument is made that *sunsum* may not fully encapsulate the Spirit's nature, as it is not expressly a "spiritual entity" but rather an emanating spiritual force. While *sunsum* exhibits characteristics of a spiritual element, it may fall short in cultivating a contextual Akan Christian pneumatology.

The concept of *honhom* is introduced as a more suitable alternative, owing to its ethereal character, representing elements like air, wind, and the principle of life. This aligns more closely with the Akan worldview and provides a robust foundation for reshaping spiritual perspectives within the Akan community, facilitating the development of contextual Christian theology and practice. This proposal inevitably raises questions about the background of the concept of *honhom* in the Akan tradition. Also, the relationship between *honhom* and *sunsum*, demands further exploration and scholarly inquiry.

In the pages of *The Spirit with Us*, the author's exploration transcends the boundaries of theological discourse, venturing into the realms of language and spirituality within Akan culture. This scholarly endeavor sheds illuminating insights on how the Holy Spirit is translated and understood in Akan languages, unveiling the nuanced interplay between language and matters of the spirit.

One of the enduring strengths of this work is its capacity to ignite not only theological contemplation but also broader reflections on the essentiality of interfaith dialogue and the importance of embracing diverse perspectives, especially those rooted in indigenous spiritual constructs. In our interconnected world, the clarion call to engage respectfully with these diverse beliefs resonates deeply.

Furthermore, the author generously offers a valuable compass of principles for those embarking on a journey to engage with different spiritual traditions. These guiding principles, steeped in respect, theological integrity, humility, and discernment, provide invaluable guidance for navigating the intricate terrain of interfaith exploration.

May this book be a catalyst for fostering deeper understanding, fostering open dialogue, and enriching our spiritual lives. Let it stand as a testament to the transformative power of exploration and collaboration as we embark on a collective journey towards a heightened appreciation of the divine presence in every facet of human existence. *The Spirit with Us* extends a gracious invitation to transcend the confines of cultural and theological boundaries, ultimately nurturing a world marked by compassion and inclusivity.

Robert Owusu Agyarko, Phd (UWC, SA)

PREFACE

The central focus in African theology has consistently been the investigation of how Christian faith and practice can be genuinely represented within the African context. An essential question arises from this: how can Africa's unique religious context contribute to and enrich theological discussions and education? This question is closely tied to the mission of African theology, which seeks to make the message of Jesus Christ relevant and significant within the African context, while upholding and respecting the recipients' authentic cultural identity.

Building on this momentous and growing consensus of African theology, my first book, *What is this Thing Called Sunsum*, delved into an in-depth study of the Akan concept of *sunsum*. *Sunsum* is an important concept within the spiritual and philosophical traditions of the Akan people of West Africa. The study explored the historiographical and philosophical dimensions of *sunsum*, providing clarity on its past, present, and potential future implications within the Akan spiritual belief system. This approach offered a thorough and comprehensive research on the concept of *sunsum*, reinforcing the importance of understanding indigenous African spiritualities in theological discourse.

Apart from the extensive research, the book delved into the complex and dynamic nature of *sunsum*. It scrutinized the *sunsum* concept through various historical sketches, emphasizing its evolution in Akan scholarship over time and its manifestation in diverse contexts and religious symbolisms.

Further, the study addressed contemporary interpretations of *sunsum* by thoroughly analyzing and engaging with a series of fundamental questions. These included inquiries into the nature of *sunsum* as per Akan philosophers, its role as a mediator between the spiritual and physical world, its influence in the practice of philosophy, and its expression in rituals and ceremonies.

By examining the multifaceted and evolving nature of *sunsum*, the book fosters a bridge between past and present interpretations, enabling readers to reconcile various understandings of spiritual phenomena within Akan pneumatology, as well as discerning insights into African spiritual worldviews, with a particular focus on the distinctive context of the Akan people of West Africa.

This volume serves as a continuation of the previous work, and for a better understanding, I highly encourage readers to acquaint themselves with the first publication before proceeding with this one. This fundamental knowledge of the Akan unique religious and philosophical landscape, as explored in the first volume, will help to contribute a broader understanding of Akan spirituality and its intersection with Christian pneumatology.

The present work constitutes an integral part of this context-based approach to Christian theology, with a particular focus on contextual pneumatology. It delves deeply into the Akan people's understanding of the spirit, with the objective of developing a fresh, context-specific pneumatology that effectively conveys the Christian concept of the Holy Spirit within the Akan cultural context.

This study seeks to provide insights into the following fundamental questions: How do the Akan people understand the concept of a spirit? How can the spiritual worldviews of the Akan inform a contextually relevant understanding of the Holy Spirit? What are the most effective ways to convey the concept of pneumatology using the diverse expressions and idioms unique to the Akan people?

With these questions, the book is written not only to enrich academic discussions in theology and religious studies, but also to bridge the gap between scholarly understanding and practical application. By integrating the rich cultural elements of the Akan people with Christian pneumatology, I aim to contribute to a more inclusive and comprehensive theological understanding. It is my hope that readers, whether they are scholars, students, or curious individuals, will find this volume a significant addition to their understanding of the interaction between Christianity and indigenous African religions, thus fostering a deeper appreciation of the diversity and richness inherent in African religious thought and practice.

Author
July 13, 2023, Lausanne, Switzerland

PART I

GENERAL INTRODUCTION

NYAME DUA
"God's tree"
Adinkra symbol of the Nyame Dua, a medicinal tree signifying healing and protection of God.

1. General Introduction

> *"The quest to integrate Christianity and African culture has been a key feature throughout African theology. From its inception in the 1950s and early 1960s, African theology has insisted that African culture should have a major role in the growth of African Christianity"* – Ezra Chitando (2009: 24).

The question of a contextual expression of the Christian faith and practice in Africa has been an ongoing discussion in African theology.[1] How can African religious ideas contribute to theological discussion and learning? This kind of theological question is commonly categorized as part of the task of African theology, which seeks to make the gospel of Jesus Christ relevant to the African context, as well as to ensure the recipients' authentic identity. The present work forms part of this contextual orientation of Christian theology as it investigates the notion of the spirit among the Akan people of West Africa in order to propose a new contextual pneumatology for the articulation of contextual Akan Christian pneumatology. The study seeks to offer answers to the following key questions: What is the notion of the spirit among the Akan people? How might the Akan spiritual worldviews inflect a contextual understanding of the Holy Spirit? How do we best articulate pneumatology in the various idioms of Akan?

My proposal takes into consideration the nature and work of the Holy Spirit and its theological expressions among the Akan Christians of West Africa. Because the doctrine of the Spirit involves both the "spiritual" and the history of humanity, the present proposal articulates a theological framework that engages Christian thoughts and theological reflections. The

---

1 I would like to make it clear that in discussing African theology, I have no intention of broadly applying regional theological perspectives to the entirety of the African continent. I fully recognize and respect the complex religious customs and traditions among African communities, which showcase a diverse spectrum of similarities and differences across the many societies in the continent. With this complexity in mind, I have consciously chosen the Akan community as the central focus for this theological exploration.

crux of this proposal revolves around an elaborate exposition of the spiritual perspective of the Akan. The spiritual viewpoint is primarily inspired by the Akan concept of *sunsum*, which means "spirit or power." The ultimate objective is to facilitate a deeper comprehension of the idea of the "spirit" among the Akan. The expectation is that acquiring an excellent grasp of the concept of the "spirit" will demonstrate how the theology of the Holy Spirit is employed, contextually, in the Akan setting. The proposal is rooted in an entirely different Akan concept, known as *honhom.* My research contends that *honhom* exerts significant influence on any reviews, discourses, or scrutiny regarding a contextual Akan pneumatology. Previous studies have proven that *honhom,* as a premise for explaining nonphysical phenomena – such as air and spirit – and meta-empirical aspects, is polysemic. Most importantly, the aforementioned nonphysical realities complement the biblical concepts of רוּחַ (*ruach*) and πνεῦμα (*pneuma*) and have a firsthand impact on the Akan interpretation of life in its entirety. *Honhom* also enables a better understanding of the functionality and character of the Holy Spirit, which in turn shapes contextual Akan Christian pneumatology.

1.1. African Concept of Spiritual Phenomena

The concept of spirit and spirits is a universal phenomenon. In several parts of the world, spiritual phenomena have been the determining factor for a cosmological and identity construct. As a consequence, it is not strange to see spiritual phenomenology as a multireligious, multilingual, and multicultural reality. This means that irrespective of our global relationality, each religio-cultural context recognizes the "spirit" or spiritual phenomena in their own unique linguistic expression, which eventually defines their worldviews and interaction with the rest of the world.

In Africa, the notion of the "spirit" cuts across all cultural lines in the majority of African societies. John Samuel Mbiti (1931-2019), an outstanding Kenyan Anglican theologian and religious philosopher who was emeritus professor at the University of Bern and parish minister in Burgdorf, Switzerland, puts the African notion of the spirit into two categories: spirits of a divine origin created by God directly, and those that became spirits because they were once human beings (Mbiti 1969: 75). Spirits in general may comprise God, lesser deities, ancestors, and evil spirits. God remains the highest spirit-being and Creator who holds absolute will and power over all creation. No one claims to have seen or talked to God.[2] God transcends our worldly confines. God created the lesser deities, known as pantheon gods, who act *in loco dei* and are thought of as children of God. Ancestors are departed family members who are thought to be living at a special place reserved for them in the spiritual realms and are ceremonially invoked for assistance in the affairs of the living. Evil spirits are said to be malevolent spirits that can orchestrate human destinies and are likewise responsible for some human tragedies. All other spiritual forces are underlings of these two broad categories.

The general understanding has been that spirits and spiritual forces do not exist exclusively outside of the natural. The spiritual and natural are interwoven, making the African cosmology an inspirited universe, i.e., all the natural objects are inspirited to exercise power and certain essential qualities. Consequently, it is accepted that the spiritual is pervasive, and not just the 'spiritual' part of the world according to Allan Anderson (b. September 21, 1949), an Anglo-Zimbabwean systematic theologian in Mission and Pentecostal studies (Anderson 1991: 101). This understanding of "spirit" or "spirits" is, according to Anderson, implicit pneumatology, i.e., a pneumatology found in the daily practices rather than in a formal theology of the spirit (Anderson 1991: 6). Life, in its entirety to most Africans, is wrapped up with the spiritual in view. It is, therefore, crucial to identify the dimensions of African pneumatology as anthropological, philosophical, theological and ecological. To fully grasp such a pneumatological cosmology is not always easy. As Anderson observed, the African notion of the spiritual is essentially suprarational, meaning beyond logical explanation (Anderson 1991: 101).

Because the spiritual pervades the material, it leaves the material agencies with little or no control over the course of events. In this respect, African religious scholars think of the traditional African worldviews as a material-spiritual unity, contrary to the dualistic cosmology of the West (Anderson 1991: 8). Many Africans believe the phenomena of reality are shaped by the spiritual. For example, the Akan proverb *Nsɛm Nyinaa ne 'Nyame*, meaning "All things are dependent upon God," expresses the divine absolute activeness in the affairs of human life. Another proverb,

---

2 Stories of creatures talking and reasoning with God are common in Akan folktales.

Onyame Nkrabea nni kwatibea, meaning "There is no bypass to God's destiny," suggests that divine predestination is unalterable (Gyekye 1987: 20). The idea of spiritual agencies affecting the material is an established belief that contributes to the rational understanding of the African worldviews of cause and effects.

1.2. Toward a Contextual African Pneumatology

The academic commitment to a contextual Christian pneumatology has evolved at a relatively slow pace in African theological discussion when compared to Christological studies. Anderson has argued that pneumatology is a neglected dimension in written African theology, and where it exists, it is regrettably eclipsed by methodological crises that adopt a Western approach to the study of traditional African worldviews (Anderson 1991). It is a paradox that Africans' spiritual worldviews, which are characterized by a suprarational disposition and a buoyant legacy of Christianity, can lag behind in pneumatological discourses in scientific research. The reasons are not obvious, but they are partly due to a historical negative view of African traditional religions among some mainstream and independent African churches. Or perhaps it stems from a lack of interest in the subject. Does a sense of worry prevail? Yes, in my opinion.

Although only a few scholars have investigated the African concept of the spirit and its relationship to Christian faith and practice, pneumatological emphasis in scholarship is not entirely futile. Things seem to have changed in recent years and there is a huge and significant contribution to this special but neglected area in recent African scholarship. Eminent scholars such as Allan Anderson, Chigor Chike, Teddy Sakupapa, and Robert Owusu Agyarko come to mind. Even though this evolution is praiseworthy, it should be noted that it has made little difference in the area of contextual pneumatology.

In the section that follows, I will highlight a few renowned studies on African spiritual worldviews to demonstrate how scholars have understood the nature of spiritual phenomena that underpin current contextual pneumatology across the continent of Africa, especially in sub-Saharan regions.

1.2.1. Placide Tempels and the Notion of Vital Force

The contribution of the Belgian missionary Placide Tempels' (1906-1977) *Bantu Philosophy* (1956) is significant. Tempels' work is known for its exposition on African cosmology and ontology, especially its contribution to African pneumatology among the Baluba people of the Democratic Republic of Congo. The central idea that Tempels grapples with is the notion of vital force. He argues that Bantu ontology is all about forces: "Force is the nature of being, force is being, being is force" (Tempels 1959: 44). Tempels understood vital force or life force as the enabling principle for the life of all beings, except God who is essentially life and the source of vital force.[3]

Tempels' work evoked strong reactions from scholars of African religions, namely Mbiti (1969: 10), Mulago (1969: 148), Nyamiti (1976: 170), Vahakangas (1999: 285), Ngong (2010: 77), and Wiredu (1998: 24). For instance, Mbiti questioned whether Tempels' theory of vital force could be applied to other African peoples (Mbiti 1969: 10). In other words, the concept of vital force is not organic to African societies. Similarly, Wiredu has accused Tempels of generalizing the Bantu concept of being as though "what is true of the Bantu is true of all Africans" (Wiredu 1998: 24). Okafor takes a moderate position by praising Tempels' approach to Bantu religion as "methodologically on the right track towards uncovering of the inner structure of African cosmology" (Okafor 1982: 89). However, Okafor rejects Tempels' application of "vital force" and proposes that African cosmology is meaningful in the context of the concept of life (Okafor 1982: 91). Whatever Okafor meant by the term "life," it is totally dependent on a vital force as understood in many African societies.

Despite the many criticisms, the very core idea of Tempels' thesis about life among the Bantus, which is interrelated because of the vital force from God, remains standing. Sakupapa observes that "a conceptual framework of vital force is one which highlights the centrality of life and the interrelatedness of beings (community)" (Sakupapa 2012: 426). He further argues that "vital force is the power of God present in all creation and without which life is not possible…[V]ital force is the Spirit of God understood as

---

3 The way Tempels expresses the concept of "vital force" bears similarities to the Akan understanding of *sunsum*. However, as I proposed in my previous book, "vital force" aligns more closely with the concept of *ɔkra* in the Akan tradition, rather than *sunsum*. In my view, equating "vital force" with "sunsum" represents a misinterpretation.

the principle of life and enabler of communion within creation" (Sakupapa 2012: 426). Nalwamba & Buitendag also come to a similar conclusion that "vital force recalls the biocentric impulse in African ontology and its potential to heighten our sensibilities to the intrinsic value of all of life (creation) in all of its interrelatedness" (Nalwamba & Buitendag 2017: 4).

After decades of criticism, the vital force has become an object of heightened interest in recent African contextual Christian pneumatology. Sakupapa has noted that "the notion of vital force provides a conceptual framework for articulating pneumatology that is relevant to the context, faithful to biblical witness and also accountable to the wider Christian community" (Sakupapa 2012: 427). Nalwamba & Buitendag conclude with a recommendation to acknowledge the concept of vital force as the basis for "a viable conceptual framework for an eco-pneumatology that is not just relevant to African Christian theology in the African context alone but a gift to Christian theology as well" (Nalwamba & Buitendag 2017: 8).

1.2.2. Moya: The Holy Spirit in an African Context

Allan Anderson's *Moya: The Holy Spirit in an African Context* (1991) is an attempt to demonstrate how different categories of African pneumatology are viable for the development of contextual Christian pneumatology. In this work, Anderson contends that a meaningful reinterpretation of spiritual concepts in light of the Biblical revelation by African Christians can only be understood and evaluated when such reinterpretations are seen in light of the traditional world view of Africans (Anderson 1991: 69). This work is a masterpiece which expresses Anderson's thought on traditional religions as the context for meaningful theological discussions. Anderson has written on African pneumatology with particular emphasis on African Initiated Churches (Anderson 1991, 2000, 2001, 2003).

Anderson argues that the notion of the "spirit" in African traditional religions is compatible with the Biblical understanding of the Spirit. The analysis he draws from the study of African pneumatology concludes that in most African traditions, "spirit" also denotes wind and the movement of air, among other connotations that are analogous to the biblical meanings (Anderson 1991: 114). From that background, he sees a theological value in *moya* or *umoya*, a Sotho-Tswana word for the spirit or breath of life, as a contextual interpretation of the Holy Spirit in South Africa.

Moya is a constituent of the human being recognized as the transcendent soul, common with God, and received directly from God (Anderson 1991: 16). *Moya* is deathless and distinct from the *isithunzi*, the personality soul, which with the *moya* becomes the *idlozi* (ancestor) after death. Anderson says *moya* traditionally means air and wind and is used to designate the very essence of human life, which is without any independent existence of its own (Anderson 1991: 17). Anderson sees *moya* as the most adequate theological term to describe the Holy Spirit as the basis for contextual pneumatology in South Africa. This perspective allows him to show that the work of the Holy Spirit is more related to the African concept of the creative spirit, which is also the vital force or life force in most African religions.

1.2.3. Chinua Achebe's Notion of Chi in Igbo Cosmology

Chinua Achebe (November 16, 1930 - March 21, 2013), the celebrated Nigerian writer and scholar, offers a critical interpretation of the African concept of the spirit by examining the notion of *chi* (pronounced as in the English *Chi*-ef) in relation to Igbo cosmology. According to Achebe, the Igbo perceive *chi* as soul, god, spirit-double, personal spirit and guardian angel, among other connotations. The Igbo also view *chi* as day or daylight and use it to denote the passage between night and day and vice versa; in this sense, *chi ofufo* represents daylight, *chi ojiji* refers to nightfall, and *mgbachi* stands for midday, a time that commands fear among children and respect among roaming spirits.

In the context of this thesis, the first interpretation of *chi* – as personal spirit, god, spiritual alter ego, soul, and guardian angel – is of great significance because of its influential, yet mysterious manifestation in Igbo psychology. Achebe argues that the Igbo generally consider an individual's *chi* to be their double in the spirit world, hence the term spirit-double. *Chi* is central to understanding Igbo cosmology and worldviews. The Igbo believe that the *chi* of a person coexists with or goes through the sun, the source of daylight, before reaching the world. This perspective is vital because Chi Ukwu or Chukwu (Great Chi), the Supreme Deity in Igbo cosmology, is intrinsically one with the sun.

Chi is also a core component of the concept of duality in Igbo psychology; for instance, something else must always straddle something. The Igbo believe that *chi*'s relationship to man is complementary rather than domineering, as exemplified by the popular phrase *Onye kwe chie ekwe* meaning that a man's *chi* submits to his wishes. *Chi* negotiates the talents that a man is accorded before birth, hence the phrase *Obu etu nya na chie si kwu*, meaning that a man who is plagued by misfortune must have made a calamitous agreement with his *chi* before he came into the world. A man's *chi,* while complementary, can also refuse to comply with his desires; this is the source of the saying *chie ekwero,* meaning *chi* has refused. *Chi* can also be obstinate or 'bad,' whereby it undermines a man's fortune or success. Perhaps the most fundamental title assigned to *chi* in Igbo cosmology is that of the creator; in other words, a man is a product of his *chi*, which is different from every other person's. According to Achebe, this belief, which confirms the power of individualism among the Igbo, is reflected in the names assigned to children at birth. For instance, Chiekezie means that balance has been restored by *chi* through the birth of that child. The logical inference, therefore, is that there is a significant relationship between *chi,* Chukwu the Supreme God, and the sun in Igbo cosmology. In particular, Achebe's analysis of the manifestation of *chi* among the Igbo establishes a sound platform for deconstructing and contextualizing African pneumatology.

1.2.4. Sunsum: The Spirit of Life by Robert Owusu Agyarko

Robert Owusu Agyarko is a native of Kumasi in Ghana's Ashanti region. He is a Pentecostal pastor who also serves as a scholar at the University of the Western Cape in South Africa.

Agyarko graduated from the University of Ghana with a diploma in theological studies and a bachelor's degree in theology from Ghana Baptist Seminary (now Baptist University College). He got a master's degree in theology from the Nigeria Baptist Theological Seminary and a master's degree in religious studies from the University of the Western Cape in South Africa, where he later earned a doctorate in religious studies.

As a result of his Pentecostal heritage, and theological studies, he is an important and enthusiastic contributor in discussions pertaining to pneumatology in Africa. He is currently the coordinator of graduate studies at Central University, Kumasi branch in Ghana. He previously served as the head of the Theology department at the Christian Service University College in Kumasi from 2013 to 2018. He also served as vice president and acting dean of Pan African Christian University College's School of Theology (now Perez University College) in 2004. Agyarko is currently an ordained minister of the Church of God in Ghana. He is credited for establishing seven Church of God congregations in West Africa, specifically in Burkina Faso, Mali, Benin, Gambia, Guinea, and Senegal (Bill, 2010: pp. 375, 381, 386).

Agyarko has conducted research on various aspects of Akan pneumatology throughout the years, including ecological theology and Christological pneumatology. A few of his articles include the following: "God of Life: Rethinking the Akan Christian Concept of God in the light of the Ecological Crisis" (2013), and "The Sunsum of Onyame: Akan Perspective on an Ecological Pneumatology" (2012).

Agyarko's contextual pneumatology begins with the Akan notion of *sunsum* as a spiritual cue for theologization.[4] At an international conference held at the University of Geneva, Agyarko presented a paper that proposes his concept and approach towards the theologization of the Akan *sunsum* as the basis for contextual pneumatology. In his presentation, "'Sunsum' The Spirit of Life: Pneumatology in the Akan West Africa Context," Agyarko announced that "The Akan notion of *sunsum* may form the basis for contextual pneumatology" (Agyarko 2014). The methodology Agyarko employed attempted to explore the ecumenical dogmatic affirmation of the councils of Nicea and Chalcedon's ecumenical creeds, in which the Holy Spirit was seen as both distinct and proceeding from God. Agyarko argues that African Christianity is largely pro-Nicaean/Chalcedonian (Agyarko 2014). This leads him to designate *sunsum* as an interpenetrating force from God in a *panentheistic* way; that means *sunsum* proceeds from God. The Holy Spirit, in Agyarko's pneumatology, is *Onyame Sunsum*: the spark of creation and life that proceeds from God, yet distinct of itself. With this proposal, Agyarko becomes the pioneer Akan theologian to work out a contextual Akan pneumatology in contemporary scholarship.

Agyarko's contextualization paves the way for a contextual spiritual formation that is not only a reflection of traditional spirituality but an integration of "Christian faith with African cultural life and thought forms" (Agyarko 2014). He believes Akan spirituality is, by and large, expressed by the term *sunsum*. Various Akan thinkers accept *sunsum* as the principle behind the essential nature of being and a force for an individual's personality, i.e., the distinctive character disposition of a person. Agyarko treats *sunsum* as a contextual framework for a Christian pneumatological discussion. Based on the concept of *sunsum*, he has further explored areas like

---

4 The translation of *sunsum* as "spirit" agrees with the consensus of most scholars studying Akan religions, and the pneumatic nature of Agyarko's character is no exception.

eco-theology and Christology in dealing with the relationship between faith and the African traditional religions to provide answers to today's ecological crisis.

Despite Agyarko's contribution to Akan pneumatology, a few questions need to be asked. Is *sunsum* the alpha and omega of the formulation of an Akan pneumatology? Could there be other ways to interpret pneumatology in Akan religion? With reference to other ways of interpreting Akan pneumatology, I will answer these questions with a categorical and firm yes. My research is introducing what seems to have been overlooked in the ongoing discussion of Akan spirituality and contextual pneumatology. Akan people have another term often used to describe a ghost or spirit, and that is *honhom* (wind, air, breath, and vital force). In this research, I will show whether the notion of the Holy Spirit in African pneumatology is more analogous to the concept of *sunsum* or the notion of *honhom*.

1.3. The Need for a Contextual Akan Christian Pneumatology

The concept of the spirit is a reality to the Akan. It is therefore important to engage Akan pneumatology in a meaningful scholarship to correctly appropriate it in dialogue with the Christian doctrine of the Holy Spirit. The reasons why I think a contextual Akan Christian pneumatology is necessary include, but are not limited to the following:

1.3.1. One Spirit but Various Names

The global phenomena of spiritual experiences make the doctrine of the spirit unlimited to Christianity. Although Christianity has enjoyed a monopoly of pneumatological studies in the past, recent studies of spirit-experience around the world is changing the perception of scholars. A number of research show that the concept of the spirit is a universal reality (Kärkkäinen & Co. 2013). For this reason, the Korean theologian Grace Ji-Sun Kim queries whether "there may be a possibility that Christianity does not have the complete answer when it comes to explaining and experiencing the Spirit" (Kim 2011: 9). In that case, the universal experience of God, and the spiritual, is emphasized in such a manner that makes pneumatological particularities in cultures point to a single source of divine experience of the spirit, but under different shades of names. One may apply the concept of a "spiritual ecumenism" to this kind of description, for instance. The current proposal for Akan Christian pneumatology demonstrates that Akan people have experienced the divine spirit in their own unique way, and this is being validated by the various linguistic expressions for the spirit in their livelihood.

1.3.2. A Response to Akan Spiritual Worldviews

In *Table Talks*, Karl Barth is quoted to have told to his students that the doctrine of the Holy Spirit would be more understandable in the twenty-first century: "I personally think that a theology of the Spirit might be all right after A.D. 2000, but now we are still too close to the eighteenth and nineteenth centuries. It is still too difficult to distinguish between God's Spirit and man's spirit" (Barth & Godsey 1963: 28). Barth identified a contemporary problem that continues to challenge today's theology of the Holy Spirit: the doctrine of the third person of the Trinity has never been an easy task for theologians. It remains one of the ecumenical creeds with numerous conundrums, and one that has maintained the rift between the churches in the East and the West. This problem is, in my view, partly the result of the neglect of rigorous research in pneumatology as compared to Christology.[5] More importantly, however, the Holy Spirit, as an experiential reality, brings divine involvement into practical life as in the case for Christology. The Spirit's impartation of spiritual gifts transforms the doctrine of the Holy Spirit from a set of theological discourses into a reality in the entirety of people's lives. Therefore, a contextual Akan Christian pneumatology is required to respond to the apparent spiritual worldviews of Akan people and their Christian experience of the Holy Spirit.

[5] Theological work in Christology has centuries of dominance and a track record in church homilies as compared to pneumatological discourses. However, there has been in recent decades a resurgence of pneumatological discussion in different quarters of theological work and ecclesiastical contexts.

1.3.2. Christian Faith and Practice in Ghana

Christianity remains a major reality in Ghana. Recent census results project that about 71.2 percent of the Ghanaian populace adhere to the Christian faith, making Christianity the dominant religion in the country. The Akan people of Ghana constitute about 47.5 percent of the general population and Christianity remains the dominant religion in this demography.[6] This pattern means the lifestyles of the majority of Akan people are now partly shaped by their new identity in Christianity. The Christian life and the Holy Spirit are indispensable since the new life in Christ is achieved through fellowship with the Spirit. Thus, we find in the book of Acts a power surge in the early church and its mission as a result of the outpouring of the Spirit. Since there is very little work being done in the field of contextual Akan Christian pneumatology, a contextual emphasis on pneumatology among Akan Christians is necessary to grasp the importance of Christian experience and the mission of the Church among Akan people.

1.3.3. African Spiritual Churches

The pervasiveness of the spiritual is analogous to pneumatological conceptions in many African churches, especially the African Initiated Churches (AICs), and the New African Indigenous Religious Movement (NAIEM) in the 1940s. These churches, often known as "churches of the spirit" or "spiritual churches," or known in Ghana as *sunsum nsɔre* (spiritual churches), emphasize the active and manifest presence of the Spirit (Anderson 2003: 178). Anderson notes that the spiritual churches often go a long way "towards meeting physical, emotional, and spiritual needs, offering a solution to all of life's problems and a way to cope in a threatening world" (Anderson 2003: 178, 179). The emphasis on faith and power healing, characterized by ecstatic manifestations such as praying in tongues, unconscious falls, and prophetic messages from their leaders, are given a pneumatological interpretation as the movement of the Holy Spirit. These characteristics led Akan people in Ghana to characterize spiritual churches as possessing

---

6 2010 Population & Housing Census, Summary Report of Final Results. Ghana Statistical Service, May 2012. http://www.webdeploy.statsghana.gov.gh/nada/index.php/catalog/51 Last visited Mar. 22, 2020.

sunsum (*tumi*=power), hence, *sunsum nsɔre* (spiritual churches). As a consequence, the Holy Spirit came to be associated with *sunsum* as *Sunsum Kronkron* (Holy Spirit). The contribution of these grassroot movements is a source for pneumatological discourse in understanding contextual pneumatology in Ghana.

1.3.4. Filmography and Pentecostalism

Pentecostalism has helped shaped African movies, especially in Nigerian and Ghanaian movie industries (Meyer 2015). It is one branch of Christianity that intersects with traditional pneumatology because of the strong emphasis on supernatural experiences of the Spirit. Pentecostalism has held the torch of the doctrine of the Holy Spirit since the beginning of the twentieth century. Pentecostals believe in the experience of salvation through the baptism of the Holy Spirit and the gifts, especially speaking in tongues.[7] Pentecostals emphasize divine movement of the Spirit as the liberating agent against all demonic agencies in the world. Recent rise in Africa's film industry has given an upsurge to a forging of technological images of the uncanny (Meyer 2015: 200). The popular spread of mystical movies about ghosts and evil spirits is a renaissance of Africa's mystical worldviews in modern technologies. Africans' spiritual worldviews over the years existed in memory and artistic visuals other than in film technology. The transition into movie industries is one of a kind and expresses the African *Sitz im Leben* of invincible realities as visual realities. This insurgence has been a forthgoing of blending religion with entertainment.

Although these films can often be sensational, the viewers, from an African point of view, are made to believe the imaginary as ordinary perceptible images. Moviemakers use concrete images to depict imaginable realities. Prior to the twenty-first century, most avengers in African movies were ancestral spirits or ghosts that intervened in adverse situations to redeem their suffering loved ones; this is also evidenced in the folklores. In the same breath, traditional priests played key roles as exorcists for individuals tormented by evil spirits. The influx of Pentecostal film writers and actors revised the traditional conception of ancestral deliverance to a divine agent

7 Pentecostalism emerged in Ghana in the mid-twentieth century although other records show that there existed indigenous Pentecostal churches (classical Pentecostalism) before its formal organization (Wyllie 1974).

of the Spirit. Whence, trained pastors joined the film industries to act as spiritual warriors against evil forces. As actors, they seized the occasion to persuade their audience of the dangers of the reality of spirits and to teach the public (Meyer 2015). Thus, pneumatological emphasis in Africa is always shaped by the African worldviews of the supernatural and how their influence can impart human lives. While filmmakers employ traditional conceptions as subject of entertainment, they typically fail to connect spiritual realities with those of the physical world.

1.3.5. Akan Traditional Religions and Practice

The Akan pre-Christian religions are widely recognized in Ghana as *Abosomsom* (the worship of *Ɔbosom*) or the Akan traditional religions in recent scholarship.[8] *Abosomsom* is best translated as "the worship of *Ɔbosom* or *Abosom* (pl.)," contrary to the pejorative translation by some Christians as "the worship of stones or rocks."[9] *Ɔbosom* is the pantheon agent who acts as an intermediary between the Akan and God. Early Western missionaries branded the religions with vulgarity, using derogatory terms such as paganism, voodooism, idolatry, fetishism, etc. to characterize it.[10] Although few adherents remain faithful to the traditional religions, their powerful impact cuts across the socio-religious and political dimensions of everyday activities in Akan societies. The religions impose certain values that tend to underlie the basis for moral and ethical expressions.[11] It is in the view of the religious tenets that inculturation theology engages as a theological

---

8 Discussing Akan religions in today's context can often attract criticism, given that the majority of the Akan people have abandoned their traditional faiths. These religions were once their only religious experience before the advent of Christianity and other religions. Nonetheless, any discussion about Akan religions should focus on its indigenous roots, its kingship traditions, and the influence of its worldviews on contemporary Akan society.

9 Stone or rock is called in Akan languages *ɛboɔ* or *ɔboɔ*. The word is homonymous to *ɔbosom*, leading to a loose description of Akan religions as the worship of stones or rocks.

10 Captain Rattray dedicated a whole chapter to expose some of these erroneous assumptions (Rattray 1923: 86-91).

11 Akan traditional religions continue to decline since the past two decades. About 8.5% of the general Ghanaian population adhered to the Akan traditional religions in the 2000 national population census report. The number decreased in the 2010 population census from 8.5% to 5.2%.

praxis to deal with the practice of the Christian faith within a given context in Africa.

Furthermore, Christianity and the traditional Akan religions have a reciprocal impact on each other. This has resulted in the challenge of reconciling dual allegiance among Christian adherents who also have a previous devotion to their traditional religion's deities. It is common for Akan Christians to seek solutions to their problems from both Christian clergy and traditional priests. Some pastors and religious leaders have been known to incorporate aspects of traditional beliefs into their churches, such as using the powers of deities.[12] The persistent fear of evil spirits and supernatural forces among Akan Christians has led to a strong emphasis on pneumatology by various Pentecostal and Charismatic churches, including independent ones. This includes practices such as faith healing, demon exorcism, speaking in tongues, and other spiritual gifts aimed at combating evil.[13] As a result, the Holy Spirit is often perceived as a powerful, active force, sometimes represented by fire, that fights malevolent forces in a similar manner to an individual's sunsum. This has led to the important theological question of the nature and role of the Holy Spirit in the lives of Akan Christians.

1.3.6. Biblical Authority

The Bible is widely regarded as the foundation of Christian faith and practice among various Christian denominations in Ghana. African Christian theology, which is practiced by the church, is largely based on the Bible, and differs substantially from traditional African theology (Muzorewa 1985: 78). The Bible remains the supreme source of any Christian theology

---

12 In 2008, an online video report surfaced detailing an incident involving a highly popular Ghanaian traditional priest, who stormed a church in Kato, a town near Berekum in the Brong Ahafo region. The priest, known as Nana Kwaku Bonsam, claimed to be retrieving an amulet that he had given to the pastor to help in establishing the church. It was implied that the pastor had failed to meet certain agreed-upon conditions, prompting Nana Kwaku Bonsam's intervention. This dramatic event took place on Wednesday, April 2, 2008. The priest intruded during the church service to reclaim his amulet. The pastor, Collins Agyei Yeboah, offered no resistance and peacefully handed over the amulet to the priest. The video documenting this occurrence can be viewed at the following URL: https://www.youtube.com/watch?v=iI_lFCutgLo. Last visited on Dec. 17, 2019.

13 These are commonly expressed in many African movies.

and African Christian theology, in particular, seeks to articulate the connection between traditional religions and the scriptures (Muzorewa 1985: 92). Hence, it would not be appropriate to take a narrow view on contextual Christian pneumatology that downplays the scriptural conception of the meaning of the Spirit. Culture plays a crucial role in giving the gospel a communicative function, making the message of Christ relevant and meaningful to the audience. In the following sections, I will elaborate further on the influence of culture on Christian doctrines for those who remain skeptical.

The Christ-gospel holds a universal mission to communicate the message of salvation to all nations, as stated in Matthew 28:18-20. The Christian message must be conveyed to all tribes, languages, and people, as noted in Revelation 14:6. This universality of the Christian message highlights its significance as a movement that transcends linguistic, cultural, and ethnic boundaries. According to Kathy Ehrensperger, the Christian movement "emerged from within the tradition of the Jewish people and developed into a movement that encompassed people of different linguistic, cultural, and ethnic traditions" (Ehrensperger 2013: 1). She further stated that "intercultural interaction and communication lie at the core of this movement and played a crucial role in shaping its self-understanding" (Ehrensperger 2013: 1). Ehrensperger's emphasis on the instrumentalization of culture in the Christ-movement serves to illustrate the importance of contextualizing the gospel in its immediate cultural context. Through this, the gospel can be presented in a meaningful and relevant manner, thereby highlighting its significance in a multicultural context.

The Bible provides several examples that emphasize the importance of cultural diversity in the spread of the gospel message. One such instance is found in Acts 2, where a multi-cultural phenomenon occurred in Jerusalem, whereby the Holy Spirit granted different tongues to the disciples, allowing them to speak to people from diverse cultural, tribal, and national backgrounds (Acts 2, 11). As noted by Ehrensperger, this linguistic diversity among Jews from the Diaspora meant that even if they were not bilingual, they were likely to negotiate their own Jewish tradition within the context of their local traditions (Ehrensperger 2013: 126). This ecstatic experience of the gospel message and cultural diversity among tribes and nationalities provides us with an effective method of understanding the relationship between culture and the Christian message in contemporary times. The ability to communicate the gospel message in various languages and cultural contexts is crucial in effectively spreading the message of Christianity.

In Athens, Paul encountered a group of Greek philosophers, which led to a speech regarding the *Agnostos Theos* (Acts 17, 16-34). In his speech, Paul emphasized the existence of a supreme deity who provides life and sustenance to all mortals (v. 25 NRSV). He was concerned with the Greek polytheistic spiritual experience, which idolized this deity through the creation of human-made images using gold, silver, and stone (v. 29). Paul sought to correct the misconception surrounding the presence of this God in the world. In doing so, he demonstrated his familiarity with Greek culture and traditions, and aimed to shed light on the limitations of these traditions in fully comprehending the realities of God.[14]

In the Corinthian correspondence, Paul had to address cultural practices that were causing problems in the Corinthian churches, including the issue of propriety in worship regarding head coverings (1 Cor. 11, 1-16). Although the text does not go into detail about head coverings, Paul's conclusion is clear: whether with a head covering or one's natural hair, Corinthian women should cover their heads and men should uncover their heads during the liturgy. Paul's argument was based on both cultural and theological analysis to bring a cultural practice into proper worship experience.

These biblical examples of cultural diversity and the gospel message highlight the importance of cultural sensitivity and understanding in mission endeavors. It is crucial that we recognize and appreciate the diversity of cultures and traditions and use that understanding to effectively spread the gospel message to people from diverse backgrounds. The scripture does not outright oppose culture, and there is a delicate balance between cultural traditions and gospel traditions that cannot be easily broken. Paul's thoughtful approach to sensitive cultural issues serves as a model for how to handle

---

[14] Kathy Ehrensperger's work on Paul at the crossroads presents Paul as a mediator between peoples, traditions, and cultures. Ehrensperger carefully examines the role that Paul played in bringing the gospel from Jewish traditions and theology and also from a Hellenistic culture to formulate his theological doctrines of Christ. Paul however becomes a perfect point of starting one's scriptural understanding of contextual theology. So, Paul's example has given space for a continuous method of theologizing and as Kathy Ehrensperger concludes in her book that "in the footsteps of Paul, there should be space for all who are interested and who wish to participate in such a conversation – 'for the Jew first and also for the Greek'" and for the African too (Ehrensperger 2013: 224).

theological dialogues in African societies, and as Kwame Bediako stated, "without injury to the integrity of the Gospel" (Bediako 1992: xi).

African theology endeavors to explore the relationship between traditional religion and scripture, with the Bible serving as a foundational source for Christian theology (Bediako 1992: 89-92). Some African theologians adopt this method in developing a theology that reflects the values of African traditional religions for the African Church.

Given all the aforementioned reasons, this proposal seeks to contribute a pneumatological exploration of the nature of the Holy Spirit from a biblical standpoint, encompassing both the Old and New Testaments. Through the inculturation methodology, which aims to achieve an authentic Christian self-expression, the research aims to identify the most suitable Akan religious term that accurately reflects the Hebrew and Greek concepts of the Spirit as expressed in the Bible. This is because the concept of God in the Bible and the Akan religions are closely intertwined, making biblical pneumatology a complementary addition to contextual Akan pneumatology.

1.4. Honhom Kronkron: A Pneumatological Proposal

The term *kronkron* in the Akan Twi language means holy. The term *Honhom Kronkron* translates to "Holy Spirit." In this study, a pneumatological construction is being advanced based on the Akan religious concept of *honhom*. The general understanding of *honhom* among the Akan people refers to all non-perceivable realities and spiritual entities, collectively referred to as *ahonhom*. Traditional Akan thinkers use the term *honhom* to describe breath, gentle wind, spirits, and other entities that reside in the spiritual realms. Notable Akan scholars who have made significant contributions to the discourse on *honhom* include Joseph Boakye Danquah and Kwame Gyekye. Danquah (1895-1965), a Ghanaian statesman and scholar trained in philosophy and law, was a political activist and not as widely known for his philosophical or legal work. He remains one of the key expositors of the Akan conceptual scheme and attempted to address conceptual discrepancies in Akan narratives in his books, *Gold Coast: Akan Laws and Customs* (1928) and *The Akan Doctrine of God* (1944). However, his contributions were partially attributed to his Christian background and non-indigenous conceptualization.

Danquah and Gyekye share similar fundamental Akan ideas, such as those related to morality, monotheism, and personhood. However, their perspectives on Akan spirituality differ significantly, particularly with regards to the concepts of sunsum and *honhom*. Gyekye's interpretation of *honhom* is monomorphic, while Danquah's is polymorphic. Gyekye thinks *honhom* is only breath and not identical with Spirit. On the other hand, Danquah defines *honhom* as an expression of the idea of breath, wind, or Spirit, as represented by the multivalent Hebrew רוּחַ and Greek πνεῦμα (Danquah 1968). Gyekye, however, critiques the pneumatic origin of *honhom* as well as the Christian influence on the Akan religion (Gyekye 1987: 88). According to my research, this critique is historically disputed, as early Akan philologists and ethnographers considered *honhom* to be the indigenous translation for a spirit or ghost (Christaller 1881; Rattray 1916). Furthermore, if *sunsum* represents the idea of a spirit, why would Christians replace it with *honhom*? A critical investigation may be necessary if there is suspicion surrounding sunsum as a spirit.

Besides philologists, later Akan Bible translators have used the term *honhom* to translate the word "spirit" from the original languages of the Bible. Akan literature started in the nineteenth century as part of the European missionary effort to reach the indigenous Akan people. The first literary works in the Akan language were produced starting in 1845 through the establishment of the Basel Mission in what was then the Gold Coast. Johann Gottlieb Christaller (1827-1895), a German missionary, translated the New Testament books into the Akan language from 1857 to 1871, and these were published by the British and Foreign Bible Society (BFBS).[15] By 1881,

---

15 Johann Gottlieb Christaller (1827-1895) was among the missionaries to Ghana who suffered illness and loss of a wife (Christiane Emilie Ziegler, 37 years), yet, he never gave up on missionary activity. He was a German missionary, philologist, and translator, sent to Ghana (then Gold Coast) by the Basel Mission of Switzerland in 1853. Information I acquired from the Basel Mission in Switzerland revealed that Ghana became the first and most successful missionary field in Africa by the Basel Mission after their first operation in the Middle East, specifically in Iran, had failed. Christaller became quite instrumental, especially in his determined use of the local language as the means of missionary work. He died on 6th December 1895 in Stuttgart, Germany. It is reported that his last words were, "My work is coming to an end and my Sabbath is coming. The marked hands and legs [of Christ] have done all of that for me" (Knispel & Opare 2006).

Christaller had completed a dictionary of Asante-Fante, which included a grammatical introduction, appendices on the geography of the Gold Coast, and other subjects (Christaller 1881). The location of the Basel mission in Akropong, the capital of the Akwapim North District in the Eastern Region of Ghana, influenced the early literature to be written primarily in Akwapim and partially in Asante and Fante languages. The first publication of the Twi Bible in 1871 used "sunsum" instead of *honhom* as the corresponding term for "spirit" in the Bible. Today, both terms are used interchangeably to refer to a spirit, but a more in-depth comparative analysis would reveal otherwise.

Given the above arguments and analyses, several questions need to be addressed, such as the difference between *sunsum* and *honhom* and their potential relationship. This study argues that *sunsum* should not be directly translated as "spirit" due to the various meanings it has received in anthropology, philosophy, and theology studies. Instead, it is suggested that the Holy Spirit should be translated as *Honhom Kronkron* rather than *Sunsum Kronkron*. The research argues that in the Akan traditional mindset, the concept of "spirit" is always expressed as *sunsum* due to a spirit's intrinsic power, not because *sunsum* is always a spiritual being. This is a response to those who reject the English translation of *sunsum* as spirit.

Again, pneumatology stems from the Greek words πνεῦμα, meaning "breath," "wind," or "spirit," and *logos*, meaning "word" or "matter." Pneumatology is the systematic study of the Holy Spirit, spirits, or spiritual forces. Christian pneumatology focuses on the nature of the Holy Spirit and its activities in the world. It is therefore theologically defensible to interpret the activities of πνεῦμα as corresponding to the Akan *honhom*, rather than *sunsum*. This does not mean that Hebrew or Greek pneumatological terms should be identical with Akan realities. The point is that the term *honhom* already exists, and its indigenous understanding reflects those of the classical Bible languages. *Honhom* is a multiform and dynamic reality that underlines the Akan's entire metaphysical worldviews of spiritual entities and forces. Additionally, *honhom* conveys the idea of a spirit and should therefore be the basis for the formulation of a contextual Akan pneumatology.

As far as the history of Christianity in Ghana is concerned, Christaller remains one of the most influential missionaries, not only in the spread of the Gospel, but his contribution to Akan literature and scholarship. Read more about Christaller on Chapter Ten.

In my previous book, *What is this Thing Called Sunsum?*, I conducted a thorough analysis of the concept of *sunsum* from a historiographical and philosophical perspective. I evaluated the strengths and weaknesses of the nature of *sunsum* by examining the various methodologies and conceptual frameworks among scholars in the field of Akan religions and cultures. This current study advances the previous research by offering a new perspective on Akan pneumatology based on *honhom* and introducing a new approach to contextual Akan pneumatology. The purpose of the research is to make the study of pneumatology relevant to Akan Christians and contribute to a deeper understanding of this topic in the African context.

1.5. Summary

Kwame Bediako, the renowned Ghanaian Presbyterian theologian and former rector of the Akrofi-Christaller Institute for Theology, Mission, and Culture (1945-2008), once stated, “Wo ntumi ne nipa nkasa a, wo ntumi nka Nyame asɛm nkyerɛ no,” to wit, “If you cannot talk to people, you cannot talk to them about the word of God.”[16] Bediako believed that theology requires human contact and is not separate from cultural influences. Thus, interaction between theology and culture should be considered a crucial aspect in Christian missiology.

The acceptance of Christianity among the Akan culture requires the integration of its doctrines within their societal context. This interaction promotes a deeper understanding of the Christian message within the Akan community, as well as fostering cultural appreciation and assessment. This research aims to help the Akan people express the Holy Spirit in their indigenous language. The study focuses on contextual Akan pneumatology, which examines the concept of spirits and spirituality in Akan cosmology.

The research aims to critically examine the spiritual worldviews of the Akan people and understand their notion of the “spirit” and how this affects the application of the doctrine of the Holy Spirit in their context. The question of how the Akan people of West Africa speak of spirits, spirituality, and the Holy Spirit is the main focus of this study.

---

16 Quote from Kwame Bediako’s speech during one of their maiden graduation ceremonies of Akrofi-Christaller Institute of Theology, Mission and Culture in Accra, Ghana. (Date unknown). https://youtu.be/cAOj5sOFbJE. Last visited March 19, 2023.

2. INTRODUCTION TO AFRICAN THEOLOGY

> *"The concept of God reveals a set of knowledge about God and how that knowledge affects humans' perception of what it means to live a meaningful life. In spite of this, the reality of God is not always a simple notion, especially when what is meant by the term "God" can be subjective. This is because the question "what or who is God?" still exists today"*
> – Clifford Owusu-Gyamfi (2023: 76).

Introduction

This chapter critically analyzes the theological systematization of contextual Christian theology in postcolonial Africa, focusing particularly on the liberation and inculturation methodologies, which are the two main contemporary approaches in African theology. African theology is a process of contextualizing the gospel in the specific geographical location where it is expressed. Context refers to the immediate surroundings where the gospel takes shape. The process of contextualization involves giving meaning to a theological discussion in a particular region.

Scholars use the term contextual theology to describe Christian missions and practices within a specific sociological context, aimed at achieving effective communication and an authentic Christian identity. This task requires exhaustive effort and has multiple systematic dimensions. The gospel, being universal in nature and Jesus Christ being the "Savior of all people" (Jn. 3:16; Matt. 28:18-19; 1 Tim. 4:10), requires contextualization as a praxis theology to address people in their own cultural context.[17]

---

[17] The use of the term "culture" within the context of theology does not imply that culture is the end of Christian theology, but rather a means to achieve a greater purpose. Theology seeks to incorporate the cultural context, or *Sitz im Leben*, into the gospel's narrative to better communicate Biblical truths. A notable example of this approach to contextualization is seen in John 1:1-3, 14 where the term *logos* from Greek philosophy is used to underline Christ's preexistence and supreme authority as the true creator and sovereign of the universe. Again, we see this approach in Acts 17:16-34, where Paul refers to

According to Bediako, Christianity is always indigenous and culture-bound (Bediako 1992: 305). This highlights the significance of culture in theological discourse, but the gospel, not culture, is the ultimate goal. The gospel has its own unique mode of expression that supersedes cultural ideas. The British theologian and missiologist Lesslie Newbigin (1909-1998) noted that "contextualization accords the gospel its rightful primacy, its power to penetrate every culture and speak within each culture, in its own speech and symbol, the word, which is both No and Yes, both judgment and grace" (Newbigin 1989: 152). Theology, therefore, finds its proper expression of the gospel within a particular cultural context.

African theology is a unique expression of biblical interpretation and theology, rooted in African traditional religions. This expression sometimes elicits negative reactions due to its rejection of Eurocentric theological interpretations. Many African theologians feel that the era of Western imperialism and mission activities was damaging to African traditional religions (Bujo 1992; Opoku 1968; Idowu 1973). It is incorrect to assume that African theology is solely a mission-oriented strategy. African theology also contains important sociological and anthropological elements related to the issue of identity and social construct. The cultural elements in African theology emphasize the significance of African realities, including traditional religions and culture, in academic and theological discourse.

2.1. The Impact of Christianity in Africa

This section delves into the historical context that gave rise to African theology. What sparked African Christians to begin discussing an African theology? There are various reasons that led to the creation of an African theology. The most significant of all is the influence of Christianity in sub-Saharan Africa during the latter half of the second millennium.

Africa was once a center of Christianity in the early centuries. Christianity spread rapidly in the northern parts of Africa in the first five centuries. Notable theologians who impacted Christianity in Africa during these times

---

the "Agnostos Theos" or "Unknown God" during a discourse. In this instance, the previously "unknown God" is revealed to be the same God of Paul. This passage illustrates Paul as a contextual missionary, capable of incorporating his understanding of Greek culture and thinking into his affirmation of the truths of the gospel.

included Clement of Alexandria (150-215), Tertullian (160-220), Origen (185-254), and Augustine of Hippo (354-430). However, the rapid expansion of Islamic colonialism in the seventh century in North Africa resulted in a gradual decline in the growth of Christianity in the region, allowing traditional African religions and Islam to become dominant in the sub-Saharan regions of Africa (Shillington 1989).[18] Nonetheless, Christianity persisted in the Ethiopian empire in East Africa. The growth of Christianity waned until its revival in the fifteenth century by European merchants and missionaries. Early settlers were merchants from Portugal, Spain, France, the Netherlands, and Italy (Sanneh 1991: 159). In 1652, the Dutch established the Dutch Reform Church in the southern regions of Africa. The arrival of colonialism by Europeans in the nineteenth century solidified the expansion of Christianity and westernization.

Since the nineteenth century, the spread of Christian missions and learning in Africa has been widespread, particularly in sub-Saharan regions.[19] According to the Pew Research Center, in 2010, Christianity was the dominant religious group in sub-Saharan Africa, accounting for 62.9% of believers in the region compared to other major religions.[20] There were several factors that contributed to this growth, including:

1. The institutionalization of Christian beliefs and learning through mission schools, health centers, and humanitarian agencies established by European missionaries.

---

[18] Rosino Gibellini believes the decline was not as a result of Islamic invasion in North Africa. He asserts that the Islamic invasion only prevented Christianity from reaching the rest of the continent. Gibellini deduces two main causes for the decline of Christianity in North Africa: first is an allusion he makes to internal heresies that plagued the North African churches as a result of Donatism and Arianism, and the second allusion he makes was to the exclusive use of Latin language unlike the Eastern churches who had translations in several languages (Gibellini 1994).

[19] The Northern regions of Africa record a slower pace in Christianity due to Islamic dominance and strict rules against the practice of Christianity. Islam and Christianity are competitive religious groups in Africa and fears of tension sometimes threaten peaceful co-habitation and relation in some parts of sub-Saharan African states such as Nigeria, Liberia, Chad, Tanzania, and other Islamic dominated areas in Eastern Africa. Islamization ideologies in Sudan and Gambia are current threats to the practice of Christianity in those regions.

[20] The same research projects that Christianity will be the leading religious group in sub-Saharan Africa by the year 2050. Source: Pew Research Center, "The Future of World Religions: Population Growth Projections, 2010-2050." http://www.pewforum.org/2015/04/02/sub-saharan-africa/163-3/. Last visited Mar. 22, 2020.

2. The translation of liturgical books such as the Bible and songs into local languages.
3. The training of indigenous Bible workers to collaborate with Western missionaries in teaching and mission activities.
4. The Africanization plan, which aimed to have Africans take leadership responsibilities in the administrative management of African churches in the twentieth century.
5. The increase in independent churches and denominations such as Pentecostalism and Charismatic movements.
6. The encounter of Christianity and African traditional religions in the mid-twentieth century.
7. The strong ties of kinship and community in Africa have largely contributed to the spread of the Christian faith, as it has become a conventional family value in many African homes.[21] Many African households now consider Christianity as part of their ancestral traditions, just like it was before in the African traditional religions.

Observably, Christianity has been the most successful and impactful religion in sub-Saharan Africa in the latter part of the second millennium.[22]

---

21 The impact of African traditional religions has been key in promoting the spread of Christianity throughout the African continent. These traditional religions, which acknowledged a Supreme Being prior to the introduction of Christianity, significantly facilitated the acceptance and propagation of the new faith. Rather than being destined for extinction as initially assumed, these indigenous religions actually formed the foundation for Christian expressions in Africa. In the early phases of Christian growth, the gospel was spread subtly alongside these religions, with Europeans preaching about their "High God." However, the acknowledgement of the significant role played by African traditional religions in shaping theological discourse has only been recognized fairly recently. This insight provides a novel angle for understanding Christianity in Africa, despite ongoing debates in academic circles about this approach.

22 If Ghana is taken as a case study, per the recent 2021 population census, the Ghana Statistical Service Report shows that about 71.3% out of Ghana's general population adheres to Christianity, followed by Islam with a percentage of 19.9 %. Others profess to be traditionalist (3.2 %) or without any religion (4.5%) (Source: https://www2.statsghana.gov.gh/nada/index.php/catalog/110). A breakdown from the 2012 census shows that the Northern region of Ghana records the highest percentage of Islam (60 %) of the population in the region. The remaining nine regions adhere to Christianity. Traditional religion is popular in Upper East (27.9%), Northern Region (16.0%) and Volta (14.1). People without religion are found in Brong Ahafo (7.3%) and Western

2.1.1. Challenges to the Growth of Christianity in Africa

Despite the success of Christianity in Africa, there is a sense of concern about theological disarray and common concerns about the depths of the faith, the proliferation of groups claiming affiliation to Christianity, Christians' lack of involvement in social life, and their silence on issues such as poverty, conflict, and terrorism on the continent. These challenges have prompted a rethinking of theological discussions in Africa. How should theology respond to these challenges and the various socio-economic and political dynamics on the continent? Does the theological content reflect the African reality? These questions are crucial for understanding what is known as African theology.

2.2. African Theology

2.2.1. What is African Theology?

African theology is a pan-African discussion of the Christian faith and practices in Africa. There are various definitions of African theology, but the All Africa Conference of Churches (AACC) defined it in 1969 as "a theology which is based on the biblical faith and speaks to the African 'soul' (or is relevant to Africa). It is expressed in categories of thought which arise out of the philosophy of the African people" (Engagement 1969: 114).

In 1977, a group of African theologians gathered in Accra, Ghana, to reevaluate the emerging pathways in African theology. This conference, known as the Pan-African Conference of Third World Theologians or Ecumenical Association of Third World Theologians (EATWOT), brought together theologians from various denominations, including Protestant, Orthodox, and Catholic. This marked a significant period in African theology,

---

regions (6.7%). In terms of gender stratification, about 73.4% of females profess Christianity compared to 68.8% of males; in contrast 18.3% are males and 17.0% are females practice Islam. Among the non-religious, about 6.7% are males and 3.9% females. The picture of Ghana's religious affiliation shows that there is at least one or two persons professing a religious faith in a single house. http://www.web-deploy.statsghana.gov.gh/nada/index.php/catalog/51 Last visited May 25, 2023.

characterized by a more diverse and inventive, yet conservative mode of interpretation.[23]

The resurgence of Christianity in the sixteenth century was fueled by the West, resulting in the earliest form of theology in Africa being heavily influenced by Western hermeneutics and lacking proper contextualization in the African way of life (Gibellini 1987: 61).[24] Bediako, in his book *Theology and Identity*, criticizes Western missionaries for their preconceived ideologies that viewed Africans as primitive and uncivilized, negating African traditional religions (Bediako 1992). This highlights the lack of understanding the West had towards Africans. As a result, African theology became reactive and apologetic, with a focus on countering Western dominance and preserving indigenous self-expression and independence (van Eck 2006: 679). African theology is eventually a process of seeking indigenous Christian self-definition from a Euro-Christian Africa.[25]

There is a missiological definition of African theology which views it as Africa's systematic contextualization of the Christian missiology among the indigenous people of Africa. This approach takes a systematic interpretation of Scripture and how Christian missiology should be applied through the lens of cultural and religious ideas to interpret Christian thoughts and learning to African Christians.

In summary, African theology is a hermeneutical approach that prioritizes the African context, creating an authentic form of African Christianity. It aims to liberate Africans from various socio-economic and political challenges such as poverty, conflicts, domestic violence, illiteracy, and poor governance.

---

[23] The term African theology was first used in the publication *Les prêtres noirs s'interrogent* (Paris, 1956) by a group of African and Haitain Catholic priests (Bujo 1992: 5). Bujo also refers to Vincent Mulago, a graduate from the Urban University in Rome in 1955, as the first African theologian. Mulago's thesis was published in 1956 with the title "L'union vitale bantu, ou le principe de cohésion de la communauté chez les Bashi, les Banyarwandas et les Barundi" (Annali Lateranensi 20 (1956), 61-263) (Bujo 1992: 58).

[24] It cannot altogether be ruled out that Europeans did not do any contextualization of the gospel in Africa. As will be seen in the discussion, Bible translations into the indigenous languages were part of the missionaries' way of internalizing the Gospel in Africa.

[25] A term used by Kwame Nkrumah in his *Consciencism: Philosophy and Ideology for Decolonization* (1970).

2.2.2. In Search of a Positive Mode of Expression

Critics of African theology take issue with the term "African theology" and question whether there should be one. Attempts have been made to discourage the nomenclature. The late Nigerian evangelical scholar Byang Kato, in his book *Theological Pitfalls in Africa* (1975), criticized the emerging theological approach that incorporates African traditional religions into theological discussions. He saw this as a betrayal of sound theology and condemned it as syncretism (Kato 1975: 16). Kato was skeptical about Mbiti's theological sympathy with African traditional religions and blatantly condemned it. Although some scholars, such as Bediako, Oduyoye, and Parrat, saw Kato as negative and unsympathetic, Kato and Mbiti shared a negative view on the various definitions of African theology. Mbiti himself refused to use the term as a designation for a distinctive form of theology, and instead described African theology as simply "theological reflection and expression by African Christians" (Mbiti 1979: 83). However, Mbiti's description did not receive enough support.

Attempts have been made to distinguish between African Theology and African Christian Theology. Charles Nyameti, a Tanzanian Orthodox Roman Catholic theologian, defines African Theology in broader terms as "*discourses on God (theo-logos)* – and on all that is related to Him – in accordance with the mentality and needs of the people in the black continent" (Nyameti 1994: 63). He creates a dichotomy between African Traditional Religions theology (non-Christian) and African Christian theology, which refers to "the understanding and expression of the Christian faith in accordance with African needs and mentality" or the "systematic and scientific presentation or elaboration of the Christian faith according to the needs and mentality of the African peoples" (Nyameti 1994: 63).

Other scholars, such as Agbeti, Tienou, Muzorewa, and Chitando, share this view and consider African Theology as the beliefs and practices of African traditional religions, while African Christian Theology refers to the interpretation of the Christian faith in Africa (Agbeti 1975; Tienou 1982; Muzorewa 1985; Chitando 2006). The Catholic theologian Bénézet Bujo from the Republic of Congo expands this further by suggesting that African Theology should be based on the basic elements of the African tradition, interpreted in light of the Bible and the Fathers (Bujo 1992: 68).

The Pan-African Conference of Third World Theologians in 1977 in Accra outlined five main sources of African Theology, namely, the Bible and Christian heritage, African anthropology, African traditional religions, African Independent Churches, and other African realities. However, the growing commitment to contextual studies among African Islamic scholars proposes a reconsideration of the definition of African Theology.[26] Should it remain exclusive to African traditional religions and Christianity?

2.3. Toward an African Contextual Theology

Both Christianity and Islam have been present in Africa for many centuries and have become an integral part of the continent's religious and cultural history. While both religions have their roots in other parts of the world, they have taken on distinct African forms and have been adapted to local cultural and religious practices. The Africanization of these religions has made them an integral part of African identity and history, and it is important to acknowledge and include their influence in the study of African religions (*See* Bediako 1989: 60; Mbiti 1969: xii). Emmanuel Martey, a Presbyterian systematic theologian from Ghana, particularly singles out the incorporation of Islam into theological discourse in Africa. This approach provides a more comprehensive understanding of the religious landscape in Africa and contributes to a richer and more nuanced theological discourse (Martey 1993: 40).

The increasing trend of more inclusive discussions in African theology should change the traditional definition of African theology. My research therefore suggests that if African theology is to be regarded as a credible field of theological study, African theologians should adopt the term African Contextual Theologies (ACT) to describe the relationship between culture and theology within the African context. This approach would allow us to "theologize in a more genuinely African way and address issues relevant to Africans" (Bujo 1992: 5). African Contextual Theologies should strive to reach the hearts of Africans through meaningful dialogue and appropriate methodologies.

Furthermore, my research suggests that Christian theologians in the field of African Contextual Theologies should use the term African Contextual

26 *See* (Palombo 2014).

Christian Theologies (ACCT) to describe Christian theology that arises from a specific African cultural context. It is imperative to re-examine the ambiguous and controversial term "African theology" unless it is used in a generic sense, as Mbiti proposes, to describe theological reflection and expression by African religious thinkers, not just Christians. Therefore, in this research, I will use African Contextual Theologies (ACT) and African Contextual Christian Theologies (ACCT) instead of African Theology.

In the following section, my research delves into the current approaches and trends in African Contextual Theologies. Two prominent approaches that are widely recognized today are inculturation and liberation theologies, both of which cater to the specific historical needs of Africans. The meaning of liberation and inculturation theologies as understood by scholars will be discussed, as well as the historical contexts that gave rise to these theologies in Africa. Furthermore, this section will examine the current trends, opportunities, and challenges associated with these theological approaches.

2.3.1. Liberation Theology

Liberation theology is expressed in Christian missiology where the Church considers the gospel of Jesus Christ as a liberating message to the oppressed from all dehumanizing forces. The Church identifies with the suffering and poses the question, "What would Christ do?"

The origin of liberation theology dates back to the colonial era in Latin America. A group of theologians saw the need to address social and ecclesiastical concerns for people fighting for liberation from colonialism. Gustavo Gutiérrez, a Peruvian Catholic priest (born 1928 in Lima), is considered one of the main proponents of liberation theology. His book, *A Theology of Liberation: History, Politics, and Salvation* (*Teología de la liberación: perspectivas*, 1971), largely focuses on liberation theology. In this book, Gutiérrez defines liberation in three interrelated meanings. Firstly, it is the expression of the aspirations of the oppressed for political, economic, and social justice – in other words, the active consciousness of the oppressed to reject oppressive systems and institutions. Secondly, it is the human being as a historical figure that "takes conscious responsibility for its own destiny" through self and social renewal (Gutiérrez 1971: 36). Thirdly, it is the revelation of Jesus Christ as a liberator who saves humanity from sin, "which is the ultimate root of all disruption of friendship and all injustices and oppression" (Gutiérrez 1971: 37). While salvation is not the same as socio-economic and political liberation in the strictest sense, liberation theologians believe that it is where human beings finally gain freedom from the oppressive consequences of evil and live in communion with God. This new life is historical and forms the basis of all social reforms.

Between 1968 and 1975, two seminal conferences marked the formative phase of liberation theology: the Medellin Conference in Colombia in 1968 and the Theology in the Americas (TIA) conference in Detroit in 1975. This period gave prominence to the emerging theology and its focus on addressing poverty and oppression through its intrinsic Christian values (Gebellini 1987).

In 1976, the creation of the Ecumenical Association of Third World Theologians (EATWOT) in Dar es Salaam reflected on the methodologies and systematization of liberation theology's various themes (Gibellini 1987). By 1977, liberation theology had gained widespread attention and swept across Third World countries, leading to its heightened assimilation as a hermeneutical approach in African Contextual Theology.

The EATWOT conference held in Accra in 1977 took the fight against oppression as a theological task and solidified liberation theology's position as a theological framework in African Contextual Theology.[27] Since then, liberation theology has continued to be widely understood and recognized as such.

---

27 The statement on oppression from the Ecumenical Association of Third World Theologians in Accra (1977) reads: "There is also oppression in the exploitation of the people through national and multinational institutions. In all these instances of captivity we need to be liberated. We recognize that there are many forms of oppression. There is the oppression of Africans by white colonialism, but there is also the oppression of Blacks by Blacks. We stand against oppression in any form because the gospel of Jesus Christ demands our participation in the struggle to free people from all forms of dehumanization. Therefore, African theology concerns itself with bringing about the solidarity of Africans with Black Americans, Asians and Latin Americans who are also struggling for the realization of human communities in which the men and women of our time become the architects of their own destiny" (Pan-African Conference of Third World Theologians, 17-23 December 1977, Accra, Ghana).

2.3.1.1 An Overview of African Liberation Theology

African Liberation Theology is a struggle for authentic theological self-definition. In its African context, this theology seeks to attain an authentic African dignity and identity that is free from any form of colonization and apartheid on the continent. As stated by Martey, "theology has always been a struggle […] against all enslaving and dehumanizing forces" (Martey 1993:7). This understanding is "based on the historical experiences of Black people under white supremacist domination" (Martey 1993: 95). However, this description is limited in its political connotations. To better understand the meaning of liberation theology in Africa today, it is essential to expand its scope to encompass the fight against any unjust structure against Africans, regardless of the perpetrator's race - white or Black.

Characteristically, liberation theology is a theology of public or social interest that differs from the traditional understanding of individualistic salvation. This shift demonstrates a theological concern for collective social well-being and can be more appropriately characterized as a commitment to socialism.[28] The scope of interest for liberationists encompasses socio-economic and political challenges such as poverty, female genital mutilation, child labor, human trafficking, HIV/AIDS, girl-child education, child marriage, and domestic violence. These prevalent social challenges in Africa provide the opportunity for liberation theology to flourish as a theological framework. In these contexts, liberation theology addresses the unjust ideological framework on which unjust structures are built, and through the application of Christian virtues, aims to dismantle these structures and promote civil equity towards a free and virtuous society.

2.3.1.2. African Black Liberation Theology (Black Cultural Theology)

Black theology, an African American socio-political theology, seeks to understand the significance of Black identity through the lens of Jesus Christ in the lives of suffering Black individuals. The roots of this theology can be traced back to the 1960s, a time of racial segregation in the United States, where African Americans faced limited civil rights and were subjected to

---

[28] Marxist praxis theory has been the underlining hermeneutics of liberation theology. *See* (Miranda 2004) and (Míguez 1976).

discriminatory policies with severe psychological impacts. The dehumanizing experiences during this period inspired the Black community to question the existence of racism and their role in challenging the existing racial structures. This awakening is often referred to as the Black Consciousness movement, which is a crucial aspect in understanding the context of liberation theologies in Africa.[29]

African Black Liberation Theology is a form of Black Theology that originated in South Africa. It represents the global struggle of Black people for self-dignity and identity and emerged as a response to the systemic oppression and white supremacy prevalent in South Africa during the apartheid era.

From 1948 to 1994, South Africa was governed by a system of apartheid, a term derived from Afrikaans meaning "separateness". It stems from the compound of two Dutch words, *apart* meaning "separate" and *heid* meaning "hood." According to the Encyclopedia Britannica, apartheid was a governmental "policy that governed relations between South Africa's white minority and non-white majority and sanctioned racial segregation and political and economic discrimination against non-whites."[30]

In his speech to a crowd of 100,000 at 125th Street and Adam Clayton Powell Boulevard in New York City on June 21, 1990, Nelson Mandela, the first Black president of South Africa and anti-apartheid hero, described the effects of apartheid as perpetuating a "the color line that all too often determines who is rich and who is poor; that all too often decides who lives in luxury and lives in squalor; that all too often determines who shall get

---

[29] The idea of Black Consciousness is a mind renaissance, i.e., an awakening of Black Consciousness to the question of being in a world that has denigrated them into inferiority and servitude. It is the period when Blacks began to see their humanity beyond the color line. This awakening started as egalitarian campaign that seeks to bridge up the color line. The initial phase rested on two major emancipation agenda (though several others may apply), namely: (1) political emancipation movements such as the civil rights and Black Power movements that pressurized the government and civil authorities to reconsider the social status of Blacks in the United States of America, and (2) Black religion which brought about several racial churches of a people struggling for self-identity in a society that has failed to recognize their humanity (Washington 1984). The emerging Black churches took solace in God as a Father whose imposed image defines authentic humanity.

[30] Adam Augustyn and Co. (Eds). "Apartheid." *Encyclopedia Britannica*. https://www.britannica.com/topic/apartheid. Last visited Mar. 22, 2020.

food, clothing, and health care; and that all too often decides who will live and who will die."[31]

Under apartheid, South Africa was divided into a social caste system with the white minority at the top, enjoying privileges not extended to other races. This institutionalized segregation perpetuated a legacy of systemic oppression and discrimination that continues to shape South African society today.

The origin of apartheid as a system of racial domination in South Africa can be traced back to three main phases. The first phase was the political-economic invasion of the country by the Dutch (Afrikaners) and the British in the seventeenth century.[32] Starting from 1652, both Afrikaners and the English colonized South Africa, resulting in a struggle for economic and political dominance in the region. This culminated in the Anglo-Boer War (1899-1902), which ended with the British emerging as the victors and the majority of the colonies in South Africa coming under British rule. The unification process that followed, through the South Africa Act of 1909, brought together the British colonies of Cape Colony, Natal, Transvaal, and Orange River, resulting in the creation of the Union of South Africa in 1910. This process involved a political compromise between the British and the Afrikaners and the adoption of a common flag, but it excluded the input of indigenous Black Africans and non-European races in South Africa, marking the rise of white supremacism in the country (Connolly 2003).

In the second phase of apartheid in South Africa, constitutional limitations were imposed to restrict non-white integration into the newly established Union of South Africa. This was achieved through the implementation of several segregation laws that laid the foundation for the apartheid regime. These laws deprived non-whites of equal rights and freedoms as compared to their white counterparts, leading to unequal distribution of opportunities and resources. For example, the most prestigious and high-paying jobs were reserved for whites, while the Mines and Works Act of 1911 relegated Blacks to low-wage labor. The Native Affairs Act of 1920 established government-appointed tribal district councils that spanned the entire country, and the Natives (Urban Areas) Act No. 21 of 1923 controlled the

---

31 Transcription by *The Militant*, vol. 54: 6 (New York, July 6, 1990), 8.

32 The Dutch were the first permanent settlers in South Africa who later came to be known as Afrikaners. Afrikaner derived its name from a Dutch-root dialect comprising of various group languages known as Afrikaans.

migration of Blacks to urban cities and towns. Moreover, the Industrial Conciliation Act No. 11 of 1924 restricted Blacks from joining trade unions, as membership in registered trade unions and registration of Black trade unions were prohibited (Meisel, 1994: 23).[33]

The National Party instituted apartheid as a constitutional principle in 1948. Following the end of World War I and World War II, the political influence of Britain in South Africa declined as Afrikaners gained greater power in political affairs. The National Party, composed largely of Afrikaners, held significant sway in parliamentary proceedings by 1948, having earned the trust of the white population through the election of D. F. Malan as Prime Minister. Under Malan's leadership, the party implemented policies limiting British immigration to South Africa and promoting Afrikaner dominance through nepotistic practices. With the ease of British imperialism, the only remaining opposition was the Black African population, against whom the Afrikaner leadership deployed apartheid as a means of suppression (Lapping 1987: 87; Martey 1993: 19).

During the apartheid regime in South Africa, the government enacted legislation that institutionalized racial inequality, as it viewed whites and non-whites as inherently unequal. This resulted in the unequal distribution of privileges in areas such as education, healthcare, transportation, and employment. The social stratification of individuals based on their skin color was a significant issue, with non-whites being relegated to a lower status. For instance, although non-whites were allowed to use public transportation services, these were segregated into separate compartments for whites and non-whites, particularly in trains. Similarly, education and employment opportunities were also based on racial categories. The non-white population was also denied the right to participate in national affairs, as they were politically disenfranchised. The apartheid regime created a barrier of racial segregation, effectively rendering the Black population of South Africa as individuals without human rights or dignity. The apartheid government exerted control over all social, political, and economic structures in the country, using the color of skin as a tool to entrench white supremacy and restrict the freedom of other races (Martey 1993: 19).

---

[33] For more on segregationist legislation in South Africa, visit: South African History Online, http://www.sahistory.org.za/topic/segregationist-legislation-timeline-1920-1929 Last visited 05. 09. 2017.

I will now move to examine the ideologies behind the institution of apartheid as it sheds light on the mechanisms and motivations that facilitated this system of racial inequality and oppression.

2.3.1.2.1. Apartheid As a Theological Heresy

The apartheid system in South Africa is often perceived as solely a political construct, but it was in fact a religio-political system that supported white monopoly. The ideology behind apartheid was rooted in theological beliefs, specifically divine predestination, with support and justification provided by the white Dutch Reformed Church (Boesak 1979:204; Maimela 1994:186; Martey 1993:18). The notion of theonomy, or the belief that God's elect are destined to dominate and subdue other nations to a life of servitude, was heavily incorporated into apartheid (Martey 1993:19).[34] The British colonial ventures were sustained through the theology of the elect, shaping human history based on their political and messianic expression (Maimela 1994:185). Cecil John Rhodes (1853-1902), a businessman and former Prime Minister of the Cape Colony, encapsulated this ideology of British supremacy when he declared, "I contend that we are the finest race in the world and that the more of the world we inhabit the better it is for the human race."[35] He is considered a representative of the theological agenda of British supremacy, as he stated that the British were "destined to help on God's work and fulfill His purpose in the world."[36] The British saw their role in human history as similar to that of ancient Israel, with a divine mandate to subdue heathen nations (Maimela 1994:185, 186). It is clear that this was a purported colonial ideology.

The British theological perspective of white supremacy was adopted by the Dutch Reformed Church, which provided spiritual sustenance to the growing Afrikaners (Maimela 1994). The church provided Afrikaners with a theological justification for preserving white dominance and superiority

---

34 The whole of the colonial adventure was justified by theological ramifications of the Papal Bull "Dum Diversas" in June 18, 1452 to enslave and evangelize third worlds.

35 Cecil Rhodes, "Confession of Faith." Written on June 2, 1877 in Oxford. (Cited in John E. Flint, *Cecil Rhodes* (Boston: Little Brown, 1974), 248-52).

36 Van Jaarsveld, F. A. *The Afrikaner's Interpretation of South African History*, pp. 3, 4. (Cited in Maimela 1994: 185).

on the African continent, and thus the theology of apartheid became entrenched in the Afrikaner National Party's manifesto of 1947.[37] The fusion of religious beliefs with politics was nothing but the sanctification of Afrikaners' nationalist agenda, which were implemented through the structural elements of the apartheid policy.[38] The insidious nature of apartheid, sustained by astute theological doctrines, greatly advantaged the white minority over the disadvantaged non-white population.

In summary, the aim of apartheid was to maintain white supremacy over non-white races. The theology of election was utilized by the white minority to validate segregation and ultimately establishing apartheid law. The Afrikaner God was viewed as a "white God" who favored the white race and was indifferent to the suffering of the majority under apartheid rule. This racial interpretation of theology resulted in both political and religious triumphalism in South Africa, but also brought forth serious issues such as: (1) westernization as a domineering movement, (2) the relevance of theological virtues, (3) the essence of church and state, (4) Christian ethics in relation to human dignity and identity, and finally (5) white supremacy. These problems were overlooked by the beneficiaries of apartheid but were the catalyst for the political awakening and emergence of Black theology among Black South Africans.

---

[37] Certain portions of the manifesto read: "the policy of apartheid, a concept historically derived from the experience of the established white population of the country, and in harmony with such Christian principles as justice and equity" (Krüger 1960). The manifesto further justified the theology of apartheid as in line with Christian values: "the party rejects any policy of oppression or exploitation of the non-whites by the whites as incompatible with the Christian character of our people and therefore unacceptable" (Krüger 1960).

[38] After the party seized power in 1948, Malan is reported to have said: Our history is the greatest masterpiece of the centuries. We hold this nationhood as our due for it was given us by the Architect of the Universe [sic!]. [God's] aim was the formation of a new nation among the nations of the world […] Indeed, the history of the Afrikaner reveals a will and determination which makes one feel that Afrikanerdom is not the work of men but the creation of God. (Cited in Martey 1993: 19).

2.3.1.2.2. Emergency of South Africa's Black Theology

The fall of apartheid was largely indebted to the politics of conscience known as Black Consciousness. This new outlook of theological anthropology emerged around the mid-1960s and was characterized by anti-apartheid movements that sought to challenge the apartheid government through Black cultural renaissance and new contextual hermeneutics of the Bible, now known as South Africa's Black theology. Steve Biko, the father of Black Consciousness Movement (BCM), was a key figure in this movement. He redefined blackness beyond color perception, interpreting the South African situation using the Hegelian theory of dialectic materialism. This theory posited that Black solidarity (antithesis) and white racism (thesis) could result in defining true humanity beyond color or race (synthesis) (Martey 1993: 24). This epistemological rationality was used to empower Black people psychologically concerning their authentic humanity.

The BCM emphasized authentic liberation as the liberation of the mind. Liberating psychological faculties was fundamental to understanding the evils of apartheid and the being of Black. This liberation was seen as a way to counter the divisive definition of being human espoused by the apartheid policy, which reduced the degree of their humanity and blackness to nothing but a syndrome of blasphemy (Martey 1993: 24; Tutu 1979: 194). In 1977, the BCM was banned, but subsequent resistance groups emerged, such as the Black Theology Task Force (BTF). The new theology aimed to liberate victims of racist policies by reversing the apartheid hermeneutics of racist demarcation, and to understand God as the Father of all through Jesus Christ in human history (Tutu 1979: 195, 196). The movement was conscious of redefining Black identity by reacting to apartheid as heretical (Martey 1993: 23, 24). Prior to this, Black Nationalist groups such as the African National Congress (ANC) and Pan Africanist Congress (PAC) had been banned in 1960 following a major massacre of blacks by whites in a nonviolent protest against the apartheid government (Martey 1993: 22).

Black theology was not only a struggle against apartheid but also a struggle towards a united humanity. Following a three-year negotiation that ended apartheid in 1991 at Kempton Park in Johannesburg, the Truth and Reconciliation Commission (TRC) was formed in 1995 to further the transition to a fully democratic South African state. Part of its mandate was to build a new society that would bury the immoral consequences of apartheid and seek acceptable moral norms for progressive reconciliation and prevention of future human rights abuse in South Africa. The role of Black theology was the promotion of authentic humanity in a communal solidarity. The Zulu word *Ubuntu*, which defines humanity as a community working together towards the interest of each other, became a utilitarian moral philosophy for reconciliation. Ubuntu takes up the socio-political dimensions of South Africans to promote peaceful co-habitation and equal human rights.

Though Ubuntu has been praised for its effectiveness in reuniting South Africa, critics perceive the concept as a means for cultural nationalism; as a consequence, whites, Indians, etc. are obliged to claim an African identity as long as they seek utilitarian good for the masses (Christoph 2002: 53). Others, such as Allan Boesak, the avid anti-apartheid activist, have criticized both Ubuntu and the TRC as ill-equipped to address the social injustices and post-apartheid ideologies that are entrenched in the social structures of South Africa. While speaking to students at Yale Divinity School, Boesak remarked that Ubuntu does not enable the doing of systemic justice or the undoing of systemic injustice (Boesak 2017: 141).[39] The reason, given by Boesak, is that no demands for remorse and repentance are made from the perpetrators of apartheid.

2.3.1.2.3. African Feminist Theology (Womanist Theology)

Women's involvement in African religious experience is essential for understanding their role in recent theological discourses. As Mbiti noted, there are more female priests (priestesses) in African Traditional Religion than male priests.[40] This background has been highly influential in the integration of African women into Christian liturgy.

The need for female integration into theological dialogue was highlighted during the postcolonial era. At the 1977 Pan-African Conference of Third World Theologians in Accra, the importance of equal integration of

---

39 Allan Boesak, "Reconciliation, Justice, and the Spirit of Ubuntu." Lecture at Yale Divinity School, April 05, 2013. https://livestream.com/yaledivinityschool/boesak. Last visited April 30, 2020.

40 John Mbiti, "The Role of Women in African Traditional Religion." http://www.africanamerica.org/topic/the-role-of-women-in-african-traditional-religion-by-john-mbiti Last visited March 22, 2020.

women into the theological task was emphasized.[41] This recognition of the qualification and qualitative significance of African women's spirituality as equal to that of their male counterparts in applicable theological expressions and reflections gave women more prominence in academic discussion and in shaping public opinions.

Following the Accra meeting, a group of women experts in religion and cultural studies met at the World Council of Churches (WCC) in Geneva in 1989 to discuss key aspects of theology that women can play within the African context. This meeting gave rise to the Circle of Concerned African Women Theologians (CCAWT), led by Mercy Amba Oduyoye, a Ghanaian theologian and director of a task force in promoting women theologies in Africa at the WCC. Oduyoye is also known as the mother of African feminist theology. The Circle has championed Africa's feminist theology through a conscious articulation of women's role in the church and society, as well as academic influence in the development of Africa's feminist hermeneutics. Over the past three decades, feminist theology has become one of the transformative approaches in shaping Christianity in Africa. It has sought to address issues such as HIV/AIDs, child marriage, slavery, clitoridectomy, domestic violence, and education for the female child.

Like all other theological approaches, African feminist theology has been met with criticism. It poses a reactive paradox in its contextual integrity. African theological agenda has been a reaction to foreign oppression and redemption of African cultures from Eurocentric ideologies, while African feminist theology has been a reaction to and liberation of women from injustice and inequality suffered by African women in some Africa's domineering patriarchal societies (Abbey 2001; Chitando 2009; Oduyoye 2001). Feminists argue that African cultural structures support the oppression of women, and African feminist theologians accuse cultural norms of

---

41 Part of the statement read: "Throughout this document, we have referred to the need to struggle against sexism. If that struggle is to be taken seriously by the church, then our seriousness will be reflected in the way we do theology. We recognize that African women have taken an active role in the church and in the shaping of our history. They have shown themselves to be a coherent part of the liberation struggle. But we cannot ignore their exclusion from our past theological endeavors. Therefore, the future of African theology must take seriously the role of women in the church as equals in the doing of theology." (Pan-African Conference of Third World Theologians, December 17-23, 1977, Accra, Ghana).

protecting men to enjoy the dividends of these structures. Critics of Feminist theology believe its adherents are articulating Africa's normative thought forms through the perception of Western feminists (Nadar 2012: 273, 276).

Feminist theologians also face the problem of ecumenical systematization of theology, especially in most conservative African churches that are basically characterized by "globalized hermeneutics" as in the case of ordination of women in the Catholic and some evangelical Protestant churches. In such instances, contextualization loses its significance and penetrating effects.

In conclusion, liberation theology seeks to confront unjust systems that tend to bring suffering or subject humanity to harsh conditions. Liberationists believe that social life and the Church's public actions are intertwined. Therefore, the gospel message of salvation and freedom should have a socio-political impact to create a free and a virtuous society for all.

2.3.2. Inculturation Theology in Africa

In this section, we are examining inculturation as an approach in African Contextual Theologies. There is a growing sentiment among many Africans that Christianity is a tool to further Western imperialism in Africa. Reference is always made to the Papal Bull *Dum Diversa*, which was issued to evangelize and colonize third world countries, leading many Africans to question the intentions of Christianity in Africa. How can this concern be addressed? How can Christianity be seen as a part of African realities, and how can it be domesticated through an inculturation theology?

Furthermore, there is the question of the depth of the gospel among Africans. Have African Christians broken away from traditional religions? Do they still consult traditional priests/priestesses? Are there issues of fear of witches, demons, and spirits? Augustine Musopole, a Presbyterian theologian from Malawi and professor in philosophy of religions, has questioned the depth of Christianity in Africa and calls for a second stage of evangelism and theological indigenization. Speaking to a group of church leaders at the eighth Assembly of the World Council of Churches in Harare, Zimbabwe, Musopole stated: "While Christianity in Africa is growing in numbers and in its geographical spread, its depth is questionable. This might be the reason it is easily overcome by forces of ethnicity, patriarchy, corruption, hatred, political manipulation, racism, classism, regionalism, and traditionalism." He further asserted that "[t]he Church in Africa, especially the mainline churches, are being called to embark on a second stage of evangelism and theological indigenization."[42] Although the term indigenization has received unfavorable criticism, Musopole shares similar feelings as several African theologians who have expressed a concern for a theology that deals with African dimensions and immediate spiritual challenges, herein identified as inculturation theology.

2.3.2.1. What is Inculturation Theology

The term inculturation became popular in the 1990s, though the Gospel and culture have always enjoyed an intimate interaction. Inculturation involves the acquisition of cultural norms to incorporate the Gospel into its immediate context. It is a contextual discipline that uses persuasive models to critically engage culture and the message of Christ for an effective missionary activity. The theology of inculturation is also an academic exploration into cultural anthropology, which is defined as the study of human societies and cultures with respect to their spiritual needs. Inculturation provides a strong foundation for both theologians and missionaries to understand the process of the Gospel in its sophisticated anthropological context.

Inculturation emphasizes Africa's religio-cultural experiences as the starting point of theological discussion (Martey 1993: 69). Several African Christian contextual theologians have accepted inculturation as a praxis technique to create an authentic African Christian identity. The security of integrated identity, thus the ecumenical identity as a Christian and one's unique cultural identity (e.g., Ghanaian Christian), in African Christianity – both mainstream and independent churches – has been a matter of deliberate concern and growing consensus. There is a growing body of literature articulating themes of inculturation theology. Additionally, more and more African churches have embraced cultural integration, especially in the liturgy, as a mode of Christian expression. With this in mind, the concept of inculturation should be spared, if possible, of further criticism that it is a

---

[42] The 8th General Assembly of the WCC in Harare, Zimbabwe on Dec. 3-14, 1998. Press Release No. 23. http://www.wcc-coe.org/wcc/assembly/pre-23.html. Last visited April 30, 2020.

theological falsification, if not heresy. Instead, African theologians should strive to stimulate an in-depth understanding of Christianity and the formulation of applicable methods of evangelism in order to inculcate in Africans the relevance of Christ's message to their actual lives and its effect on the socio-economic and political sectors in society.

In the following sub-sections, I shall examine the events that led to the development of Africa's inculturation theology.

2.3.2.1.1. Contextualization of Ecclesial Models

The attempt to contextualize the gospel was liturgical in the early years of missionary activities. The resurgence of Christianity in Africa in the fifteenth century saw European expansion of the faith in Africa. Already established, both Catholics and Protestants carried out missionary endeavors in Africa. Early missionaries focused on indigenizing the liturgy to facilitate the reception of Christianity (Sanneh 1991: 160). Western philologists enhanced the transition of African indigenous languages from oral communication to literature. The effort to translate the Bible into indigenous languages became a prime agenda of the missionaries. By the end of the nineteenth century, many Africans could read the Bible in their own indigenous languages and could also defend their faith by the same means.[43] The training of indigenous missionaries and later translation of liturgical hymns into indigenous languages prepared the ground for the renewal of cultural ideas in the growth of the church in Africa.[44]

---

43 The Ugandan Luganda Bible was completed in 1894; the Malagasy of Madagascar Bible in 1830. The Oromo of Ethiopia New and Old Testaments Bible was completed between 1893 and 1899. The Bible was translated into Sotho, Xhosa, and Zulu South African languages between 1837 and 1883. The Yoruba Bible was first published in 1884 followed by later republication by the BFBS in 1900. The Akan Twi New Testament books were translated by Johann Gottlieb Christaller from 1857 to 1878 and published by the BFBS. Others such as Bemba (Zambia), Chinyanja (Malawi), Igbo (Nigeria), etc. were completed in the early twentieth century.

44 The assimilation of indigenous languages into missions became one of the most successful channels to legitimate Christianity in Africa. Further reading on Christianity's encounter with African indigenous languages and cultural values can found in Lamin Sanneh's book *Translating the Message: The Missionary Impact on Culture*, 157-208.

2.3.2.1.2. African Anthropology as a Rebirth of Africa's Cultural Values

Missionaries and colonial officials have made valuable contributions to African anthropology. Africans esteem their cultures, but they were never studied until the twentieth century when a heightened interest in Africa's social structures and cultural values emerged as worthy for documentation. The works of European historians and anthropologists on Africa laid the foundation for later indigenous anthropologists and also provided a roadmap for constructive cultural patterns and appreciation. African inculturation theology leans heavily on early Western anthropologists as their works provide a source for critical observation and "a theoretical basis for transforming traditional religion or, at least, for using some of its elements in the process of adapting Christianity" (Ilesanmi 1995: 58). Their descriptive studies of African cultures and religions, besides the criticism and biases, have helped shaped contemporary contextual studies.

2.3.2.1.3. The Rise of Africa's Nationalism

The struggle for liberation from colonization and neo-colonization paved the way for what has come to be known as the theology of cultural liberation or inculturation theology as it is technically known. Martey has identified politics, culture, and religion as significant stimulants for the emergence of African Contextual Theology, although other factors may apply (Martey 1993: 9). The struggle for independence from colonialism created socio-political and economic concerns that led to the rise of pan-Africanism and African nationalism. Pan-Africanism is an intellectual vigilant movement that aims at frustrating Western imperial influence in Africa. It has several modes of expression such as in Negritude by Léopold Sédar Senghor, a Senegalese poet, writer, and statesman. Negritude was an African solidarity movement against French imperialism. Ghana's philosophy of *sankofaism* is another example of pan-Africanism that seeks to return to Africa's past traditions to critically retrieve relevant traditions for the future. Several anti-apartheid movements in South Africa were sub-movements of pan-Africanism, such as the Pan Africanist Congress (PAC) and Black Consciousness Movement (BCM). Pan-Africanism, with its ideology of redeeming an authentic African identity and cultural experiences, has been a contributing factor to Africa's cultural renaissance.

2.3.2.1.4. Philosophical Decolonization as a Philosophy of Identity

A major influence of Africa's inculturation theology was the rise of theological philosophies and philosophies that began to question and to unearth Africa's cultural values through critical reflection. Ghanaian J. B. Danquah's classic work, *The Akan Doctrine of God* (1944), explores Akan anthropology, philosophy, and theology. African literary and artistic philosophers such as Ngũgĩ wa Thiong'o (Kenya), Wole Soyinka (Nigeria), Chinua Achebe (Nigeria), Okot p'Bitek (Uganda), and Taban Lo Liyong (Uganda), contributed significantly to the definition of an African personality. African philosophers like Kwasi Wiredu, Kwame Gyekye, and others have all called for a philosophical decolonization of African epistemologies which they think are more or less contaminated by Western ideas. These philosophers do not reject everything Western, rather, they call for the reclamation of authentic African epistemologies as a way of reconciling the spirituality of Africans with their cultural values. This endeavor thus raises questions regarding who or what is responsible for shaping the worldviews of Africans.

2.3.2.1.5. African Theological Hermeneutics as Inculturation

The rise of African theology and its hermeneutics of Africa's pre-Christian religion and culture as a source for theological discussion reached its zenith with the publication of *Des prêtres noirs s'interrogent* in 1956 (Martey 1993: 16; Bujo 1992: 5). This book is a collection of reflections on the churches in Africa by some African priests studying in Europe and is widely accepted as the starting point of modern African Contextual Theology. The greatest feat of this movement came from the Pan-African Conference of Third World Theologians in 1977 in Accra, during which African cultural realities and African traditional religions were considered sources of theology, as seen in the pioneering works of Charles Nyameti (Tanzania), Stephen Mulago (Congo), John Mbiti (Kenya), Kwesi Dickson (Ghana), and Bolaji Ndowu (Nigeria). By the early 1980s, the term inculturation had become widespread. The earliest usage of the term was in 1962 by Professor Joseph Masson of the Gregorian University in Rome, but it became popular after its definition by Father Arrupe, Superior General of the Jesuits, in

1978. Consequently, the term became a theological phrase in contemporary theology (Martey 1993: 67-68).[45]

In summary, African Christian contextual theologians have embraced the inculturation approach in order to define an African Christian identity more accurately. This identity transcends beyond religion and culture to incorporate political, educational, and literary ideologies of Africans. As a result, the inculturation agenda provides a framework through which theologians can effectively carry out Christian missions in Africa.

2.3.2.2. An Appraisal of the Theology of Inculturation

An appraisal of the theology of inculturation reveals that it is subject to criticism from both past and contemporary theologians. These critics can be divided into two main groups: universalists and progressivists. Universalists possess a static and unitary view of Christianity, rejecting the inculturation theology and insisting that it is a misguided effort (Ilesanmi 1995: 58, 59). Progressivists, on the other hand, criticize the methodologies and content of inculturation, not to reject it entirely, but to consider what is called inculturation theology for the present and future (Ilesanmi 1995: 59, 60). It is important to discuss these criticisms in their respective contexts to gain a better understanding of the theology of inculturation.

2.3.2.2.1. Universalists Criticism of Inculturation

The intellectual effort to explore the past religions of Africa with an eye to theologizing Christianity's assimilation in Africa was misconstrued as a resurrection of African traditional religions (Ilesanmi 1995: 59). This view was contested by the Qua Iboe Church of Eastern Nigeria, Pentecostal, and Charismatic movements, who adhered to the stance that the inculturation agenda represented a "heathen gospel," satanic doctrine, and an overt nationalist sentiment (Ilesanmi 1995: 59).

---

[45] Inculturation is defined by Father Pedro Arrupe as, "[T]he incarnation of Christian life and of the Christian message in a particular cultural context, in such a way that this experience not only finds expression through elements proper to the culture in question, but becomes a principle that animates, directs and unifies the culture, transforming it and remaking it so as to bring about a 'new creation'." Pedro Arrupe, "Letter to the Whole Society on Inculturation," AR 17 (1978), 230. Cited in Martey 1993: 88.

One of the most significant critics of inculturation theology was Byang Kato. Bediako, in his Theology and Identity, refers to Kato as a dissenting voice in modern African theology (Bediako, 1999: 391). Kato fervently promoted Scripture as the absolute word of God, enquiring, "Must one betray Scriptural principles and God's dealings with man in the name of any regional theology?" (Kato 1975: 16). Prior to his conversion to Christianity, Kato had been raised in a traditional religious (Jaba religion) family, which initiated him into the role of a traditional priest. This formational experience contributed to his vehement hostility towards traditional religions, which he saw as providing no "redemption or evidence of direct divine revelation" (Kato 1975: 44). It is because of this background that Kato takes a universalistic approach against African theology and branded the inculturation methodology as syncretistic universalism (Kato 1975).

However, it is not evident that Kato is entirely opposed to African realities; rather, he simply did not perceive a relationship between the traditional religions and the gospel (Kato 1975: 25). In his opinion, such an effort would lead to syncretism and invalidate the singular salvific power of Christ (Kato 1975: 175). Many African theologians of the inculturation school have viewed Kato as an attacker and rejectionist (Bediako 1992; Oduyoye 1986). Bediako, who reviewed Kato's response to African Theology, suggested that Kato had not successfully confronted "the identity problem of the modern African Christian" nor had he provided a suitable theological interpretation and insight into the religion and spirituality of the Jaba people (Bediako 1992: 386-387). Regardless of this criticism, Kato acknowledged the heightened appreciation for African theology, which has indisputably been successful (Kato 1975: 16).

Besides Kato, other early African authors like the Ugandan Okot p'Bitek, and Ali Mazrui (who wrote the epilogue of p'Bitek's book in 1970) have nicknamed both Mbiti and Idowu as "intellectual smugglers" who treat African traditional religions as subjective to contain Christian revelations without recognizing its unique spiritual experiences (p'Bitek 1970: 88).[46] P'Bitek did not only see inculturation theology as a threat to the

---

[46] Cited in Bediako 1992: 9. p'Bitek's intellectual smuggling could have best been descriptive if his argument was geared towards an acculturation agenda, which does not seem to be the case here. The expression of one's own contextual realities in the Christian faith cannot be smuggling unless one perceives Christianity as another culture; such characterization has been the struggle for African Contextual Christian Theology, which

uniqueness of the African traditional religions, but inappropriate to Christianity itself. Hence, Mazrui posits: "Why should African students of religion be so keen to demonstrate that the Christian God had already been understood and apprehended by Africans before the missionaries came?" (p'Bitek 1970: 127).[47] Bediako considers p'Bitek as by far the most incisive critic of the Christian interpretation of the African traditional religions (Bediako 1992: 9). However, Bediako also believes p'Bitek and others demonstrate the success of the essential thrust of the African theological enterprise (Bediako 1992: 9).[48]

2.3.2.2.2. Progressive Criticism of Inculturation

Besides the critical "objectors" (if the term "attackers" is too strong), progressive critics identify three main shortcomings of the theology of inculturation: 1) lack of methodological rigor, 2) naivety concerning definitional issues, and 3) disciplinary solipsism.[49]

1) Lack of Methodological Rigor

Although African theology has its own mode of expression and primary theological purpose, the quest to recast African traditional religions is often faced with a methodological crisis (Bediako 1996: 4). Jesse Mugambi, a Kenyan scholar of African Christianity and phenomenology of religions, has noted that African theology "is in a methodological crisis, owing to the lack of methodological consciousness" (Mugambi 2000: 69).[50] One such

is already the subject of a detailed discussion in Bediako's book *Theology and Identity* (1992).

47 Cited in Bediako, 1999: 9

48 Okot p'Bitek had feared the death of African traditional religions from the rushing floods of Eurocentric philosophies and ideologies that pose a threat to both Christianity and the traditional religions. He wrote: "Will the African deities survive the revolutions in science and philosophy which have killed the Christian God? I doubt it" (p'Bitek 1970: 112).

49 Ezra Chitando in discussing African traditional religions in African Contextual Christian Theology brought out these three main issues in the theology of inculturation (2006: 105).

50 Cited by (Chitando 2006).

methodological problem is the conceptual confusion between religious phenomenology and reductionism. Religious phenomenology is indispensable from inculturation theology since one need adequate knowledge about African traditional religions before proper inculturation can be achieved. However, phenomenology is descriptive and lacks theoretical criticism; it is religious studies by direct experience. Inculturation on the other hand uses a theological approach. It also employs reductionist approach to construct a theological thought for Christian missions.

Correctly understood, inculturation is not just another form of religious studies. Neither is it without religion. Inculturation is a theology seeking 'landing' within a given context. Hence, rigorous interpretation, reinterpretation, and criticism of the culture are embarked through the lens of Scripture to produce an inculturation theology. In this case, one would have to appreciate Kato's contribution to African theology that Scripture should take primacy as it communicates its mode of expression and authority over culture in order not for Scripture to become "one of many revelations rather than special revelation" (Kato 1975: 173).[51] Mbiti likewise affirms categorically that "nothing can substitute for the Bible" (Mbiti 1986: 59).[52]

---

51 God's revelation as explained by Kato is not only through Scripture. Like all evangelicals, Scripture is the special revelation of God. Kato maintains that there are revelations in nature which he terms as natural revelation.

52 Lesslie Newbigin (1909-1998), the British theologian and missiologist, had warned against starting contextual theology with culture. Newbigin has been a staunch European contextual theologian in the twentieth century, whose endearing legacy of 'missionary encounter with Western culture' to the Western church provides in-depth understanding of culture and contextualization. To Newbigin, biblical stories provide a useful context for dealing with culture. There is nothing more important than the primacy of Scripture in the contextualization of the Gospel. He emphasizes that scriptural truths are absolute and, therefore, superior to cultural ideas. This understanding is contrary to the Platonic understanding of truth as related to ideas. For Newbigin, the authority of Scripture must be surpassing all forms of societal ideas. This knowledge penetrates through the church that carries the Gospel to world societies. It is the church that is endowed with the judgment of both "No" and "Yes." He says: "True contextualization accords the Gospel its rightful primacy, its power to penetrate every culture and speak within each culture, in its own speech and symbol, the word which is both No and Yes, both judgment and grace." It is therefore not some cultural element that legitimates the contextualization of the Gospel. The Gospel has its mode of expression that pronounces its authority over cultural ideas. (*See* Newbigin 1989: 151-152).

Another methodological problem is critical engagement with African cultures. In one hand, inculturation is used as a means of criticizing Eurocentric hermeneutics that for so long has been the basis for theologizing in Africa.[53] On the other hand, inculturation shows that the fabrics of African cultures are worthy and compatible with the Christian message (Ilesanmi 1995: 52). These two are essential to the discipline of inculturation. However, they are not sufficient, particularly if inculturation is to be employed as a tool for retrospection. African Contextual Theologies must be willing to challenge African cultures, determining which aspects are appropriate for theologization and which are detrimental to modern social formations. African feminist theologians have, over the course of decades, engaged in the process of eradicating negative predispositions, such as aspects of patriarchy that are contrary to human rights and equality, though their efforts are often met with strong resistance from their male counterparts.

Further, inculturation hermeneutics face the problem of homogeneous synthesis of African cultures. Is there a thing called an "African culture?" Or we should start talking of plurality of cultures? Chitando draws attention to the fact that a homogenizing approach to African culture persists irrespective of alert-calls from feminists and other interest groups (Chitando 2006: 106). Africa is a huge continent comprising of about 54 internationally recognized states with each state diversified with complex socio-cultural experiences. Homogenization discourses ignore this complex diversity that also carries in itself implicit unique revelations. It is true that a lot has changed over the last few decades. Several African theologies have focused on regional hermeneutics rather than continental homogeneity.[54] Constructive inculturation approaches free from homogeneity are engaged in recent African theological works (Burton 2000; Aye-Addo 2013).

Lastly, African theologians are confronted with the challenge of present-day social dynamisms. The frequent reference to Africa's "past" has generated a static view of culture, which should not be the case because culture

---

53 Bediako discusses this in "Christianity as "Civilisation": The legacy of "The Third Opportunity" and Making of a Modern Identity Problem" in his *Theology and Identity* (Bediako 1992: 225-266).

54 Recent African contextual studies, such as Musopole's *Being Human in Africa: Toward an African Christian Anthropology*, systematize the *munthu* concept of Malawi in developing an African theological anthropology. Robert Agyarko's "'Sunsum 'The Spirit of Life: Pneumatology in the (Akan) West Africa Context" explores the spiritual worldviews of the Akan people.

is dynamic and ever evolving. Each generation is faced with its own socio-cultural questions, such as those relating to post-modernism, sexuality (LGTBQI), the ordination of women, scientism, transhumanism, etc. These inevitable trends in the global sphere should inform the methodological consciousness of African theologians, prompting them to adapt their methods to meet contemporary questions.

2) Concerning Definitional Issues

The question asked here is whether African theologians have a definite mode of semantic expression. Chitando thinks African theologians are wobbling in a definition crisis and further remarks that there is lack of clarity concerning the meaning, nature, and task of African theology (Chitando 2006: 106). Several arguments exist in the usage of the various terms employed. Over the decades, African theologians had to struggle with terminologies such as adaptation, enculturation, indigenization, and acculturation, until inculturation became preponderant as a missiological approach (Byrne 1990). Again, several names have been proposed in place of the term "African theology." I do not take this problem for granted. African theology, herein referred to as African Contextual Theology (ACT), has been proposed to define the reinterpretation of the gospel in a specific cultural context. Chitando had proposed "African Christian theology," but this trademark is too vague and broad to define what is understood as an African theology. Up to this time, the term "African theology" is not too awkward to use – although insufficient to define what is referred to in my present work as African Contextual Theology. The present terminological variances or contradictions point towards the fact that a rigorous preoccupation of the discipline is a work in progress other than "a discipline that is unsure of itself" (Chitando 2006: 107).

3) Lack of Disciplinary Solipsism

Critics accuse African theologians of lack of disciplinary solipsism as a result of too much focus on African traditional religions. Chitando, for instance, argues that African theologians should gear towards multidisciplinary approaches that will help to reposition Christian theology in the academy and to help it to attain relevant significance. One relevant problem

Chitando raises is the threat of "thoroughgoing criticism of Christianity in Africa by African intellectuals and creative writers" (Chitando 2006: 107). Given this observation, African churches stand accused of lack of Christian apologetics. Again, African theology has been mainly a discipline of systematic theology and ethics. Other areas of theological concentration, such as the history of Christianity and the study of the Old and New Testament, have received comparatively little attention, and when this focus is maintained, it is often characterized by denominational biases. African Bible scholars like John Mbiti and Bolaji Idowu have taken contextual interpretation that leaves the historical and critical analysis of biblical text to suffer. African theologians should take serious consideration to Western scholarship as a source of theological engagement in the wider ecumenical spheres of multidisciplinary and interdisciplinary theological scholarship to avoid being accused of "sequestrating and ghettoizing African Christian theology" (Chitando 2006: 107).

2.4. Summary

This chapter has looked at the phenomenal growth of Christianity in sub-Saharan Africa that has given way to a neo-scholastic engagement between theology and culture. What has come to be known as African Theology, herein referred to as African Contextual Theology or African Contextual Christian Theology, is Africa's theological contextualization of religious faith and practices in Africa. The primary purpose of African Contextual Christian Theology is to express the Gospel in terms that are consistent with the various African worldviews, in order to facilitate Christian practice and ecumenical dialogue. The academic driving force behind this has been keen in current African theological discourses. Several African theologians accept that the Gospel should be communicated in ways that become relevant to Africans. Proponents such as Mbiti, Idowu, Nyameti, Dickson, and Bediako, after examining African traditional religions, have pointed out that African religions are resourceful for the practice of Christian faith. Their overall theological works show that African cultures and religions are worthy and compatible with the Christian message, and therefore should be a medium for Christian missiology in Africa.

Two main approaches have been identified in the African theological enterprise: liberation theology and feminist theology. Liberation approach addresses socio-economic and political injustices in Africa and is most predominantly practiced as a response to apartheid in South Africa. Encompassed within liberation theology, theologians seek to speak of Jesus Christ as the liberator of the oppressed, using the Christian faith as the foundation upon which to address unjust concerns. This approach is often reactive to Eurocentric and patristic ideologies prevalent in African societies.

The second and oldest approach is inculturation theology, widely accepted by African contextual theologians as an incarnation of the Gospel in a particular cultural context. However, some critics view this concept as syncretistic universalism, or an attempt to create a common world faith combining elements of different religions. While I do claim that inculturation methodology is not a form of syncretism, I have also identified certain tendencies within some inculturation circles. If the incarnation of Christ is taken seriously to define the substance of inculturation, African contextual theologians must consider Christ in all aspects of His humanity, yet, as the Son of God (Philippians 2:6-8). In that way, the Gospel can be expressed in the worldviews of those in reception without losing its salvific power or missiological intent. By following such a methodologically conscious approach, Christianity can maintain its presence in Africa.

PART II

THEOLOGICAL DISCOURSE ON SUNSUM AND A PROPOSAL TOWARD A NEW CONTEXTUAL AKAN PNEUMATOLOGY

GYE NYAME
"Except God"
Adinkra symbol of Akan theology signifying the supremacy of God

3. Sunsum Pneumatology

> *"God's Spirit, the Holy Spirit, is not only a power by which God once upon a time intervened in past worlds and made Godself knowable. God's Spirit, the Holy Spirit, is also the power and the force by which God intervenes in constantly new ways in the present world and makes Godself knowable to people living in the present and in the future"* – Michael Welker (1994: 4).

3.1. Introduction

Before we delve further into any discussion of *sunsum* in this volume, it is important for us to reflect on the meaning of *sunsum*. Akan pneumatology is largely based on the concept of *sunsum*, which has been translated in various ways such as spirit, soul, character, and conscience, among other terms. It has been described as the essence of being, the inner spark that animates life and inspires one's experiences. The concept of *sunsum* is deeply rooted in traditional Akan cosmology and worldviews and plays a central role in the interpretation of life and the spirituality of the Akan people. *Sunsum* is inseparable from the traditional Akan value system, principles, and ethics. Thus, at the core of the Akan cultural ethos lies an inherent respect and reverence for the *sunsum*, which is seen as the source and determinant of a person's character, self-identity, and behavior. *Sunsum* is a unique concept, as it transcends the physical and material aspects of life. It is considered to be the all-encompassing, transcendent, and ultimate source of the good life. To comprehensively understand *sunsum*, it is important to first categorize its various characteristics.

The first characteristic of *sunsum* is its cosmological or ecological nature. It is believed that everything created possesses *sunsum*, which is a mystical and non-empirical vital force. This means that *sunsum* is present in all living and non-living things. The Akan people perceive *sunsum* as a kind of force, or the Akan word "tumi" which means power. *Sunsum* is also believed to animate the elements of the universe, from natural objects like trees and mountains to every spiritual existence in the Akan worldviews. It is thought that *sunsum* operates from the non-physical realm and can be affected by both the spiritual and physical environment. It is also believed to be a form of energy that exists at the heart of all organic forms and is deeply connected to the unborn before their entrance into the universe.

The second characteristic of *sunsum* is its theological aspect, which considers the Akan God, Nana Onyankopon, as the highest Spirit-being, all-powerful, all-pervading, and all-penetrating through the creation in the form of *sunsum*. This aspect of *sunsum* was enhanced in various ways by the emergence of "spiritual churches" and Pentecostal churches in Ghana in the mid-twentieth century, who saw *sunsum* as the power and Spirit of God. The concept of *sunsum* has since been adopted by some Christian scholars as the basis of Christian pneumatology, referring to the Holy Spirit as Onyame *Sunsum*. Besides God, all the spiritual entities in the Akan worldviews, such as deities and spirits of the living dead, are referred to as *sunsum* because of their essence as non-perceptible.

The third and most common understanding of *sunsum* is its anthropological aspect. This view believes that *sunsum* is an essence of human beings, an intrinsic dynamic that shapes one's character and life. The primary expression of the *sunsum* is associated with the individual's physical and spiritual health. Therefore, the *sunsum* has the power to determine one's well-being and prosperity in the physical world. Thus, the concept of *sunsum* is often seen as something that not only has the potential to shape one's destiny, but also cast an individual's destiny in a larger cosmic context. Beliefs in fate, luck and superstition are heavily informed by the concept of *sunsum*, in which the individual's spiritual and material destiny is considered to be intertwined with the power of the *sunsum*. In addition, *sunsum* is associated with various other metaphysical, esoteric, and spiritual aspects of life. For instance, it is believed to be responsible for prophecy, divination, and various other forms of spiritual healing. Further, the *sunsum* is believed to be the most fragile and vulnerable part of a person subject to spiritual attacks. As such, it is believed to require the utmost respect and delicate handling in order to ensure that the individual's life is enriched and fulfilled. The *sunsum* predisposes each person to take care to maintain the balance between the physical and spiritual aspects of life. This is done by engaging in both spiritual and physical practices such as religious practices and socialization to maintain a healthy *sunsum*.

The Akan have various ways in which they seek to incorporate the power of the *sunsum* into their daily lives. For example, certain rituals, invocations, and prayers are used in an effort to appease the *sunsum*, and many traditional Akan religious activities are performed in an effort to appease the *sunsum* and ensure that its benevolent influence is at work in an individual's life.

3.2. Toward a contextual Akan Christian pneumatology

The current contextual Akan Christian pneumatology is the work of the Ghanaian theologian Robert Owusu Agyarko. So far, he is the pioneer scholar to contribute a systematic contextualization of the Holy Spirit to Akan studies and research. His background as a Pentecostal, combined with theological scholarship, has made him a passionate and valuable contributor to pneumatological discourses in Africa. He has researched several dimensions of Akan pneumatology, ranging from ecological theology to Christological pneumatology.

Agyarko's contribution to African pneumatology is a theological reflection on Akan religious ideas. The value of his works, in fact, lies in his positive attitude towards traditional Akan religion and his hermeneutical approach, which is an inculturation methodology, towards the construction of a contextual Christian pneumatology. Agyarko uses Akan religion as a raw material for theological reflection, something from which early missionaries and subsequent theologians have shied away. By this approach, he braced with the late Kwame Bediako who championed the need to treat Africa's pre-Christian religion as a hermeneutical principle for Africa's contextual theology to define an African Christian identity. Bediako always believed that there are revelations in African traditional religions that speak profoundly of African identity, and therefore he urged African theologians to retrieve them to deal with the question of identity on the continent. The thrust of Bediako's proposal leads to the creation of a distinctive Christian identity that will depend largely on the right of Africans to own and maintain their identity against any Eurocentric assimilation (Bediako 1992,

1995). Agyarko's attempt to develop a contextual Akan Christian pneumatology reflects these methodological insights to recast Africa's implicit pneumatology into a coherent theological discourse for Christian faith, practice, and learning.

In the next sections, I will review Agyarko's contextual pneumatology as it is necessary to ensure a better understanding of his Akan pneumatological construction. The appraisal begins by looking at the basis of his contextual understanding of pneumatology. This will comprise the definition and nature of spirits and the spiritual in Akan cosmology, and further, an analysis of his methodology for the construction of a contextual Christian pneumatology for Akan people.

3.3. *Sunsum* as Onyame *Sunsum*

The basis of Agyarko's pneumatology is the Akan concept of *sunsum*. In the introduction of his paper, "'Sunsum' The Spirit of Life: Pneumatology in the Akan West Africa Context," he pinpoints that the "Akan notion of *sunsum* may form the basis for contextual pneumatology" which intends to "enable one to speak of the Holy Spirit and its relation both to God and to nature" (Agyarko 2014: 1). Thus, Agyarko takes a positive approach towards Akan religions, and dares to claim that biblical pneumatology can have a contextual reinterpretation to suit the context.

Agyarko treats *sunsum* as the essence of natural objects which enables the being or object to exercise power and to function in its characteristic manner. To Agyarko, *sunsum*, "so necessary to existence, is not conceived as an indwelling spirit foreign to the object in which it resides. Rather, *sunsum* is the very essence of the object; it is its intrinsic activating principle" (Agyarko 2014: 7). Agyarko's understanding of *sunsum* as the principle of an intrinsic activation follows that of Gyekye, who defined the principle of activation as an active force that causes natural objects to exercise activity. Or, as Gyekye puts it, "activity is a property intrinsic to matter, that is, natural objects; it is the essence of natural objects to be active, to possess power" (Gyekye 1987: 75). Thus, to the Akan, natural objects are not just material or inert. They are, rather, inspirited. This conception of inspirited objects leads Gyekye to characterize the Akan worldviews with *panpsychism*, i.e., everything, being animate or inanimate, is conscious.

Unlike Gyekye, Agyarko prefers to describe the Akan worldviews with *panentheism*, i.e., the immanence of God in all-things or what he terms as "a conscious vitality" (Agyarko 2013: 10).

The idea of a panentheistic cosmology is central to Agyarko's spiritual conception of Akan realities. He categorizes his spiritual understanding into three main aspects: "the *Sunsum* of *Onyame*, the *sunsum* of human beings, and *sunsum* of non-human nature" (Agyarko 2014: 7). The *Sunsum* of Onyame (spelled with a capital "S") or the Spirit of God, is the ultimate source of all *sunsum*.[55] Thus, the *Sunsum* of *Onyame* is divine, whereas that of humans and non-human forms embodies sparks of the divine. The distinction Agyarko makes captures Akan's cosmic perspective and realism of the pervasiveness and interpenetration of *sunsum* which "expresses how the 'one' (*Onyame*) and the 'many' (nature including human beings) are related" (Agyarko 2014: 7). All these justify his conception of *sunsum* as panentheistic, and further designate the *Sunsum* of *Onyame* as distinct yet inseparable from *Onyame*, an eternal and absolute Being manifesting its nature in individual creatures (Agyarko 2012, 2014). Thus, *sunsum* becomes the basis of the relationship between creation and the Creator because all things belong to God. In that regard, Agyarko emphasizes the distinct nature of *sunsum* to come to terms with Helaine Minkus' categories of *sunsum* of the exclusively spiritual (*ye sunsum*) comprising God, lesser deities, ancestors, spirits, etc. and the inspirited (*wɔ sunsum*) comprising human beings and non-human objects (Minkus 1980). Agyarko does not confuse the two categories.

Against this background, one can understand the pneumatological context that shapes Agyarko's contextual pneumatology. He comes to the following conclusion:

> The concept of *sunsum* therefore enables one to speak of the Holy Spirit and its relation both to God and to nature. This may also enable one to understand the Holy Spirit as cosmic in nature and as divine in being. *Sunsum* as an anthropological and also as ecological concept will help our understanding of the *Sunsum* of *Onyame*. The reason is that the Akan speculate less about the *Sunsum* of *Onyame* than about *sunsum* in human and

55 *Sunsum* of Onyame is equal to Onyame *Sunsum*, the well-known expression modern Akan people use to speak of the divine power or Spirit.

> nonhuman nature. Nonetheless, the Akan usually infer the nature and operations of the *Sunsum* of *Onyame* from *sunsum* found in nature and, more particularly, the *sunsum* found in a human person (Agyarko 2014: 7, 8).

The Holy Spirit, in Agyarko's pneumatology, is *Sunsum* of Onyame, the spark of creation and life that proceeds from God yet is a distinct being.

3.4. *Sunsum* in Agyarko's Anthropology

The established understanding of the divine nature of *sunsum* as *Onyame Sunsum* explains why human beings also have *sunsum*, a notion that describes the spiritual part of every human being. The *Sunsum of Onyame* is the locus to trace the extent of God's sovereignty over the entire creation. Thus, *sunsum* serves as the ultimate conduit through which the omnipotence and omnipresence of God interpenetrate the creation, and for the creation itself to depend on the *Sunsum* of God. Agyarko's anthropology seeks to extract from this divine transcendence to establish the fact that human beings are not in isolation from the dynamic nature of *Sunsum of Onyame*.

Agyarko understands the Akan concept of the human being to consist of two principal entities or substances, namely: spiritual or non-material, and material. The spiritual consists of *ɔkra* (the soul or bearer of destiny), *sunsum* (spirit or personality) and *ntorɔ* (fatherhood), while the material consists of *mogya* (blood) from the mother. Here, Agyarko does not list the *nipadua* (body) as a material component of the human being for unspecified reasons. He refers to *ɔkra* and *sunsum* as descending directly from God, whereas *ntorɔ* is derived from the biological father and *mogya* from the biological mother. In previous analysis, some scholars have identified both *ntorɔ* and *mogya* as biogenetic physical elements making their roles more social than spiritual contrary to Agyarko's conception of the *ntorɔ*.

I think Agyarko's grouping of *ɔkra*, *sunsum*, and *ntorɔ* as spiritual is correct although *ntorɔ* has a physical presence as the semen that a male transmits during sexual intercourse with a female. For the most part, however, the majority of scholars have linked *ntorɔ* directly to the pantheon deities (Rattray 1927: 154; 1929: 8; Meyerowitz 1951a: 24, 25; Busia 1954: 196-198; Ephirim-Donkor 2016: 82). Agyarko ascertains this fact with a more vivid explanation: "From the myth of the first *ntoro* ever bestowed upon the Akan the *Bosommuru ntoro* – it could be deduced that *ntoro*, though genetically associated with human fatherhood, is a spiritual entity that originated directly from God" (Agyarko 2014: 9).[56] Busia thinks all spiritual power derives indirectly from God (Busia 1954: 198, 100).[57]

As for the meaning of the *sunsum*, the characteristics given to it, according to Agyarko, are based on his own "reconstruction and adaptation of traditional Akan thinking on how *sunsum* may be understood" (2014: 8). Why he does that is his attempt "to lay a foundation to help reinterpret the status and position of *sunsum* as a dynamic equivalent of the Christian concept of the Holy Spirit" (2014: 8). There are more characteristics of the *sunsum* given by Agyarko within the scope of Akan anthropology.

3.4.1. The Meaning of Sunsum in Agyarko's Anthropology

The basic idea of *sunsum* in Agyarko's anthropology is a pneumatic character, i.e., spirit or personality. That means one must see it as an intangible element or the spiritual part of each human being (also in all forms of life). As a personality, it accounts for the character disposition and intelligence of the individual (Agyarko 2014: 8). A person's individuality is thus established by *sunsum*, his spiritual disposition. In spite of this, there are variations to this spiritual disposition due to the dynamic nature of *sunsum*. Agyarko writes: "*Sunsum* is subject to change, for it is capable of being trained from the state of being 'light' (*ne sunsum ye hare*) to a heavier weight (*ne sunsum ye duru*: literally, his *sunsum* is heavy)" (Agyarko 2014:

---

56 *Bosommuru* is a compound of *Bosom* (god) and *Muru* (name of a river), together meaning the god of the River *Muru*. The location of the river is disputed. Rattray, for instance, located it in the Akyim area (Rattray 1923: 47). Meyerowitz identifies *Buru* or *Muru* with the god of the great river in Niger, where she thinks the royal Oyoko clan in the Ashanti region first settled. According to Meyerowitz, Danquah thought "the Bosommuru River cannot be found on this earth but it is with Adu Gyamfi, god and king of the nether world." (Meyerowitz 1951: 30). Danquah's account traces the river to Bodwesango, a town in the Asante region during Adu Gyamfi's lifetime. Danquah's account has been contested by Meyerowitz as an invention (Meyerowitz 1951: 30).

57 By linking *ɔkra*, *sunsum*, and *ntorɔ* directly with God, Agyarko suppresses the role of the *Abosom* in the conception of children, a fundamental idea in Akan anthropology. Not only that, but he also seems to take a backseat on the role of the *Abosom* in Akan religious ideas.

8). The vice versa is also true as the majority of Akan will say, *Ne sunsum so ate*, literally, "He is low-spirited."

There are other characteristics of *sunsum* that Agyarko affirms, including the nightly peregrination of a person's *sunsum* during sleep. Agyarko remarks that the *sunsum* can take leave of the body while a person is asleep and may not return for some time (Agyarko 2014: 8). It can also be knocked about by evil forces; this happens because the *sunsum* is the vulnerable part of the human being that is subject to attacks of witchcraft. The pneumatic emphasis of *sunsum* enables it to survive death. Agyarko agrees with the fact that the final departure of *sunsum* signifies the death of the person. However, he thinks *sunsum* does not perish with the dead person, but returns to Onyame (God), its source (Agyarko 2014: 8). I think this latter account is Agyarko's own reconstruction (if not a Christianized account of Akan realities) and is contestable against the positions of the majority of Akan scholars who unanimously do not relate the departure of *sunsum* with God.

In summary, Agyarko sees the interrelatedness of *ɔkra*, *sunsum* and *ntorɔ* as inseparable, although each represents a distinct vital force in the human being. They work in harmony and there is no subordination between them. Such non-subordination is expressed in the fact that the "permanent absence of any one of these connotes the death of a person. To the Akan, one is a human being only when one possesses all these three components together with *mogya*" (Agyarko 2014: 9). The overall study of *sunsum* by Agyarko leads to the conclusion that unlike *ɔkra* and *ntorɔ,* which are identical to human beings, all individual creatures possess *sunsum* – this makes *sunsum* a cosmic reality. The cosmic reality of the eternal *sunsum* and the creation "suggests not juxtaposition but interpenetration;" this makes "nature as *necessarily* open to the dimensions of transcendence" (Agyarko 2014: 9).

With this conclusion, Agyarko offers a new pneumatological proposal for African churches and theological schools, herein identified as contextual Akan Christian pneumatology based on *sunsum*. The identification of *sunsum* with the essence of God and as the basis of Akan spirituality leads Agyarko to theologize the Holy Spirit as Onyame *Sunsum*. The question we need to consider is: how does Agyarko arrive at this conclusion? In the following sections, I will present a review of his methodology for developing a contextual Akan Christian pneumatology based on the concept of *sunsum*.

3.4.2. Agyarko's Methodology

The basis of Agyarko's methodology is grounded in the Nicene and Chalcedon Creeds; he argues that African Christianity is largely pro-Nicene/Chalcedon. Although Agyarko points out key theologians such as Piet Schoonenberg, Edward Schillebeeckx, Hans Küng, Ellen Flesseman-van Leer, William Robinson, Wolfhart Pannenberg, James Dunn, and others for rejecting the Chalcedon Christology, he is convinced that the Nicene/Chalcedon confessions permit a responsible engagement of theological reflection on Christology and pneumatology for Africa churches. Therefore, Agyarko argues that "the church in African would gain much by standing with Nicene/Chalcedon which is duly represented in the tradition of mainline Christianity rather than an individual Christian Christological and Pneumatological proposals which are in conflict with the ecumenical councils" (Agyarko 2014: 3). He dismisses any personal proposal that may potentially conflict with these dogmatic creeds, which he touts as firmly rooted in scripture, especially the pneumatological affirmation of the Holy Spirit in the Nicene/ Chalcedon Creed.

How biblical is the Nicene/Chalcedon affirmation of biblical pneumatology? This is the question that Agyarko grapples with to strengthen his methodology, particularly the explanation of the ambivalent usage of "God as Holy Spirit, and God the Holy Spirit," which to him "requires a historical account of the Biblical and patristic developments" to set out a "systematic exposition of pneumatological doctrine" (Agyarko 2014: 3). He makes the two approaches compatible and complementary as he employs the Old Testament pneumatology of "'the Spirit of God' or 'the Spirit of the Lord'" to indicate "a distinction-in-identity that will eventually allow the Christian church, after the coming of Christ and the Pentecostal outpouring of 'Holy Spirit', to elaborate its doctrinal in a Trinitarian direction" (Agyarko 2014: 3, 4). The other approach entails the patristic Trinitarian affirmations of the nature of Christ and the Holy Spirit in the Nicene/Chalcedon/Constantinople councils, which also became the basis of Christology and pneumatology in Africa for the early missionaries. Consequently, "the church in West Africa has subsequently remained largely pro-Nicene/Chalcedonian," which is why Agyarko interrogates, "would it not be more appropriate, if one wants to engage in responsible theological reflection, to set the Nicene/Chalcedon confessional definition of the person of Christ as the appropriate point of reference for a contextualised Pneumatology?" (Agyarko 2014: 3). Agyarko answers with a firm yes since he thinks that the pneumatology of the Nicene/Chalcedon confessions is firmly rooted in the Scripture. Indeed, this conclusion confirms his dogmatic methodology even if it is against the consideration of widely varying contextual, historical, or situational influences of the Hellenistic culture in patristic traditions.

3.4.2.1. Niceno-Constantinopolitan Creed on the Holy Spirit

The strength of Agyarko's methodology comes from his analysis of the Niceno-Constantinopolitan Creed in 381. The Nicene Creed in 325 "had been content to confess belief in the Holy Spirit by the simple affirmation 'and in the Holy Spirit'" (Agyarko 2014: 5). The mention of the Holy Spirit in the Creed was more of an affirmation of a fundamental belief without much theological clarity; this is because the doctrine of the Holy Spirit was less of a concern to the Church fathers than the threats of Arianism concerning the incarnation of Christ. The expansion of the Nicene Creed occurred at the Council of Constantinople with the objective and purpose of renewing the Nicene Creed due to the emergence of further heresies in post-Nicene about the personality of Christ and the Holy Spirit. The Niceno-Constantinopolitan Creed added "certain phrases functionally equivalent to defining the deity of the third person of the Trinity in the way that Nicaea had done in respect of the second, the Son" (Agyarko 2014: 5). The Creed reads:

> And in the Holy Ghost, the Lord and Giver of life, who proceeds from the Father and the Son, who with the Father and the Son together is worshiped and glorified, who spake by the prophets.[58]

The Niceno-Constantinopolitan Creed "is clear that 'the Holy Spirit' is a Name, or an element in the Triune Name of Father, Son and Holy Spirit in which baptisms took place (see Matthew 28:19)" (Agyarko 2014: 5). Beyond that is the ontological union between the Spirit and the Father: τὸ ἐκ

[58] "and the Son" a later addition by the Western Catholic Church.

τοῦ Πατρὸς ἐκπορευόμενον, "Who proceeds from the Father."[59] The Spirit is identified with the Father and the Son as a personality by the exclusive attributes of "the Lord" and "giver of life." The assumption can be made that the Spirit is not created but is one in substance with the Father and the Son. The Nicene phrase ὁμοούσιον τῷ Πατρί, "of one essence with the Father" is not used in connection with the Holy Spirit, but as Agyarko suggests, "the implication is that the Paraclete also is 'consubstantial with the Father'" (Agyarko 2014: 5).

This leads to the next assumption, which is the distinctive nature of the Spirit from the Father and the Son. The Spirit is worshiped and glorified in the same way as the Father and the Son. Agyarko writes: "To worship is to regard as divine, and the only proper recipient of worship is the one true God. Here, then, is a further confession of the Holy Spirit's divine being and personal character" (Agyarko 2014: 5). The hypostatic character of the Spirit makes it capable of receiving worship. The character given to the Father, the Son, and the Holy Spirit unites them in one consubstantial reality,[60] in agreement with Athanasius' Creed: "all three Persons are coeternal together and coequal, so that in all things, as said before, the Unity in Trinity and the Trinity in Unity is to be worshiped."[61] Hence, Agyarko concludes:

> Within mainstream (Trinitarian) Christianity the Holy Spirit is one of the three *persons* of the Trinity who make up the single substance of God. As such the Holy Spirit is personal, and as part of the Godhead, he is fully God, co-equal and co-eternal with God the Father and Son of God. He is different from the Father and the Son in that he *proceeds* from the Father (or from the Father and the Son) as described in the Nicene Creed (Agyarko 2014: 6).

59 The phrase corresponds to the Christological affirmation of the Son in the Nicene Creed: ἐκ τοῦ Πατρὸς γεννηθέντα, meaning "begotten of the Father."

60 The "consubstantial" theory of the Holy Spirit was first introduced by Gregory Nazianzus in 380 in defense of the divinity of the Spirit. He claimed the Holy Spirit is God though distinct (*Orationes theologicae*, 31, 10). Tertullian had earlier associated the Spirit with God, even as same as God (*Prax*. 4.1, 13. 6).

61 Athanasius was an outspoken figure in the debate over the person of Christ against the Arians during the council of Nicene in 325.

From this background, Agyarko contends that "the concept of spirit as person and active force is encountered in many African societies" (Agyarko 2014: 6). In response, he sees the need to articulate a theological reflection that emerges from a (re)-reading of biblical texts, Christian tradition, as well as from the African cultural context as an essential theological task "in order to develop an indigenous African Christian Pneumatology that will directly relate to Christology and Trinity" (Agyarko 2014: 7). Consequently, his constructive Akan pneumatology has sought "to retrieve and reinterpret concepts in African traditional culture from a Christian perspective" to theologize the Akan notion of the *sunsum* "as a contribution towards ecumenical discourse on pneumatology" (Agyarko 2014: 7).

3.4.3. *Sunsum* as a Christian Theological Concept

Agyarko argues in favor of *sunsum* as a Christian theological concept since it is the dynamic equivalent of the biblical notion of πνεῦμα, making the concept of *sunsum* not alien to the Judeo-Christian tradition (Agyarko 2014: 10). However, he does not base his argument on how adequate *sunsum* is semantically to articulate biblical pneumatology. Much of his argument is an ecumenical approach based on the Niceno-Constantinopolitan Creed's definition of the Holy Spirit.

Agyarko draws much inspiration from the consubstantial notion of the Holy Spirit as God to lay a Trinitarian foundation for contextual Akan Christian pneumatology. His proposal follows that the "creation as the sparks of God's *sunsum* highlights the activity of God the Holy Spirit (*Onyame Sunsum*) that is inseparable from God the Father (*Onyame Ntoro*) and the Son (*Onyame Okra*) in creation and redemption" (Agyarko 2014: 12). Therefore, "[b]y way of *perichoresis* (the essential interrelatedness of okra, sunsum, and ntoro) sunsum has a trinitarian character. By joining the three 'persons' in creating, everything becomes interwoven with relationship, interdependencies, and webs of inter-communication" (Agyarko 2014: 12). Thus, Agyarko concludes, *sunsum* is "consubstantial" with the Father (*homoousios to Patri*), and hence, the Holy Spirit should be best known among Akan people as Onyame *Sunsum*. With regards to that conclusion, Agyarko indicates that African religious doctrines shed light or meet with Christian doctrines.

In summary, Agyarko is a precursor of contextual Christian pneumatology in postcolonial theology in West Africa. I find his contextual pneumatology genuinely impressive. He studies and theologizes *sunsum* as a pneumatological concept to define Akan ontology and cosmology and, more importantly, for Christian faith and practices. Agyarko argues that the majority of Akan people believe *sunsum* is a vital force, power, spirit, and signifies purity and everlasting. Everything that exists in its natural state possesses *sunsum*, which enables the object to exercise power. Onyame, the Akan God, is *Sunsum* because Onyame is the highest spirit-being. Onyame transcends time, is all powerful, all-pervading, and all-penetrating, making Onyame the source of life who endows all the creation, including human beings, with an activating principle called *sunsum*. There is no life without *sunsum*. Onyame's *sunsum* permeates the creation and makes Onyame sensible to human beings. From this background, Agyarko uses the concept of *sunsum* to suggest solidarity in terms of community of the whole creation – both solidarity between God and nature and solidarity within nature (Agyarko 2014: 12). The communal ontology results from the unifying force of *sunsum* which is also analogous to the work of the Holy Spirit in the world. Therefore, the Akan concept of *sunsum* permits a responsible discussion of contextual Akan pneumatology where the Holy Spirit is known as *Sunsum* of Onyame.

3.5. The future of Agyarko's Contextual Pneumatology

Agyarko has proposed and formulated a pneumatological doctrine that makes one speak of a contextual Akan Christian pneumatology. His proposal articulates a "pneumatological ecumenism" whereby God, being the source of all things, interpenetrates and bonds the universe together through His eternal spirit, herein *sunsum* in Akan cosmology. In doing that, he has shown an awareness that the Akan culture and religion can engage Christian thought and practice. Agyarko's commitment to scholarship and to the church is important for two key reasons:

First, Agyarko has given the field of the doctrine of the Holy Spirit a renewed focus in Africa. Over the years, the study of the Holy Spirit has been neglected, and now that Agyarko has helped to draw it back into the theological discourse, pneumatology has seen an upturn. My first encounter with Agyarko was at the International Conference on Pneumatology and Contextual Theology held at the University of Geneva in 2014. When he introduced the concept of *sunsum* as a theological subject, I was intrigued to learn more. And because of the strong possibility of future prospects in this area, I made the decision to specialize in Akan pneumatology.

Second, the work of Agyarko is of benefit to African churches in understanding the operation of the Spirit. Most African cultures consider reality to originate in spirit phenomena rather than ordinarily experience. Many continue to hold on to the idea of an inspirited world. Thus, the belief in God, pantheon deities, ancestors, and other spirits are not just abstract concepts, but reality to the Akan. This has changed the African way of thinking when it comes to Christianity. Many Christians exhibit characteristics of faith commonly associated with the African traditional religions. Agyarko's adeptness in working on the work of the Holy Spirit from an African context provides African Christians with greater understanding of God's involvement among their lives.

3.6. Summary and Critique of *Sunsum* Pneumatology

This chapter has offered an appraisal of Agyarko's contextual Akan pneumatology. The purpose has been to express an appreciation for his recent contribution to contextual Akan pneumatology, and to the overall pneumatological discourse in Africa. In view of the foregoing contextual pneumatology, I propose a few suggestions to be considered in future studies.

First, Agyarko was able to do justice to his ecumenical methodology. However, the ecumenical characterization of the Holy Spirit is not sufficient to construct a contextual pneumatology for reasons that it disregards other confessional definitions of the Holy Spirit. For example, Jehovah's Witnesses disregard the personage of the Holy Spirit and regard the Spirit as an extension of God's power, his active force (www.jw.org). Likewise, the Church of Jesus Christ of Latter-Day Saints (LDS) regards the Holy Spirit as "a personage of spirit, without a body of flesh and bones." Even though the LDS Church are Trinitarians, their teaching about the Godhead differs widely from traditional Christianity or Catholicism. They reject the Holy Spirit as being one in substance with the Father and the Son though they believe in subordinationism, affirming the unity of the three as "fully one in love, purpose and will" (www.churchofjesuschrist.org). The problem is to what extent can the current proposal for contextual pneumatology be ecumenical.

Second, it can also be noted that the nature of the Holy Spirit, as a personality from the ecumenical creed, makes its work more specific than being a substance in creation. Agyarko seems to sympathize with the assumption that the Holy Spirit is a substance in creation in the same manner as *sunsum* is active or the principle of activation in natural objects. If so, then why does the prophet promise an outpouring of the Spirit? The famous prophecy of Joel 2:28 – concerning the future fellowship of the Spirit with "all flesh" – signifies that the *modus operandi* of the Spirit is neither ontological relationality nor substantial. In both the Old and New Testament, we find specific activities of the Spirit such as alighting, i.e., a foreign spiritual agent descending on an individual. This experience is also true of the Akan religions where instances of spirit alighting throw the *Ɔkɔmfoɔ* (traditional priest) into a trance status. It suggests that even in the Akan religions, some aspects of spiritual experiences are specific.

Third, given the nature of the spirit from biblical pneumatology as רוּחַ and πνεῦμα, one should question whether *sunsum* can capture the essence of the spirit as wind, breath, or moving air. The basis for the *Sunsum Kronkron* pneumatology is the fact that the Spirit proceeds from the Father and the Son, and that the Spirit is consubstantial with the Father and the Son just as a person derives *sunsum* from the father, or from God according to Agyarko. However, such an approach is theologically inadequate for theologizing the biblical concept of the Spirit since it relegates to the background the overall understanding of the nature of the Spirit. It should be a theological imperative to give serious considerations to the biblical languages, namely, רוּחַ and πνεῦμα, to theologize the Spirit within the Akan *Sitz im Leben* if theologians really want to make sense of biblical pneumatology.

Fourth, is *sunsum* the alpha and omega (the be-all and end-all) for the formulation of Akan pneumatology? Might there be other ways to speak of pneumatology in Akan theology other than *sunsum*? Regarding other ways of speaking of pneumatology in the Akan religions, the answer is a categorical and firm yes. Akan people have another term often used to describe a ghost or spirit, and that is *honhom* (wind, air, breath, and vital force). Agyarko's *sunsum* pneumatology did not inquire about the question of *honhom* and Christian pneumatology. The term does not appear at all in his contextual pneumatology. It seems he does not show interest in the subject. The general idea of *honhom* among the Akan is multifaceted, and one needs to understand its various aspects or characteristics for a theological discussion. Current literary references to *honhom* are chiefly found in Twi Christian literature books such as the Twi Bibles, hymn books, and other Christian books. The term appears in several lyrical contents of Ghanaian gospel musicians, and it has also captured the imagination of filmmakers, making *honhom* a contemporary reality. Prior to my research in *sunsum* and *honhom* pneumatology, I never came across any theological work that justified the pneumatic character of *honhom* as a spirit or spiritual phenomenon. Neither did any research demonstrate that it is theologically incorrect to interpret Akan contextual pneumatology using *honhom*. Therefore, I take it as an appropriate theological task to give it a theological justification.

4. In Search of A Contextual Akan Christian Pneumatology

> *"But Pentecost is not the only Pentecostal event in the narrative of Acts. Surprisingly, a Pentecost-like event is repeated twice: at the meeting of the apostle Peter in the house of Cornelius (10:44-48) and the Johannites of Ephesus baptized by Paul (I9:6). Such recurrence, typical of the Lukan vision of history, shows how God drives his community in order to enlarge the Pentecostal nucleus to worldwide dimensions"* – Daniel Marguerat (2013: 117).

4.1. Introduction

Undoubtedly, the concept of "spirit" and "spirits" holds a central place in Akan culture and religion. For the Akan, beliefs in God, pantheon deities, living dead, and other spirits are not mere abstract ideas, but rather an actual reality. This phenomenon is not unique to the Akan but is observed in many other societies across the world. The question at hand is how Akan pneumatology can contribute to current research in contextual theology for the Church in Akan societies. However, this process is not straightforward. There is a tendency to limit contextual Christian theology to the theologization of the context rather than the gospel. Contextualization is the process of theology seeking interaction, which requires a comprehensive understanding of both the Bible and the context of reception. It allows one to examine how much of the Bible can interact with the context and how much the context can contribute without compromising the integrity of both the Bible and the context. This endeavor necessitates a thorough grasp of the Bible and the context to enable effective engagement.

4.2. In Search of Linguistic Expression

In Louw-Nida's Dictionary of the Bible, the difficulty of finding a suitable term to describe the Spirit of God in some languages is discussed. This challenge arises from the diverse ways in which spirits are understood in local languages. If a term that usually identifies local supernatural beings is used, it tends to carry with it connotations of evil or mischievous character, as noted by Louw-Nida (1989: 12.18). This phenomenon is particularly common in African churches, where traditional terms continue to be rejected due to their former associations. Examples among the Akan people include "Ɔkomfoɔ" (traditional priest) and "Ɔbosom" (pantheon deity). The use of such terms in liturgy can be viewed as syncretism in certain Christian circles.

The root of the problem dates back to the era of the early Christian missionaries, who disregarded and stigmatized African traditional religions. However, this attitude should be challenged. African traditional religious concepts can have a transformative effect on the reinterpretation of traditional ideas and provide perspectives for the reception and adaptation of Christian doctrines. This engagement does not amount to the mixing of traditional religions with Christianity or syncretism; rather, it is an application of gospel truths.

Taking into account all these complications, finding the right terms to describe what a spirit means in a given context becomes difficult. Louw-Nida observes:

> The solutions to the problem of 'Spirit' have been varied. In some languages the term for Spirit is essentially equivalent to 'the unseen one,' and therefore the Spirit of God is essentially equivalent to 'the invisibleness of God.' In a number of languages the closest equivalent for Spirit is 'breath,' and in a number of indigenous religious systems, the 'breath' is regarded as having a kind of independent existence. In other languages the term for Spirit is equivalent to what is often translated as 'the soul,' that is to say, the immaterial part of a person. There is, of course, always the difficulty of employing a term meaning 'soul' or 'life,' since it often proves to be impersonal and thus provides no

> basis for speaking of the Spirit of God as being a person or a personal manifestation of God.

The apparent difficulty highlighted in this discussion underscores the crucial importance of recognizing the theological significance of language as a medium of communication within any contextualization. This challenge is not a new one, as scholars of the Septuagint had to confront similar semantic and theological issues within the Hellenistic tradition. It is worth noting that the Greco-Roman cultural context was also instrumental in shaping the New Testament Scriptures.

Today, as we navigate the complexities of diverse cultural contexts, we must grapple with the doctrine of the Spirit and its linguistic revision and clarity. In the subsequent sections, I will explore the various characteristics of the Spirit as depicted in the Old and New Testaments of the Bible. By categorizing these characteristics, we can gain insights into the different ways the Spirit operates in specific contexts.

One pertinent question that arises in this context is: how does Akan pneumatology influence our understanding of the concept of the Spirit as presented in the Bible? Furthermore, how do we contextualize the Biblical pneumatology to effectively communicate it to Akan Christians?

In answering these questions, it is crucial to take a well-balanced approach that takes into account the rich cultural and linguistic heritage of the Akan people. By exploring the unique perspectives and insights offered by Akan pneumatology, we can enrich our understanding of the Spirit and better communicate its teachings to Akan Christians.

4.3. The Bible and the Concept of Spirit

The concept of the Spirit of God, also known as the theology of the Spirit, is a widely discussed theological concept that has its roots in Scripture. However, given that Trinitarian theology only emerged in the first few centuries of Christian theology, the Bible does not provide us with any explicit debates over the doctrine of the Spirit. Consequently, our search for the Spirit in Scripture must confront the challenge of "heterogeneity and the pervasiveness of the occasions on which the Spirit appears" (McIntyre 1997: 29). To better understand the Spirit, we must examine the trajectory of references to the Spirit in Scripture, while keeping in mind the socio-cultural traditions and particularities of the root usage of the terms for the Spirit in both the Jewish and Greek traditions of the Scriptures. A superficial reading of pneumatological themes in Scripture could lead to unexpected conclusions due to the lack of clear references to the Spirit in Scripture. However, as McIntyre suggests, biblical terms are the starting point for thinking in this direction (McIntyre 1997: 30).

Therefore, the purpose of this study is to explore the various trajectories of the Spirit, or the notion of "spirit," in the Bible to provide a better theological foundation for the development of contextual Akan Christian pneumatology. By examining the use of the term "spirit" in Scripture, we can identify key themes and trajectories that have shaped pneumatological thinking throughout history. Through this approach, I aim to provide a more comprehensive understanding of the Spirit and its significance for the development of contextual Akan Christian pneumatology.

4.3.1. The Spirit in the Old Testament

The Old Testament pneumatology is rooted in the Hebrew word רוּחַ, meaning "wind" and "spirit." The word appears 389 times (378 Hebrew, 11 Aramaic) in the Old Testament (Kubat 2016: 290). It conveys, in its most fundamental form, the idea of the expulsion of wind or breath, the idea of air in motion, or the life-breath of the individual (Ferguson 1996: 16, 17). For the time being, we can readily think of the wind as an act of God, "invisible, immensely powerful and sometimes catastrophic in its effects…[It] is also of mysterious origin, transcendent and quite uncircumscribed in its activity" (Bourke 1959: 538). While on some occasions רוּחַ may denote a gentle breeze (Gen. 3:8), Ferguson implies that "the dominant idea in the Old Testament is that of power" and when רוּחַ is used of God, it emphasizes "his overwhelming energy; indeed, one might almost speak about the violence of God. 'Divine Spirit' thus denotes 'the energy of life in God'" (Ferguson 1996: 17). These cosmic realities are used symbolically or metaphorically as illustrations of the divine reality of the Spirit (Pierre Miguel 1998: 5, 6). רוּחַ is translated as "spirit" in English, and it is the basis of several pneumatological themes around the world. Besides its primary usage as "wind" and "spirit," Kubat says the Old Testament "reveals different uses of the word in different kinds of texts and at different times." These may involve "conceptual and linguistic contexts" such as "blowing, breath, meaning, reason, will (bearer of will), the personal pronoun 'I', and so forth" (2016: 290). The word as a spirit or Spirit "often connotes the power of God, as well as dynamism and activity in general" (Kubat 2016: 291). It may as well refer to the immaterial faculties of the human being (Gen. 45:27; 1 Sam. 30:12) or of God (Ps. 33:6; Is. 11:4; 40:13). רוּחַdesignates the power of God or that which proceeds from God in the history of the world (Maldamé 2009: 55; McIntyre 1997: 34).

In a more general sense, there is a theo-anthropological usage of the term רוּחַ, where the relationship between human beings and God is described in a dynamic relationship (Wolff 1974:32, 39; Kubat 2016: 291). Job 27:3: "...as long as my breath is in me, and the רוּחַ of God is in my nostrils." Job does not only identify his breath with God but also refers to it as a principle of life. The term רוּחַ in this verse emphasizes vitality, the spark of God, and the source of life and energy, as opposed to deadness. The identification of the word with the nostrils recalls the physical dimension of the breath of life in living organisms, contrary to a nonliving object (Gen. 2:7; Jer. 10:14; 51:17). Kubat makes several allusions to support this fact in the Old Testament. He writes, "God gives 'the breath of life, to everybody (Num. 16:22; 21:16). A human being's רוּחַ is her spirit'" (2016: 294). He further notes that רוּחַ is the manifest force of movement identical with inhalation and exhalation and that works within and without a person. In a similar sense, Maldamé identifies רוּחַ with נֶפֶשׁ to suggest that the human being is not an inert organism, but he lives "life," that is to say, he is in the world to interact with his fellows and with his creator. Therefore, Maldamé sees the function of רוּחַ as a vital force of communication between the human being and God, and that which alone survives death (Maldamé 2009: 51, 52).

The Spirit is a person's life force, created by Yahweh "who stretched out the heavens and founded the earth and formed the human spirit within" (Zech. 12:1). רוּחַ, from an anthropological perspective, is a sign of life upon which human life is solely dependent (Job 33: 4; Ps. 104:29-30; Ez. 37:6, 8-10,14). This pneumatic ignition from God to the human being establishes the theo-anthropological notion of the operation of רוּחַ, makes us conclude that life is dependent on an impersonal life-force, herein identified as רוּחַ, and affirms that without it, there is no life: "the dust shall return to the earth as it was: and the spirit shall return unto God who gave it" (Eccl. 12:7). The separation is a disembodiment activity. What is earthly goes to the earth, and what is spiritual goes to God (West 2011).

Besides the theo-anthropological aspect of רוּחַ, Kubat identifies an epistemological dimension of the usage of רוּחַ, where it is linked to wisdom and understanding in the Old Testament. The texts in Neh. 9:20, Num. 27:18 and Dan. 5:11 are examples of how רוּחַ is closely related to the power of cognition. In other instances, רוּחַ is the spirit that enlightens and "enables a person to perceive realities that are beyond the scope of normal human thinking;" thus, רוּחַ becomes "a mediation of God's revelation" to humankind (Kubat 2016: 298). Examples include Joseph and Daniel, who could interpret dreams by the spirit of God (Gen. 41:38; Dan. 5:12). The gift of prophecy is another avenue through which God activates the mind of the prophet to actualize His will or to reveal the intents of human thoughts. Ez. 11:5 reads, "And the Spirit of the Lord fell upon me, and he said to me, "Say, Thus says the Lord: So you think, O house of Israel. For I know the things that come into your mind" (ESV), and Micah 3:8 reads, "But as for me, I am filled with power, with the Spirit of the Lord, and with justice and might, to declare to Jacob his transgression and to Israel his sin" (ESV). The charismatic influence of the Spirit renders a human being powerful. "Without the spirit of God, a human being's spirit is powerless" (Kubat 2016: 299). Other related allusions include the spirit of creativity, wisdom, and understanding (Ex. 28:3; 31:3; 35:31; Is 11:2). The Spirit inspires epistemic principles that mirror the divine presence in a person (Wood 1998: 24).

Another dimension of the use of רוּחַ in the Old Testament is noted by Kubat as the metaphysical-cosmological perspective. The phrase the Spirit of God or Spirit of the Lord often occurs in the Old Testament. Here, Kubat makes a distinction between a Stoic understanding of God from the Jewish theological concept of God. While Stoics maintain a pantheistic conception of God as a pervasive spirit, Jewish traditions see God as present in the world through His spirit (Is. 42:5; Ps. 139:7-10). The biblical traditions present a panentheistic conception of God. Kubat argues that the pervasiveness of the spirit in the Old Testament is implicit rather than explicit. רוּחַ is an instrument of God in the created world. Kubat writes:

> The spirit is a creative force of God that not only created the world also rules it. God creates the world through the

> spirit: "By the word of the Lord the heavens were made, and all their host by the breath [*ruach*] of his mouth." (Ps 33:6) This verse reveals that *ruach* relates to the "word" as a synonym because both come out of the mouth of God. In this scene, the spirit is the mediating force that makes God present (2016: 301).

רוּחַ makes God immanent in creation. God is not identical with creation as understood in stoicism, but His spirit is active in and out of creation. We can also conclude that רוּחַ, in its panentheistic conception, establishes a relationship between the material and immaterial, i.e. the universe is inspirited. The activity of God's Spirit in the creation reveals God's regard for the creation and human beings; more importantly, "order and existence come about as a result of Yahweh's work through the agency of the *rûach*" (Hildebrandt 2019: 19).

The last usage of רוּחַ, as mentioned by Kubat, is the theological aspect where רוּחַ is identified as a divine hypostasis in the person of the Holy Spirit. Although there are rare appearances of the phrase Holy Spirit in the Old Testament writings, the few appearances indicate strong support for this conception. Ps. 51:10-12 reads:

> Create in me a clean heart, O God, and put a new and right spirit within me. Do not cast me away from your presence, and do not take your holy spirit from me. Restore to me the joy of your salvation, and sustain in me a willing spirit.

רוּחַ appears three times in the text as the *modus operandi* for David's restoration to God. David suggests a theological dimension of the theo-anthropological aspect of the spirit for the basis of personality formation, that is, a charisma contrary to his present spiritual lethargy. The permanency of the divine hypostasis of the Holy Spirit is emphasized in the text as parallel to the presence of God. Kubat makes this clear:

> The Holy Spirit is parallel to the face of God. These phrases suggest that the Holy Spirit establishes a kind of rapport with God and meditates the presence of God. The Holy Spirit is the one who enables a person's spirit - that is, a

> human being - to sustain life in communion with God. It is the force of God by which a person is released from sin and enabled to fulfill the will of God. The Holy Spirit is a guarantor of belonging to the community of God (2016: 304).

Kubat further discusses the Holy Spirit by considering the textual variations between the Septuagint (LXX) and Masoretic Text (MT) in Dan. 5:11,12; 6:3. While the MT uses "excellent Spirit" in Dan. 5:12, the LXX uses "Holy Spirit." The same translation follows for Dan. 6:3. Kubat thinks that the translation "Holy Spirit" is identical with "excellent Spirit" in both the LXX and MT. In this context, the Holy Spirit is seen as a remarkable spirit of God that stands in a special relationship with Daniel (Kubat 2016: 304). Kubat touches on a more striking text where the Spirit is seen as a mediating hypostasis in Is 63:10-11:

> But they rebelled and grieved his holy spirit; therefore, he became their enemy; he himself fought against them. Then they remembered the days of old, of Moses his servant. Where is the one who brought them up out of the sea with the shepherds of his flock? Where is the one who put within them his Holy Spirit?

As Kubat noted in the text, the Spirit, to some extent, is "personified and represented as a hypostasis," a spiritual agent "who resides in Israel" (Kubat 2016: 305). We know this because of the anthropological sentiments alluded to the Spirit in this context. The theological usage of רוּחַ makes us understand how God permeates the universe through the mediation of His Holy Spirit.

To sum up, the usage of רוּחַ in the Old Testament is multiform and has several meanings. The various dimensions discussed include the theo-anthropological aspect where רוּחַ is identified with the breath of life, i.e., the breath of humankind. Its usage concerning epistemology is identified with wisdom and understanding. רוּחַ has a metaphysical-cosmological dimension in which the mystic presence of the spirit is emphasized. As a mediating hypostasis, רוּחַ is used to justify the theological characterization of the Spirit of God as the Holy Spirit. These literary and theological motifs of Old Testament writers are going to shape the New Testament pneumatology.

4.3.2. The Spirit in the New Testament

The New Testament Bible teaches about the spirit in a variety of contextual meanings; more importantly, the narratives present the spirit as an active participant in the early Christian community. It is normal to readily think of the spirit as the Holy Spirit in the New Testament. However, the idea of spirit entails other conceptions in the New Testament. In this section, I will conduct a careful examination of the nature of the spirit in light of the New Testament and how some of the characteristics given to the spirit affected early Christian thoughts on pneumatology.

Πνεῦμα is the Greek word for spirit, and it is the root word underlining the neologism pneumatology, i.e. the study of spirits or spiritual phenomena.[62] Its primary meaning is "wind" or "breath." In Jn. 3:8, Jesus identifies the work of the Spirit (*pneumatos*) with the wind (πνεῦμα). He does not seem to assume that the Spirit is identical with the wind; neither are both analogous. The only assumption we can deduce is that the Spirit is an invisible object or entity that manifests its presence like the wind.[63] Few examples include the Spirit that comes upon Mary (Matt. 1:20; Lk. 1:35). It is invisible although it has a decisive impact on her existence and life, which also explains the unique status of the Son (Marguerat 2013: 144). Jesus is driven to the desert by the Spirit (Lk. 4:1). The Spirit speaks to, with, and through people while remaining invisible (Acts 8:29; 11:12; 13:2; 21:4; 28:25) (Karakolis 2013: 90). Concretely, however, πνεῦμα is used to denote the movement of the wind or air (Heb. 1:7). It is also used to parallel the

---

62 For many years Christian theologians thought of pneumatology as the study of the Holy Spirit. Recent scholarship, however, seems to challenge that notion as pneumatology also expresses the notion of spirit and spirits in other faith and belief systems. For that matter, one does not need to limit the study of pneumatology to only the Holy Spirit. For further details read Kärkkäinen & Co. (2013).

63 Jesus conveys the idea of the wind to let Nicodemus understand the supernatural movement of the Spirit, and its power to regenerate newness of life in a person without the person necessarily going through a biological recycle of birth. The analogy of wind and birth are more akin to the process of life that makes the Spirit an enlivening entity.

breath of life in a person's nostrils (2 Thess. 2:8; Rev. 11:11). Πνεῦμα is the category that is opposite of the flesh (Clark-Soles 2006: 35).

Another link between the wind and the Spirit is the metaphorical description of the coming of the Spirit at Pentecost. Luke's narrative describes the theophanic coming of the Spirit "as of a rushing mighty wind" (2:2). He does not use the term πνεῦμα in this context but another synonymous Greek term, πνοῆς, which means both breath and wind. The use of the metaphor is Luke's manner of differentiating between the actual Spirit and the phenomena that declare or symbolize its presence (Karakolis 2013: 90). Similar descriptions of the apparition of the Spirit are mentioned on two occasions in the Gospels. First, both Matthew and Luke record the Spirit descending on Jesus "in bodily form like a dove" (Matt. 3:16; Lk. 3:22 cf. Jn. 1:32). The second occasion occurred on Pentecost when tongues like flames of fire descended upon the heads of the disciples (Acts 2: 3). These visible manifestations are described in metaphors and therefore should not be understood as the actual essence of the Spirit. The nature of the Spirit remains invisible like the wind or air even when it is said the disciples were all filled with the Holy Spirit (Acts 2:4) like "the air or wind, which can be inhaled and fill the interior of a person in an invisible way" (Karakolis 2013: 90). The semantic notion of wind underlining the idea of spirit is quite substantive, and it provides the basis for grasping the essence of πνεῦμα in the New Testament. The Spirit, as in the wind, "is powerful, it can be felt, and it has an impact upon people's lives and their way of thinking and acting. On the other hand, it normally cannot be seen but only sensed" (Karakolis 2013: 90).

There is the anthropological dimension where πνεῦμα is seen as the vital principle in the human being. According to Matthew, Jesus yielded up His spirit to signify his final breath or death (27:50). Πνεῦμα is identical with life in human beings, and without it the body is dead (Lk. 8:55; 23:46; Jn. 6:63; 19:30; Acts 7:59; Ja. 2:28). It is used to define the rational and emotional aspect of mankind as opposed to the body (Matt. 26:41; Mk. 14:38; Rom. 8:10; 1 Cor. 2:11; 5:5; 6:17, 20;7: 34;2 Cor. 7: 1; Col. 2: 5; 1 Pet. 4:6). The apostle Paul differentiates πνεῦμα from the body and soul (1 Thess. 5:23). The spirit of the human being is a substance rather than an indwelling spirit foreign to the body; it defines the essence of being. "Tó πνεῦμα is the rational part of man, the power of perceiving and grasping divine and eternal things, and upon which the Spirit of God exerts its influence" (Mk. 2:8; 8:12; Lk. 1:47; Acts 17:16; Rom. 1:9; 8:16; 1 Cor. 5:4; 16:18; 2 Cor. 2: 13; 7: 13; Gal. 6:18; Phil. 4:23; Philem. 1:25; 2 Tim. 4:22).[64] According to the Gospel of Luke, John the Baptist is presented as acting in the spirit and power of Elijah (Lk. 1:17). The joy of Mary is presented as a rejoicing of her spirit (Lk. 1:47). John the Baptist's spirit is presented as being strengthened while he was growing (Lk. 1:80) (Karakolis 2013: 90).

Πνεῦμα is again used to describe an entitative spiritual being, often as a generic term for a spirit. In this context, we are talking about the qualities of a being that is essentially spiritual, "a simple essence, devoid of all or at least all grosser matter, and possessed of the power of knowing, desiring, deciding, and acting" (Thayer 1889: 520). For example, God is πνεῦμα (Jn. 4:24) means that God is essentially spiritual. This definition means He is not subject to material constraints or the confines of what could be considered as physical. Spirits may have anthropomorphic descriptions, but such depictions are only perceptions that belong to human beings. Such anthropomorphism exists as far as spirits are conceived in the memory of human beings, which also tends to evoke a belief in spirits that are higher than human beings but inferior to God. Examples include angels, ghosts, and demons (Matt. 8:16; Mk. 9:20; Lk. 4:33; 11:26; 24:37,39; Heb. 1:14).

Another area of interest concerning the use of πνεῦμα in the New Testament is the πνεῦμα ἅγιον, or "Holy Spirit." The phrase appears about eighty-nine times in the Greek New Testament Bible. Similar names and motifs include πνεῦμα θεοῦ (Rom. 8:9, 14), πνεῦμα τὸ ἅγιον τοῦ θεοῦ (Eph. 4:30; 1 Thess. 4: 8), πνεῦμα τοῦ κυρίου (i.e., of God Lk. 4:18), πνεῦμα τοῦ κυρίου (i.e., of Christ 2 Cor. 3:17,18). There are Christological categories of the Holy Spirit to point out: in the incarnation (Lk. 1:35; Matt. 1:18-20), during the baptism of Christ (Matt. 3:16), Jesus being led by the Spirit (Matt. 4:1), Jesus' messianic announcement of his ministry (Lk. 4:18), and the Holy Spirit as the Spirit of Christ who resurrected him (Rom. 8:9, 11). We can also emphasize its soteriological dimension in the salvation of believers (Eph. 1:13; 4:30). Salvation is materialized in the heart and life of the believer through the mediation of the Holy Spirit.

---

64 J. H. Thayer, *A Greek-English Lexicon of the New Testament: being Grimm's Wilke's Clavis Novi Testamenti*. New York: Harper & Brothers, 1889, p. 520.

It is theologically noteworthy and semantically revealing to see the nature of the Holy Spirit in the New Testament narratives as an active divine personality (hypostatic) that is "with" and "within" believers rather than an impersonal force. In his commentary on Jn. 14:16, Andreas Dettwiler perceives the abiding presence of the Spirit among the community of disciples as the most basic goal. He writes: "The fact that this presence is "forever" (εἰς τὸν αἰῶνα) indicates the qualitative gap between the time of the earthly Jesus and the time qualified by the Spirit-Paraclete, a presence unlimited in time or space" (Dettwiler 2016: 157, 158). Similarly, Zumstein underlines the omnipresent activity of the Spirit as everywhere and for everyone (Zumstein 2007: 73).[65] The presence of the Spirit makes Jesus "simultaneously enter in full authenticity into environments that are far removed from each other, and foreign to each other, in time and space" (Welker 1994: 224).

Fotopoulos describes the presence of the Spirit as an active agent within Christians: "the Spirit acting; the Spirit in action; or the Spirit energizing believers to act in various ways" (Fotopoulos 2016: 181). He refers to Paul's usage of action words to express "the on-going action of the Spirit, as well as the Spirit-inspired action of Christians" (Fotopoulos 2016: 181). Notable Pauline texts, as compiled by Fotopoulos, include: leads (ἄγονται, Rom. 8:14); helps us (συναντιλαμβάνεται, Rom. 8:26); intercedes (ὑπερεντυγχάνει, Rom. 8:26; ἐντυγχάνει ὑπὲρ ἁγίων, Rom. 8:27); searches (ἐραυνᾷ, 1 Cor. 2:10); comprehends (ἔγνωκεν , 1 Cor. 2:11); speaks (λαλῶν, 1 Cor. 12:3); activates (ἐνεργεῖ, 1 Cor. 12:11); distributes (διαιροῦν, 1 Cor. 12:11); gives life (ζῳοποιεῖ, 2 Cor. 3:6; "eternal life", Gal. 6:8); transforms from glory to glory (μεταμορφούμεθα ἀπὸ δόξης εἰς δόξαν, καθάπερ ἀπὸ κυρίου πνεύματος, 2 Cor. 3:18); communes (κοινωνία, 2 Cor. 13:14; Phil. 2:1); and manifests itself in a variety of gifts (φανέρωσις, 1 Cor. 12:7) (Fotopoulos 2016: 182, 185).

Significant allusions to the activeness of the Spirit in the New Testament may also include: feelings (Eph. 4:30); He wills (Acts 16:6-12); does miracles (Acts 8:39); can be lied to (Acts 5:3)[66]; can be insulted (Heb. 10:29);

---

[65] Also cited by Dettwiler (2016: 158).

[66] In Acts 5, a mutual conspiracy between Ananias and his wife Sapphira brought about an instant judgment of death upon the couple. Peter reveals the sin as lying to the Holy Spirit (Acts 5: 3). In verse 4, he also states that Ananias lied to God. In verse 9, Peter confronts Sapphira for testing the Holy Spirit. Based on this incidence, Karakolis makes

teaches and directs (Lk. 12:12; Jn. 14:26; Acts 8:29; Acts 13:2); convicts (Jn. 16:8); Holy Spirit as God (Acts 5:3,4); can be blasphemed (Matt. 12:31; 12:31-32); is the Spirit of life (Rom. 8:2); and co-equal with the Father and Son (Matt. 28:19; 2 Cor. 13:14). The Holy Spirit represents a personification of the triune God who participates in the immanence of God in the world.

Although the personality of the Holy Spirit may seem elusive, it is not entirely conclusive until the question of the nature of the Holy Spirit is discussed in the broader context of the New Testament. Is the Holy Spirit an impersonal force?

The Lukan corpus (Luke-Acts) makes a clear distinction between the Holy Spirit and God's impersonal powers, even though some of the terms Luke uses, such as the most distinctive term that denotes the power of God – δύναμις – may sometimes give "the impression of a synonymic *parallelismus membrorum,* implying an identical meaning expressed in two different ways" (Karakolis 2016: 99). Luke presents δύναμις as a mystical power from God exerted upon individuals by the Holy Spirit. Examples include the conception of Jesus Christ by Mary. In Luke 1:35, the angel tells Mary: "The Holy Spirit will come on you, and the power (δύναμις) of the Most High will overshadow you." Karakolis seems to assume that the Holy Spirit could be "understood as being another word for God's impersonal power" (2013: 99). John Zizioulas thinks of δύναμις differently as the creation of the Holy Spirit for the community of believers (Zizioulas 2010: 78). The angel's statement parallels Jesus' words to the disciples after His resurrection, "But you will receive power (δύναμις) when the Holy Spirit comes on you." In this context, Karakolis suggests that the "reception of God's power is not identical with the coming of the Holy Spirit but only the result of its coming" (2013: 100). It is so clear that Luke associates the impersonal power with the Holy Spirit, but the two are not identical and neither are they synonymous. Δύναμις appears in the ministry of Jesus Christ as an intrinsic power of the Holy Spirit, ἐν τῇ δυνάμει τοῦ πνεύματος, translated as, "in the power of the Spirit" (Lk. 4:14). The impersonal power is a character trait of the Holy Spirit through which we understand its essential potentiality and the channel of its executive work in the world. Δύναμις is unlike the Holy Spirit. It does not bear the vital properties that characterize

a strong case "to imply that the Holy Spirit is indeed a narrative character, since tempting and lying can only have a narrative character as their object" (2013: 99).

the Holy Spirit in the New Testament, such as talking, deciding, convicting, communicating, interacting, prophesying, guiding, etc. The overall character of the Holy Spirit is beyond the category of an impersonal power for reasons that are linked to its hypostatic nature in its identification with the Godhead.

In summary, both רוּחַ and πνεῦμα present similar ideas to understanding the nature of the Spirit and spirits. Etymologically, both רוּחַ and πνεῦμα mean wind or spirit. From that background, scholars refer to the metaphorical conception of the spirit as wind or breath as invisible though active in natural objects, just as one cannot see the wind but can only feel it. There is no single and straightforward meaning of the term spirit. The term spirit is elusive, and this is the reason why רוּחַ and πνεῦμα mostly appear in different categories and metaphors in the Bible. In general terms, the various conceptions of רוּחַ and πνεῦμα include the anthropological dimension, where רוּחַ and πνεῦμα are understood as the breath in the human being. The theo-anthropological dimension is understood as the spiritual force or the vital principle in humankind, as in the sense of the breath of life given by God that creates the distinction between the body and the spirit of a person. Their epistemological conception lies in cognitive qualities such as wisdom and understanding. רוּחַ and πνεῦμα underline the metaphysical-cosmological definition of the immanence of God through which we understand the relationship between God and the material world. The most important usage of רוּחַ and πνεῦμα is the theological conception of God as spirit, and the person of the Holy Spirit.

All these categories reflect the multifaceted understanding of רוּחַ and πνεῦμα in the entire Bible. This background is also true of the English term "spirit." Hence, the quest for a contextual pneumatology, herein referred to as contextual Akan Christian pneumatology, should seriously consider the medium of expression in the Twi language in order to have a better interaction between the Bible and traditional notions of the spirit.

4.4. Summary

In this chapter, I have examined the diverse aspects of the Spirit in both the Old and New Testament, which demonstrate a varied application of the terms to specific activities of the Spirit. Rather than being centered on the terms themselves, the biblical understanding of the Spirit is predominantly concerned with the theological adequacy of the terms to address different activities of the Spirit. However, the substitution of πνεῦμα for רוּחַ in the Septuagint and the Greek New Testament highlights the potential convergence of each cultural tradition with the Bible.

As the Akan concept of *sunsum* is insufficient for the purposes of theologizing biblical pneumatology, I aim to contribute to the discourse by proposing an alternative viewpoint based on the Akan concept of *honhom*. I am firmly convinced that *honhom* is a theologically suitable term for addressing the Holy Spirit and, more importantly, that it is analogous to the Hebrew רוּחַ and Greek πνεῦμα. In doing so, I will offer a broader perspective for understanding the nature and activity of the Holy Spirit, which is known in the Twi language as Honhom Kronkron.

It is worth noting that the Akan concept of *honhom* is not a mere translation of the English word "spirit," but rather a term that encompasses a broader range of meanings, including breath, life force, and vital energy. As such, *honhom* is a deeply rooted aspect of Akan culture, and its theological significance has long been recognized within the context of Akan religions.

Drawing on the works of various scholars studying Akan religions and culture, I will demonstrate how the Akan concept of *honhom* provides a rich and nuanced framework for understanding the Holy Spirit in a contextually relevant manner. By exploring the historical and cultural significance of *honhom* and its relationship to the biblical concept of the Spirit, I hope to contribute to the ongoing dialogue on the development of a new contextual Christian pneumatology.

5. Honhom Kronkron: A Pneumatological Proposal

> *"Since Christianity rejects the notion of a special sacred language and instead affirms the Scriptures in whatever language to be the word of God, it is reasonable to expect that the rich linguistic heritage of Africa should provide singular opportunities for developing indigenous Christian theologies"* – Kwame Bediako (1989: 64).

5.1. Introduction

The objective of this chapter is to engage in constructive theological inquiry in order to develop a new contextual Akan Christian pneumatology based on the concept of *honhom*, which denotes air, breath, or spirit. The Akan understanding of *honhom* is a multifaceted concept that requires an appreciation of its diverse characteristics for theological discussions. The extant literature on *honhom* is primarily limited to Twi Christian literature, including the Twi Bibles, hymn books, and other Christian texts. The term also features prominently in the lyrics of Ghanaian gospel musicians, and it has captured the attention of filmmakers, thereby establishing *honhom* as a contemporary phenomenon.

Despite the popularity of *honhom* in various cultural expressions, there is a paucity of theological scholarship that validates its pneumatic nature as a spiritual phenomenon. Furthermore, there is no evidence that interpreting Akan contextual pneumatology using *honhom* is theologically untenable. Accordingly, this chapter seeks to provide theological justification for such an interpretation.[67]

---

[67] Baffoe Antwi in his doctoral dissertation titled *Creation in the Image of God: Human Uniqueness from the Akan Religious Anthropology to the Renewal of Christian Anthropology* attempted to justify a *Honhom Kronkron* pneumatology in some sections of the thesis. His work is plausible even though contextual pneumatology was not the focus in its entirety.

It is essential to appreciate that the Akan understanding of *honhom* is not a singular concept but a composite of various ideas that are often intertwined. *Honhom* can be understood as the breath of life that animates human beings, as the life force that permeates all living things, and as the spiritual dimension of existence that connects humans to the divine. These various aspects of *honhom* provide a rich foundation for a contextual Akan Christian pneumatology that acknowledges the diverse ways in which the spirit is perceived in the Akan cultural milieu.

My proposal draws from the previous discussions on the Akan notion of the "spirit" and the spiritual, by taking into consideration the nature of the Holy Spirit and its theological expressions among the Akan Christians of West Africa. Since the doctrine of the Spirit involves both spirituality and history of humanity, the new proposal will critically recast Akan pneumatology in order to formulate a theological framework that can help articulate Christian thoughts and theological reflections within and specifically for the Akan context. To achieve this objective, I will examine the existing literature on *honhom* and contextualize it within the broader theological framework of Christian pneumatology. This will involve a critical analysis of relevant biblical passages and an exploration of the relationship between the Holy Spirit and the Akan understanding of *honhom*. The study seeks to offer answers to the following key questions: What is *honhom*? How does the notion of *honhom* impact a contextual understanding of the Holy Spirit?

While I embark on this theological study, I would like to clarify whether this pneumatological proposal is parallel to the *sunsum* pneumatology. It is not my intention to parallel this pneumatological construction with the *sunsum* pneumatology. Since *honhom* and *sunsum* are not synonymous terms, it follows that the two cannot be parallel. Nevertheless, my research does not rally against *sunsum* pneumatology, for reasons relating to the linguistic complexities existing among the different Akan subgroups, especially between the Twi-speaking and Fante-speaking Akan peoples. Concerning my previous investigation of *sunsum*, its pneumatic nature has been emphasized as a spiritual force/element rather than as being entitative. What concerns me at this point is proving that *honhom* is theologically more qualified to define the Holy Spirit, and therefore, should be the basis for a contextual Akan Christian pneumatology.

5.2. Etymology, Origin, and Meaning of *Honhom*

The spirit is understood among the majority of the Akan people as *honhom*. Traditional Akan thinkers use the term *honhom* to speak of breath, wind (a mild, gentle wind), spirit, life force, and all non-physical realities. However, the meaning of the term has much wider applications. *Honhom* denotes any meta-empirical being or spiritual state (Platvoet 1982: 73). The plural form of *honhom* (spirit) is *ahonhom* (spirits). Other root words include *ahum* (strong wind) and *ahom* or *home* (breath). In this chapter, I propose that *honhom* should form part of the basis of all Akan pneumatological and theological discourses now and in the future.

5.2.1. Etymology of Honhom

The etymology of the term *honhom* is a conundrum. A few Akan religious scholars of outstanding memory have argued the etymology of *honhom* from different viewpoints. The first attempt is found in the writings of the Basel missionary Gustav Arthur Jehle.[68] Although he connects the word *honhom* with *home* (breath), Jehle felt the appropriate etymology should be *ahung* (atmosphere), i.e. *honhom* as something from the air, something invisible (Jehle 1907: 415). The connection with the atmosphere also makes it pervasive and invisible like the air in the atmosphere. This etymology relates *honhom* to something intangible or invisible, whether as atmosphere, air, life force, or breath.

The second attempt comes from Danquah. We encounter an exhaustive interpretation of *honhom* in Danquah because the concept forms the basis of his pneumatology. The greater part of what we know about *honhom* comes from him. Danquah takes a multifaceted approach to the meaning of *honhom*. He traces the etymology of *honhom* to *ehon*, i.e. the marrow in the bone, or brain, the pith, the essence of mind. He concludes that *honhom* is understood to have derived from the repetition of the word *ehon* of the ehon (*ehon-mu hom*). He explains it as: "the pith of pith, the essence of the essence, the quintessence of the quintessence, the ineffable spiritual

---

68 Gustav Jehle entered the Basel Mission in 1899 and worked on the Gold Coast (Ghana) from 1900 to 1918 (Hauser-Renner 2008: 261).

principle or soul of ultimate reality" (1968: 171).[69] Danquah provides the most profound understanding of the Akan concept of *honhom* more than anyone else.

5.2.2. Origin of Honhom

Gyekye argues that "*honhom* has come to be used interchangeably with *sunsum* (spirit), so that the phrase *honhom bone* has come to mean the same thing as *sunsum bone*, that is, evil spirit" (1987: 88). His observation is right; Akan people use the two terms interchangeably without any nuances in their meaning. Gyekye accuses foreign missionaries of introducing *honhom* due to the radical translation of the Christian Bible into the various Akan languages. This observation was first made by Diedrich Hermann Westermann (1875–1956). He associated *honhom* with breath and further remarked that its transcendental usage in the Bible was "only a deepening, as it were, of the original material" (Jehle 1907: 415). Westermann concludes that this was due to the influence of the Christian translation of the Greek πνεῦμα as *honhom* in the Twi Bible. His observation is correct because *sunsum* was never used in the first and later editions of the Twi Bibles. Both the רוּחַ and πνεῦμα are all translated in the Twi language as *honhom* to mean "spirit." Consequently, the argument follows that the term *honhom* was a Christian, and hence, recent invention. Why did the early editions of the Akan Twi Bibles, published by the British and Foreign Bible Societies (BFBS) in 1871, use *honhom* instead of *sunsum* for the spirit? Did the foreign missionaries invent the term *honhom*? How do we respond to this question of invention? These questions lead to further analysis of the term *honhom* and its significance to Akan theological discourse.

---

69 Danquah is right on the word *ehon,* which is the Akan word for the brain. Its connection to the soul or spirit has been sustained by Kwame Gyekye. Gyekye asserts that Akan people believe the soul (*ɔkra*) is lodged somewhere in the head. The Akan expression *Ne ti ye* (His head is good) is synonymous to *Ne 'kra ye* (His soul is good). Gyekye concludes that "the soul acts on the brain in a specific locality, but it is itself not actually localized" (Gyekye 1987: 100). Another concept that is closely related to the brain is *tiboa* (conscience). For further reading on this latter concept, see Gyekye 1987: 142-143, 126.

5.2.3. Fundamental Meaning of Honhom

The oral linguistic, semantic, and grammatical structure of Akan languages were transformed into written or printed texts by early Christian missionaries. Christaller, the key philologist in the development of the Twi grammar, spent more than twenty-five years studying the Twi language and preparing manuscripts and materials collected through contact with natives of various places and cultural groups of the Akan ethnicity. He particularly mentions David Asante – his co-missionary – and other trained indigenous missionaries as contributors and reviewers of his publications (1881: vi). We can trace the meaning of *honhom* back to two of Christaller's dictionaries. The first was *A Dictionary, English, Tshi (Asante), Akra; Tshi (Chwee) Comprising as Dialects: Akan and Fante; Accra connected with Adangme; Gold Coast, West Africa*, published in 1874.[70] The original version of this dictionary was a compilation of English-Ga vocabularies by the Basel Society missionary Rev. Christian Wilhelm Locher from 1850 to 1869. The earlier Ga vocabularies had been compiled by Rev. Johannes Zimmermann and containing some notes by indigenous Ga catechists.[71] The Twi vocabularies were the contribution of Christaller. The term *honhom* appears three times in this dictionary; in all appearances, it is associated with something intangible or spiritual.

First, the diction on "breath" is translated as *ahome*, *ahuhuw*[72], *ahohow*, *honhom*, *nkwa*[73], *mfare*, and *mframa*[74] (1874: 37).[75] Second, the word "ghost" is translated as *honhom*, *sunsum*, *sãsã*, and *osaman* (1874: 112).

---

70 The language of the Ga people of Ghana.

71 See the preface to Christaller's *A Dictionary, English, Tshi (Asante), Akra; Tshi (Chwee) Comprising as Dialects: Akan and Fante; Accra connected with Adangme; Gold Coast, West Africa* in 1874.

72 From this word also comes *huhu* meaning blowing of air from the mouth to quench something, i.e. fire, hot water or food, etc.

73 *Nkwa* literally means "life."

74 The Akan word for "air" or "wind."

75 *Honhom* appears on this list as an alternative description of breath rather than a synonym. Akan people do not often use *honhom* in ordinary conversations as another word for breath or breathing. For example, if Akan want to say, "He is breathing heavily," the proper Twi translation will be "*Ne home kɔ soro*." To say, "*Ne honhom kɔ soro*" will mean his *'kra* or soul is gone to heaven. *Honhom* in connection with breath seems preponderant only when a person is dying or dies.

The third appearance occurs under "soul" and is translated as *ɔkra* and *sunsum* (*honhom*) (1874: 226).[76] *Honhom* appears in all instances as an ontological description of something intangible or spiritual. *Sunsum* does not appear under the various Akan terms for "breath" as indicated. I see this as a theological deficiency in terms of the term *sunsum* fully defining the theo-anthropological aspect of biblical pneumatology where aspects of רוּחַ and πνεῦμα parallel the breath of living organisms.

Christaller gives further elaboration on *honhom* in his *A Dictionary of the Asante and Fante Language Called Tshi (Chwee, Twi)* (1881), which was also the standard Twi dictionary for the Basel German Evangelical Mission of West Africa. The diction on *honhom* is rendered as (footnotes are mine):

> *honhom*, *(pl.)* a-, *a spirit; the spirit of man* [ah. =osaman a.s. sunsum, ahunmu ade nen[77]; sunsuma na tetefo fre no sa(se)[78]: ne h. asore no so akye (orebewu nen)[79]; onipa wu a, ne h. fi no mu ko soro[80]]. Onyame h., *the Spirit of God*; Honhom kronkron, *the Holy Ghost*; honhom ahoto, *spiritual joy or happiness*; honhom-mu-ade, *spiritual things* (1881: 189).

---

[76] Christaller does not translate "soul" as equivalent to *honhom*. The emphasis here is in reference to soul as an intangible object.

[77] The expression *ahunmu ade nen* is a blend of Twi and Fante which means "an invincible thing." *Saman* (ghost) is an invincible entity. *Honhom* is thought of in Christaller's interpretation as something invincible or from the atmosphere. For years, this has been the Akan position with respect to spiritual realities and objects. See also Christaller 1881: 197.

[78] The expression *sunsuma na tetefo frɛ no sa* (*se*), means "The ancestors used to call *sunsuma* (shadow) as *sa* (follow)." The statement seems to give credibility to those who perceive the derivation of *sunsum* from the Akan word for shadow (*sunsuma*), and also to those who think the *saman* is the *sunsum* of the deceased. None of these can fully grasp the meaning of *sunsum*.

[79] This expression: *Ne honhom asore no so akyɛ (orebewu nen)* means, "His spirit has withdrawn from him for a long time (he is about to die)."

[80] *Onipa wu a, ne honhom fi no mu kɔ soro*: "When a person dies, his spirit flits from him to heaven;" not heaven per se but *Asamando* (place of abode for the ancestors) as recognized in the Akan religion.

Christaller used both *honhom* and *sunsum* for the “spirit of man.” For example, he defines *sunsum* as “the soul or spirit of man” almost like the definition of *honhom* given above (1881: 464).

While it may seem confusing to see both *sunsum* and *honhom* expressing similar ideas, it is also important to grasp what Christaller meant by the phrase “spirit of man” in context. First, he used *sunsum* often in relation to the *ɔkra*, the intrinsic property of life, also referred to by Christaller as the “soul” or spirit of man. This is also true of his use of *honhom* for the *ɔkra*. For example, Christaller assumed that “the *'kra* is considered partly as the soul or spirit of a person (cf. *sunsum*, *honhom*)” (1881: 255). Second, his use of *honhom* and *sunsum*, as the *spirit* of man, referred to the entitative “spirit,” which Akan people call *Saman* (ghost). Although we find overlaps in his usage of *sunsum* and *honhom*, there is little evidence to assume that Christaller used the two terms synonymously.

5.3. Characteristics of Honhom

Characteristically, the concept of *honhom* is a polysemy as it has various related meanings. This section aims to outline some of the characteristics that Akan people use to define the concept of *honhom*.

5.3.1. Honhom as Breath or A Mild Wind

Honhom is the Akan term for breath or air. Other alternative terms include *mframa* (wind) or *ahom* (breath). Whereas *mframa* may be best translated as wind, *honhom* or *ahom* is used technically in relation to inhalation and exhalation of air. Breath, air, and wind are appropriate English translations of *honhom* because both express the idea of invincibility and life force. All living creatures breathe air in order to grow and stay healthy. Air is a mysterious force of nature; it is formless, shapeless, and invincible. Air or wind is beyond human control since it is unseen and can only be felt. It is a universal reality which has no specific source or end. Therefore, the Akan concept of *honhom* brings out the idea of vitality, pervasiveness, and the non-perceivable realities that form part of Akan ontology and cosmology.

Gyekye relates *honhom* to breath or spirit. The reason, he explains, is that the word seems to have been transformed from the Akan Twi word *home* or *ahom*, which means "breath" (1987: 88).[81] Ephirim-Donkor comes to a similar conclusion and associates breath (*ahom*) with life, that is, the air that a person breathes in and out as evidence of the life force in the individual. In other words, Ephirim-Donkor sees the *ahom* (breath) as the *ɔkra* that a child inhales at birth and gives out at death (2010: 45). Gyekye does not see *honhom* and *ɔkra* as synonymous; however, he considers them to be relative. He makes references to the following Akan sayings to buttress his assumption: *Ne honhom kɔ,* "his breath is gone," and *Ne 'kra afi ne ho,* "his *ɔkra* has withdrawn from his body." The two expressions suggest that a person is dead. The cessation of breath and the departure of the *ɔkra* are non-identical to Gyekye. Nevertheless, he sees a spontaneous phenomenon expressing the idea that it is the *ɔkra* that *causes* breathing (1987: 88). I will revisit all these assumptions later.

5.3.2. Honhom: The Ultimate Source of Being

Among the Akan, *honhom* is a universal reality because it is Onyame's *Honhom*. According to Agyarko, "Onyame stands as a rational, eternal, and absolute Being." He continues to argue that the Akan people do not regard Onyame as their tribal god. "Rather, *Onyame* is seen as the Supreme Being whose benevolence extends to all people. The creation of the universe is attributed to *Onyame* and this Being is regarded as the governing principle of the universe" (Agyarko 2014: 10). Thus, Onyame is a universal reality, "the Honhom of ultimate being… the cause of all being, of all existence and value, Odomankoma Borebore, the interminable Creator" (Danquah 1968: 170). The universal reality of Onyame *Honhom* is metaphorically represented by *honhom* (air), which is a universal principle circulating in all aspects of life and a universal experience of life in all living things.

Danquah thinks the concept of *honhom* is the "roof and root to the entire edifice of the Akan doctrine regarding God" (1968: 110). Onyame as *Honhom* becomes "the source of reality and the potential entelechy of all being, multiform in function, uniform in nature, infinite and interminable, which was, and 'went before any one came,' the timeless, spaceless, all inclusive

[81] "To breathe" and "breath" have the same word spelling in the Akan language. It is the context that designates its tense. For example, "*Nipa bi ara home*," meaning "Each person breathes." A second example: "*Ne home rete*," literally meaning "He is suffocating" or proverbially means the person is under severe stress.

reality" (1968: 172). God (Honhom) is "the end-cause of all being" (1968: 172). What are the implications of all these pneumatological conceptions of God to Danquah?

In Danquah's view, life is cyclical, a quest to become part of the ultimate reality, God, who is a direct representation of the Nana (ancestor), who each individual should seek to reach. Akan ancestral cult is constructed on this ideology. The ancestors share in divine attributes of spirituality (*honhom*), perfection, and possess the qualities of divinity. To achieve ancestorship is the ultimate end of life, the fulfillment of the moral life. These are the motivations for *sunsum* and *ɔkra* to achieve *honhom*, the being that is accountable after death. This is because, as Danquah puts it, life is "one grand continuous effort, one grand desire to get things done, [and] to answer the practical questions of how to live well" (1968: 152). Both *sunsum* and *ɔkra* are said to objectify these practical ideals. In practical terms, what matters, according to Danquah, is that the Akan "attains full maturity of completed incarnation, whereby man becomes God's, is absorbed into the interminable Odomankoma (Creator), and shares in divine immortality" (1968: 152). Thus, life continues in the spiritual.

5.3.3. Honhom as Spirit

Several Akan people regard the essence of spirits to be *honhom*, i.e., non-physical and permeating. The Akan proverb, *Nipa bɔnefo nti na yɛto pono mu na ɛnyɛ ɔsaman ho hu nti*, literally, "Doors are meant to protect from bad people but not because of the fear of ghosts," reinforces the nature of spirits as wind or air. In the same manner doors are not meant for ghosts, spirits are not constrained by physical objects because of their permeating nature as *honhom*. In both of Christaller's dictionaries of 1874 and 1881, the term "ghost" is translated as *honhom*. In its plural form, *ahonhom* tends to describe the myriads of entities whose nature is exclusively spiritual. A traditional priest described the nature of *Ɔbosom* (a pantheon deity) to Rattray as *Onyankopon honhom* (God's spirit) (Rattray 1916: 22). Besides Rattray's intention to connect Akan religion to the Supreme God, the relationship between the *Ɔbosom* and God is an ontological filiation because Akan people regard the *Abosom* as children of God (Rattray 1923: 145, 146). As Danquah notes, *Honhom* (God) "is the spirit of ultimate being realizing the conditions of its own existence for its highest or most intelligible expression or actualization" (1944: 171). The underlining theology makes God common to reality. *Honhom*, the spirit of God, characterizes all entities that share in the divine nature. The pantheon deities and ancestors are all *ahonhom* (pl.), and their essential characteristics have been noted as *sunsum* as well. The malevolent spirits are known among Akan people as *ahonhom bɔne* (evil spirits).[82]

5.3.4. Honhom as the Pervasive Spirit

The Akan designation of God as *Honhom* (spirit), means God is neither non-composite nor limited by time and space. Because Onyame as *Honhom* is a universal reality, Onyame's *Honhom* extends to the entire creation. Danquah views *honhom* as the ultimate reality, "the centre of all reality, pervading and informing every part of existence,... an urge or vitality" (1968: 170). It is God's *honhom* that gives reality to all forms and matter; hence, matter exists in God.[83] All things created, including the universe itself, are permeated by the *honhom* of God. Danquah sums up his ideas with the Akan maxim, "*Nsem nyinaa ne Nyame*," meaning, "'All matter is God,' or of God; all that exists or becomes is God. It is not exclusive, but common, all universally, ultimately, and absolutely, for beyond it there is no matter, neither cause nor end. It is common. All in common is Honhom, or of Honhom, the energy and power of being" (1968: 172). As a consequence, all that becomes a *honhom* becomes part of God. If *honhom* is a pervasive spirit and vitality, then it follows that many of life's realities are dependent upon it and may have a significant role to play in understanding the whole essence of life.

---

82 Witches are not spirits in the proper sense of the word. As already stated, witches are superhumans who exercise spiritual powers.

83 Danquah uses *honhom* to denote the ultimate essence of essence that contains all reality. The assumption makes the Akan concept of *honhom* the cause and essence of all reality. The Latin *ex nihilo nihil fit*, which means "out of nothing, nothing comes," cannot be contained in the Akan conception of the *honhom* since all things exist in spirit before being materialized. This explains why *honhom* captures the fundamental and essential activities of the Hebrew רוּחַ and the Greek πνεῦμα in the Bible better than *sunsum* as it will be shown later.

5.3.5. Honhom as Life Substance

Gyekye remarks that what is real in Akan ontology and cosmology is the spiritual. He does not discard the reality of the world of natural phenomena. However, he is convinced that "in ultimate terms the nonperceivable, purely spiritual world is more real, for upon it the perceivable, phenomenal world depends for sustenance" (1987: 69). This description of Akan worldviews cuts across majority of Africans' worldviews. The Akan empahsis of *honhom* as the ultimate source of reality makes *honhom* the substance of every existence. Like God, it far predates any matter and form; it also far exceeds the beginning of time. It is the *honhom* that gives reality to all forms and matter, because the matter exists in it. This suggests that everything created, including the universe, is permeated by this informing energy called *honhom* (Danquah 1968: 171).

A broad range of practical applications can be deduced from all these. The nature of *honhom* could very well be identified with life or an animating force because it is life itself. Whatever has *honhom* has life while the vice versa is death. The concept of *honhom*, as a life substance, explains how God permeates the creation and how every life is united with its source, God. For that matter, the destiny of all life is dependent on the vivification of the *honhom*.

5.3.6. Honhom: The Life force of the Human Being

Of fundamental importance is how Akan people use *honhom* to describe the life force in every human being. Akan anthropology postulates that every human being has a life principle from God called *ɔkra*. Christaller, in his first Asante-Fante dictionary in 1881, links the *ɔkra* to *honhom* based on two Akan statements: *Ne honhom asɔre no so akyɛ* (His spirit has withdrawn from him for a long time), and *Onipa wu a, ne honhom fi ne mu kɔ soro* (When a person dies, his spirit flits from him to heaven) (1881: 189). He gives further similar expressions with alternative explanations: *Ne honhom nsene no mu*, meaning: "he is beside himself with impatience, ready to leap out of his skin." Or *Ne honhom asore no so,* "his soul or spirit has left him." Christaller observes these expressions in relation to a dying person or when a person has died (1881: 451). He further commented that the *ɔkra* of a dying person leaves the body gradually before the person's last breath (1881: 255). The literal statement to describe a dead person is, *Ne home ate kɔ*, literally, "He has stopped breathing." The Akan will not say "His breath left him" because breath does not go anywhere. The equivalent of the Hebrew "breath of life" in Akan is the *ɔkra,* which is responsible for life in the individual and it is that which takes leave after death.

Danquah associates *ɔkra* with *honhom*. I have discussed Danquah's evolutionary conception of the human being in chapter six. Life begins with the *esu* (nature), followed by *sunsum* (personality), and finally *ɔkra* (soul-mind), the ideal to be lived or experienced to become *honhom* (spirit).[84] In this case, the *ɔkra* is nothing but a *honhom*, the spirit of pure ethereality that identifies or links human beings to the Ideal Spirit or *Honhom*, which is God (1968: 67). There is an ascendency towards perfection that makes the *ɔkra* qua *honhom* capable of traveling through space after death. In this state, Danquah refers to *honhom* as a *spiritus realitas* (spirit in reality), describing the Akan notion of a transfiguration of the *ɔkra* to become a spirit. The *ɔkra* is a fully developed *honhom*, the ultimate reality, that shares the same spiritual attributes with God, and the rationale behind the deathless nature of the *ɔkra*. Danquah observes that unless the *ɔkra* contains in itself the capacity of a divine nature, it cannot be identified with God (1944: 171).[85] This is the reason why the departed *ɔkra*, as *honhom*, has the potential to return to life to achieve its highest and noblest destiny.[86]

---

84 Danquah does not see *honhom* as a "thing," but as a state of being (1968: 67).

85 Danquah and several Akan scholars think the *ɔkra* returns to God. The idea of a return to God is basically absent in Akan religion. This is a purely Christian doctrine. It does not, however, make void the ability of the *ɔkra* to return to God because it has obtained spirituality. The point is the majority of Akan people believe that the *akra* (pl.) travel to *Asamando*, their final place of abode, from where also libations are poured to invoke their presence among the living.

86 Akan religion has concepts to consider the mysteries of death. One of them is reincarnation – the re-entering of the departed *ɔkra* into the mundane life. Akan people do not see life as endless cycles of reincarnation. The idea of reincarnation is for special circumstances. Reincarnation is closely related to the Akan concept of *nkrabea* (destiny). It is a common belief among Akan people that individuals do not chart their own destiny. Destiny is predetermined by God before birth. Legend has it that the departing *ɔkra* from Nyankopɔn also took its destiny from Him. Destiny determines the various facets of temporal events and occurrences in the course of the individual's whole life. The Akan understanding of destiny is positive, good luck, and is determined by the *ɔkra*. However, destiny is also unconscious, which is why the Akan will inquire about their destiny in situations of vicious cycles of misfortunes in a person's life. This

Other scholars like Meyerowitz and Gyekye are skeptical about the identification of *ɔkra* with *honhom*. Meyerowitz sees the *'kra* and *honhom* as relative but nonindentical. She identifies *honhom* as the "breath of life" in the *ɔkra*, the eternal soul or life-giving power. She says "*honhom* is always coupled with the *ɔkra*" but the two are not same (1951: 25). The distinction she draws follows that "after death the *kra* labours up a steep hill in order to reach heaven, there to submit to the judgement of Nyankopon, the *honhom* flies back to Nyame in the shape of a bird" (Meyerowitz 1951: 25). In this conception, one is made to believe that judgment in heaven after death is compatible with Akan religion. However, I cannot think of any such doctrine in the Akan religion other than what I know in Christianity and Islam.

Gyekye, like Meyerowitz, does not identify *honhom* with *ɔkra*, and neither does he agree with Meyerowitz's perception of the former as the equivalence of the "breath of life." Gyekye thinks the phrase, *Ne honhom kɔ* would best be translated as: "his breath is gone." He translates *honhom* as "breath" because he neither accepts the interpretation of the word as "spirit" nor identifies it with the *ɔkra* as a synonymous term. Gyekye says "the *honhom* is the tangible manifestation or evidence of the presence of the *okra*" (Gyekye 1987: 88). His statement creates a dichotomy between *honhom* and *ɔkra,* although both terms are closely related. I do not think this should be so. The statement *Ne honhom kɔ* is synonymous to "His spirit is withdrawn," where the "spirit" is in reference to the *ɔkra*. All these agree with the Akan notion of the *ɔkra* as a foreign entity apart from the body upon which depends life and destiny. Christaller referred to the *ɔkra* as the *honhom* (spirit) of a person, and the consequent rationality underlining Danquah's evolutionary process of life where *ɔkra* takes leave as *honhom*. The *ɔkra*, a spark from God, needs to realize its experience in life in order

---

statement in no way implies that there is an inherent evil associated with *nkrabea* (destiny). Certainly not. After all, the *nkrabea* came from Nyankopɔn, and Akan people do not associate evil with God. Misfortunes are carried out by malevolent forces that have the potential to affect lives with evils such as sicknesses, accidents, bareness, untimely death, and all other ailments suspected to be the working of evil spirits. This is where the Akan concept of reincarnation comes in to particularly stress the importance of destiny. When people die through any of these misfortunes, the *ɔkra* is reincarnated into the world to achieve its full destiny before it can enter into the spirit world of the ancestors (*Asamando*).

to express its potentiality, become an ancestor, and earn participation in divine immortality (*honhom*).

5.3.7. Epistemological Dimension of Honhom

Epistemology is widely recognized as the theory of knowledge. However, both the meaning of and the way epistemology is formulated differ or are determined culturally. Wherever significant cultural differences exist, one should expect corresponding epistemological discrepancies, and this advances the claim which distinguishes Akan's theory of knowledge from that of the rest of the world (Okrah 2003: 9). In the Akan sense, epistemology finds expression in the mythology, proverbs, idioms, festivals, and ceremonies that are repertoires of their thought process and experience of life. The concept of *honhom* forms part of the epistemic principles in the phrases of everyday life. For example, *honhom bɔne* (evil spirit) is a common phrase Akan people use to describe a malignant spirit or witchcraft. Another popular adage is *honhom fi* (unclean spirit or demon). *Honhom* appears in two Akan idioms, already mentioned, to express a state of death: *Ne honhom kɔ* (His spirit is departed), and *Honhom nni ne mu* (There is no spirit or soul in him). These expressions, as religious as they may be, are also philosophical ideas used to define Akan worldviews.

I will outline further characteristics of *honhom* in the next section to reveal the differences between *honhom* and *sunsum*. Drawing the differences between the two terms is of great concern in this chapter because they will reveal how Akan people use the terms interchangeably to speak of or describe specific experiences.

5.4. The Differences of Between *Sunsum* and *Honhom*

Sunsum and *honhom* are not always synonymous, even though there is a close relationship between the two. In most cases, it is the context of their usage that determines their meaning. The usage of *sunsum* has been suggested in my research in two views. First is the inspirited (*wɔ sunsum*), which defines *sunsum* as a principle of inherent power (force) in natural objects. The second is the exclusively spiritual (*yɛ sunsum*), referring to spiritual entities. My research proposes a third view, which is the exclusively anthropological *sunsum* (*wo sunsum*). This third view is not so different from the inspirited, but for the sake of convenience and in order to differentiate the *sunsum* of the human being from all other *sunsum*, I will employ these three aspects of the usage of *sunsum* in comparison to *honhom* to draw the differences between the two terms, and to further reveal more characteristics of *honhom* as shown in the tables below.

Table 5: The differences between wɔ sunsum and honhom

***Wɔ Sunsum* (Inspirited)**	***Honhom***
Natural objects such as trees, stones, rivers, animals, *suman*, etc. are not *sunsum* but inspirited (*wɔ sunsum*). It means they exercise power. The same applies to the Golden Stool of the Asantes, which contains the *sunsum* of the Asantes.	To say an object has *honhom* means there is life in it, i.e. the object breathes. Or, it can imply that a foreign spiritual agent has taken residence in the thing. *Honhom* is all-pervading, constant, uniform, infinite, interminable, and multifunctional.
Sunsum is a dynamic force in natural objects.	*Honhom* is not a dynamic force but a vital force. It possesses its own dynamic force from God.
Sunsum is a substance of natural objects whose absence renders the object powerless.	*Honhom* is the breath of natural objects. When used as an entity, a *honhom* (spirit) may take temporary residence in an object and leave without any damage to the object, unlike *sunsum* which may render the object powerless.

Table 6: The differences between wo sunsum and honhom

Wo Sunsum (Exclusively Anthropological)	***Honhom***
Generally, *wo sunsum* proceeds either from a being or an object, e.g., father, pantheon deity, etc. in the same way one's body throws a shadow (*sunsuma*) on the ground.	A man may transmit his *sunsum* but not his *honhom. Wo honhom* (Your spirit) is analogous to your *ɔkra*, which is not transferable, unlike *sunsum.*
Wo sunsum (Your *sunsum*) is not an entitative (spirit) but a spiritual force. To a Fante, *wo sunsum* is equivalent to one's *ɔkra.*	*Honhom* most often refers to spiritual beings or objects that are exclusively spiritual. This is so because the essence of spiritual beings is like the wind. *Wo honhom* directly refers to the *ɔkra.*
Wo sunsum is measurable either as weak, light, or strong. There is also the *sunsum pa* (good *sunsum*) and *sunsum bɔne* (evil *sunsum*).	*Wo honhom,* i.e., *ɔkra* is not measurable as either weak or strong. Akan people believe that there is *honhom pa* (good spirit) and *honhom bɔne* (evil spirit).
Wo sunsum is versatile to education. It can be transformed from bad to good, or weak to strong.	*Wo honhom,* i.e., *ɔkra* cannot be educated because it possesses its own divine predetermined destiny.
Wo sunsum does not go to *Asamando* after death according to my analysis.	*Wo honhom* is the apotheosized *ɔkra* that flits out of the body to journey to *Asamando.*
Wo sunsum is responsible for morality, charisma, personality, etc.	*Wo honhom*, being the *ɔkra*, is only a bearer of destiny. However, *honhom* as a spiritual agent can manipulate a person's *sunsum* or imparts its own *sunsum* to the individual. *Akɔmfa* (mediumship) is a typical example where a spiritual agent alights on an individual.
Wo sunsum is not related to breath, air, and wind.	*Honhom* is identified with breath, air, and wind.

Table 7: The differences between yɛ sunsum and honhom

Yɛ Sunsum (Exclusively spiritual)	***Honhom***
Yɛ sunsum involves God, Asaase Yaa (Earth goddess), *Abosom*, *Nananom* (ancestors), etc. They are *sunsum* because of their dynamic nature as force-beings.	All the entities mentioned are *ahonhom* because their very nature is spiritual, like the wind or air. The word is applied to their very essence as ethereal.
Sunsum is not a generic term to describe what is invincible; unless it is specific. It is only used to describe spiritual existents and objects.	Akan people have come to designate all entities in the spiritual realms as *ahonhom* (spirits). In this case, the term *honhom* is used synonymously or interchangeably with *sunsum*.
Sunsum, when used for a spirit (especially among Fantes), is a generic expression for a spiritual being.	*Honhom*, when used for a spirit, expresses the state of being that defines an object as spiritual.
The nature of *ɔkra* is not *sunsum*. To use *sunsum* to describe the spirituality of the *ɔkra* will amount to tautology.	*Ɔkra* is the *honhom* of an individual. *Honhom* is not synonymous with *ɔkra*; instead, it is a description of it as a foreign spiritual component in the body.
Sunsum mu is the Akan expression for the mystical world.[87]	The phrase *honhom mu* describes the invisible spiritual world.

The comparison reveals the different categories a majority of Akan people ascribe to both *sunsum* and *honhom*. It also shows the non-identical nature of the two terms. Their point of convergence explains how at times the two terms can be used synonymously; this is why Gyekye noted the interchangeability of the two terms (Gyekye 1987: 88). The synonymity only occurs in specific instances of their usage. For example, both *sunsum mu* and *honhom mu* are synonymous phrases used to describe the spiritual world. *Sunsum* and *honhom* often overlap each other to describe a spiritual

---

87 The term "mystical" is used here to express the general Akan notion of *sunsum mu* as involving mysticism since it involves an interplay of humans, superhumans (witches, medicinal men), and spiritual beings.

being without any misunderstanding among Akan people. However, *sunsum* and *honhom* diverge on their usage to describe the essence of natural objects. Whereas *sunsum* describes the essential quality of natural objects, *honhom* is the vital force of natural objects.

Although both terms have a pneumatological value, I see a much broader polysemy in *honhom* expressing the biblical conception of רוּחַ and πνεῦμα. It has been argued earlier that contextual Christian theology is not about the theologization of cultural concepts since such an attempt will amount to cultural theology. Instead, it is the use of scriptural principles that are informed by the cultural context. As a result, there is the need for a faithful interpretation of the Bible and a whole cultural dimension of its application. In the next section, I intend to offer a theological justification for *honhom* in the Twi Bible.

5.5. *Honhom* and the Akan Twi Bible Translation

The first Twi Bible was published by Johann Gottlieb Christaller in 1871.[88] A copy of this original work can be found in the archives of the Basel Mission 21 in Switzerland. This illustrious work represents the evolution of the oral Twi language, which later became the standard text for Akan scholarship in written form. If the term *honhom* is a foreign invention, it is none other but Christaller and his co-workers who worked out a translation of the Twi Bible.

To answer the question of invention, Christaller did not invent the word *honhom*; neither did he nor any of his translators temper the originality of the Twi terminologies, since such would constitute sacrilege against the civilization of the Akan people. His task as a philologist was to translate and to transform the Twi language from its oral traditions into a literary form. Nevertheless, Christaller left traces of how some foreign words were adopted into the Twi Bible:

> Foreign words adopted in Tshi (about 20 from Ga, Guan, Marewa, nearly 100 from European languages) have been

[88] The translation of the Bible from its original languages into the Twi language of Ghana was spearheaded by Rev. Johann Christaller in collaboration with other local missionaries. Refer to chapter five for more details.

> marked as such by indicating the language from which they are taken in brackets. Above 100 more foreign words found in the Tshi Bible are registered in Appendix A.—New words derived from words already existing in the language and introduced by the Basel missionaries, are partly marked by a dagger (†); many such as well as modern terms, used in teaching the various sciences, are not found in this dictionary, because not as yet sufficiently approved. Nearly a hundred of them are contained in the appendix to Mr. Bellon's Instruction in Arithmetic (1881: ix, x).[89]

The appearance of *honhom* in the Twi Bible does not carry any of the annotations mentioned above. There is no evidence or details given anywhere concerning a purposeful coining of the term. If for argument's sake, the word *honhom* was invented for use in the Bible to complement the original languages, then we ask the question, why should Christaller and his crew do that against the use of *sunsum*? The answer lies in the question of whether *sunsum* is the most adequate theological term to articulate a contextual Christian pneumatology for the Akan people.

Christaller does translate the Holy Spirit as *Honhom Kronkron* instead of *Sunsum Kronkron*. It can be noted further that he does not use *Sunsum Kronkron* as an alternative to *Honhom Kronkron*.[90] Writing thirty-six years later, Jehle attempts to solve this dilemma in the following comments:

> In the South the people say that the word honhom was formerly used for sunsum; so it would be the more ancient

---

89 Christaller lists the categories of instances where foreign words or terms taken from European languages are used in the Twi Bible language in Appendix A. These categories included: proper names of persons and places, foreign names of personal beings, names for religious objects, names of times, European months, names of some Christian festivals, names of animals, plants and productions of plants, minerals and precious stones, and measures, weights and coins (1881: 633, 634). It is obvious from the quote above that the issue at stake is not about the adoption of foreign languages or modifying indigenous terms or coining some new others to meet a theological agenda, but a question of terminological convenience for foreign names and terms recreated for the Twi languages.

90 The Fante New Testament Bible applies *sunsum* to the soul; in the other dialects *ɔkra* and *honhom* are used instead (Jehle 1907: 414).

> word. But in out-of-the-way places where the people had not been touched by civilisation at all; the people used only "sunsum." The connection of the word with "home" to breathe is apparently right; the natives have the euphemistic expression for death: he has ceased to draw his "kra." But the *popular* etymology connects the word with ahung = atmosphere and explains honhom as something from the air, something invisible [...]. A very intelligent native told me that honhom was quite different from okra and meant an influence from outside, from an invincible agency. So Christaller was right to take the word for the *Divine* Spirit (1907: 415).

Though Jehle's statement is too scanty to unravel the mysteries over the use of *honhom* in the Twi Bible for the "spirit," he does offer us a cue to discard the argument of the invention of *honhom* by former Western missionaries. *Honhom* is an Akan indigenous term for describing invincible realities, which may also include air, wind, and breath. In today's application of the term, it will describe all other invincible objects such as radio waves, electromagnetic forces, etc. that are verifiable only through scientific methods. I respond to the allegation of the invention of *honhom* as not convincing and an attempt to give credence to the pneumatic conception of *sunsum* as a spirit, which my research has contested. The use of *honhom* in the Twi Bible was accurate and theologically agreeable. Christaller's choice of the word for the spirit, though partly due to the theological implications underlining the original languages of the biblical text (which is nevertheless an influence of the use of *honhom*), is both traditionally and theologically expedient. I will give more details later. For now, the most critical question to ask is: why are some Akan people more familiar with *sunsum*, others *honhom*, and others both? Could both *honhom* and *sunsum* form the basis for contextual Akan pneumatology? These questions lead us to the most crucial issue in my research, whereby the nature of *sunsum* as a "spirit" has been called to question and, in another instance, *sunsum* becomes the basis of spiritual realities. The confusion arises when one fails to understand the complex social setup within Akan ethnicity.

I mentioned earlier in chapter six that there are two main Akan subgroups, namely, the Twi-speaking Akan, and the Fante-speaking Akan. The two subgroups are known at face value for their linguistic-accent differences, a common differentiating trait among the Akan ethnicity. The Fante dialect, as well as some vocabularies, is slightly different from the other Twi dialects even though they are mutually intelligible. *Honhom* and *sunsum* are two terms in Akan literature that often seem interchangeable among Twi-speaking and Fante-speaking people. The reason follows that Fante pneumatology is chiefly based on *sunsum*. We recall this from my previous discussion of Ephirim-Donkor in chapter six. Fante Bible translators used *sunsum* to translate both רוּחַ and πνεῦμα throughout the entire text. The term *honhom* is infrequently used, if not absent at all among Fantes. We find the same trend in the writings of Ephirim-Donkor, who seems to refrain from the word *honhom*. In his discussion of the essence of the *Abosom* (pantheon deities) as "air" or "breath," he used the Fante term *ahom* for "breath," which he explains the ethereal evidence of the *ɔkra* (2016: 64, 65). *Ahom* (breath) is known among the Twi-speaking Akan as *home* or *honhom*. All these suggest how the term *honhom* is not preeminent among the Fante, even if it once was, according to Jehle. Of significance is how the Fante never use *sunsum* to translate "air" or "breath." Meanwhile, both "air" and "breath" are analogous to the essence of the spirit in the Bible and therefore should, as a theological principle, be factored into contextual Christian pneumatology.

In this section, the evidence presented allows us to conclude that both *sunsum* and *honhom* form the basis of Akan pneumatology. To neglect this diversity is a disservice to Akan religion, but it is also true that *sunsum* cuts across almost all Akan societies. It has a significant presence in the writings of Rattray about the Asantes, although the word never appeared in his early 1915 book *Ashanti Proverbs*. Similar trends exist in other commentaries on Akan religion from the other tribes. The meaning of *sunsum* contains a universal principle within the Akan ethnicity and provides the basic spiritual framework upon which the inherent qualities of natural objects or the spiritual properties of an agent are measured.

The argument follows that if *sunsum* forms the basis of Akan pneumatology, why then is the need for a new proposal of an Akan Christian pneumatology based on *honhom*? My answer remains the same: *honhom* captures all the essential characteristics of biblical pneumatology – breath, wind, air, spirit, and soul – and should be the basis of contextual Akan

Christian pneumatology. The next section shows how *honhom* is analogous to the biblical concepts of רוּחַ and πνεῦμα.

5.6. Theological Justification for *Honhom* in the Akan Twi Bible

I will now delve into the Bible to analyze some pneumatological texts in light of a contextual reading of the Bible in the Twi language. In doing this, I will proceed with the most considerable caution to focus on a faithful exegesis of the original texts and how they apply to the theological interpretation of *honhom*. The idea here is to show how *honhom* can adequately define the meaning of the spirit in the Twi Bible. I will apply the various dimensions of the Spirit from our previous discussions in both the Old and New Testament.

5.6.1. Theo-anthropological Dimension of *Honhom*

The theo-anthropological dimension of the spirit relates both רוּחַ and πνεῦμα to the breath of life, i.e., the breath of human beings from God's breath. In both the Masoretic and Septuagint traditions, the breath of life in Gen 2:7 is analogous to the spirit in Job 27:3. This is the same for the Twi translation of the texts. Let us analyze the texts below:

English: "…and breathed into his nostrils the breath of life, and the man became a living creature." (Gen 2: 7 ESV)
Twi: "*…na ohuu nkwa home guu ne hwene mu na onipa yɛɛ ɔkra teasefoɔ*" (Gen 2:7 Asante)
English: "as long as my breath is in me, and the spirit of God is in my nostrils" (Job 27:3 ESV)
Twi: "*na m'ahome nyinaa da so wɔ me mu, na Nyankopɔn ahome da so wɔ me hwene mu yi*" (Hiob 27:3 Asante).[91]

---

[91] The רוּחַ/πνεῦμα in Job 27:3 is translated in this context as *ahome* in the Asante Twi Bible. Christaller used the term *ahohow*, and the modern Akuapim Bible uses the term *honhom*. All these terms are translated as "breath" (Christaller 1874: 37). The exception is the Fante Bible which uses *sunsum* in this context.

The texts attribute the origin of life solely to an external principle in God. It is the breath of life that quickens the body to be active. Hence, one does not expect to equate the breath of life to mere "air" in a person's nostrils. It is the רוּחַ /πνεῦμα/*honhom* of God. It is typical of Akan religion that *honhom* is related to the principle of life (*ɔkra*) in an individual. The Jewish principle of life and that of the Akan are related. Life is a divine spark, and death is a reversal of that spark. The absence of the רוּחַ/πνεῦμα/*honhom* (*ɔkra*) means death or lifelessness (Jer. 10:14; 51:17).

We are here introduced to why Akan people will say *Ne honhom kɔ*, "His *'kra* is withdrawn from the body," or *Honhom nni ne mu bio,* "No vital breath is in him anymore." Denteh thinks this "perhaps justifies the use of "Honhom" in the Twi Bible to mean the God-spirit part of Himself, and that in men called the soul. The 'Okra' therefore is virtually the 'Honhom' personified" (Denteh 1967: 93). A majority of Akan scholars, including Agyarko, believe the *ɔkra*, rather than *sunsum*, is the spark of God in human beings and shares the same qualities with God. It is deathless, and no evil is associated with it. Ephirim-Donkor shares similar thought and says, "God, then, is the first to enter a child (abofra) as Ahom (breath) in order to make it a living being. By the same token, the Ahom is the last essence to depart a living entity to cause a death" (Ephirim-Donkor 2016: 66). The breath of life is the *ɔkra*, the determining principle of life and death in living things.

Matthew 27:50 is another theo-anthropological dimension of the use of πνεῦμα to describe the death of Jesus on the cross. The text says Jesus "yielded up his πνεῦμα," which means he breathed his last and died. Almost all the Twi Bibles read: "*Ogyaa ne honhom mu.*" The statement agrees with the Akan euphemistic expression, *Ne honhom kɔ,* "His *'kra* is withdrawn from the body." The Fante Bible, exceptionally, uses *sunsum* in place of *honhom* in Matt. 27:50. To say, "*Ogyaa ne sunsum mu*" to the Twi-speaking Akan may engender contradiction. It will mean the person is separated from his *sunsum,* which according to the majority of Akan people does not necessarily define death because, in sleep, it is believed a person's *sunsum* can take voyage and return. Ephirim-Donkor frequently translates *ɔkra* as soul; I have not yet come across his translation of *sunsum* as soul.[92] The complex

---

92 Why does Ephirim-Donkor translate *sunsum* as soul? Because he thinks *sunsum* survives death and becomes an ancestor to form the basis of ancestor worship (2016: 78). I do not think he uses *sunsum* in this case in a manner that is synonymous with the *ɔkra*. He

usage of *sunsum* among the Fantes justifies why Christaller translated "soul" in his dictionary as both *honhom* and *sunsum* (1874: 226).

There is more sustainability of the *ɔkra* as the breath of life. The Twi Bible translates "a living creature" to "*ɔkrateasefo*," that is, the *ɔkra* incarnate. *Ɔkrateasefo* is related to life and means "a living being" as opposed to *owufo,* "the dead." Agyarko explains the notion of *ɔkrateasefo* to denote "that the divine spark (*okra*) has become a human being (*teasefo*). Thus, *okra* as a divine spark has the capacity to become a human being without any confusion with human nature" (Agyarko 2009: 172). The breath of life is the *ɔkra*, the principle of life, which most Akan identify with *honhom*. The views of Ephirim-Donkor support breath "as an intangible attestation to the presence of the *okra* in the person" (Ephirim-Donkor 2016: 107).

Further, Eccles. 12:7 illustrates the disembodiment of the human being at death. The Bible reads, "the dust shall return to the earth as it was: and the רוּחַ/pneuma/spirit/*honhom* shall return unto God who gave it."[93] The description is in direct relation to Gen 2:7. The material returns to the material (Earth), and the spiritual returns to the spiritual source, God. Jewish anthropology sees death as a reversal of Gen 2:7. This is also true of the Akan, who see the departure of the *ɔkra* as death. The concept of the return of the רוּחַ to God can only be identified with the *ɔkra* – not the *sunsum* that perishes or remains in the family according to my investigation – which a majority of Akan people believe came from God and returns to the spirit world (*Asamado*).

The theo-anthropological dimension of the spirit in the Bible corresponds well with the concept of *ɔkra-honhom* analogy among the Akan. By implication, the spirit is a life-giving principle in human beings. It defines humanity's numinous nature while at the same time accounting for the mysteries of duality of the human being in both biblical and Akan anthropology. It also establishes the interconnectivity with God, underlining the Akan maxim, "All human beings are the children of God." To call the breath of life "*nkwa honhom*" or *ɔkra* of God is not a tautology but a genuine understanding of the contextual application of biblical pneumatology among the

---

considers the survival of the spiritual components of the body at death. He again commented on the Golden Stool as containing the soul of the Asantes (2016: 116). By the term soul, he meant *sunsum* since it is widely held that the Golden Stool contains the *sunsum* – rather than the *ɔkra* – of the Asantes.

93 Emphases are mine.

Akan people. The breath of life, as the *honhom* of God, shows why the presence of the Spirit is vital to the existence of life.

5.6.2. The Theological Dimension of the Spirit as Honhom

The Gospel of John offers us one of the most substantial reflections on the Spirit within the New Testament literature. One of its pneumatological affirmations is John 4:23-24, which, in the narrative context of Jesus' dialogue with the Samaritan woman, speaks about true worship in spirit since God himself is Spirit (Dettwiler 2016: 149, 168). Several English Bible translations apply an essentialist definition of God as spirit, i.e., non-material and omnipresent to the text. The question now is whether an essentialist definition of God exists in Akan socio-religious ideas.

Akan traditional theology postulates Onyankopɔn (God) as the highest Spirit-being. In other words, God is not material, and Akan people do not have iconic representations of God as one may find for the pantheon deities. The Akan maxim, "Nobody teaches the child to know God," makes God a reality. God is self-revealing and accessible just like the air in the atmosphere. God's invisibility is not remote, but immanent within and without the Akan cosmology. Religious officiants, relics, shrines, and arts are all visible expressions of faith in the reality of the invisible God.

There are further concrete expressions of the essence of God as air (*honhom*). An Akan maxim says, "If you want to say something to God, say it to the wind." Gyekye thinks the proverb is an analogy used to express the invisible and all-pervading nature of God. As "the wind is invisible and intangible – yet its effects are seen everywhere – so is Onyame invisible, intangible, and omnipresent" (Gyekye 1987: 70). Nevertheless, he firmly holds that the wind can be felt, unlike God who can neither be seen nor be felt (1987: 70). Ephirim-Donkor holds a similar idea by relating the essence of God to the wind, "God is *mframa* (wind) in the sense that one must: 'converse with the wind when intending to speak to God'" (Ephirim-Donkor 2010: 28). He again writes, "God is the air, because air is synonymous with God forming the basis for the saying: "To speak with God, converse with the wind" (2016: 108). Does Ephirim-Donkor adhere to an essentialist description of the nature of God? It seems he does. He sees the wind analogy as an "acknowledgment of God's omnipresence, ubiquity, knowledge, and nature in Akan socio-political and religious life and thought" (Ephirim-

Donkor 2016: 65). His essentialist definition views "the essence of God as air or wind (*Mframa*)" (Ephirim-Donkor 2016: 66).

The identification of God with the wind is an essentialist ideology that compares the essence of the omnipresent God with the invisible wind, not that God is the wind. Agyarko sums them all up this way: "God is likened to the wind, which is also invisible and everywhere...*Onyame* is everywhere and can be called upon anywhere" (2013: 3). Therefore, the Akan understanding of God as invisible is not an abstract notion, but a reality expressed in concrete objects and terms. God is not the *mframa* (wind) per se, although one may be tempted to draw such a conclusion from a superficial reading of Ephirim-Donkor's words: "God (Nyame) is *Mframa* because the Akan equate God with wind (*Mframa*)" (2016: 65).[94]

Given the Akan view of the nature of God as wind, it agrees largely with πνεύμα ο θεός in Jn. 4:24. The wind is also *honhom* in Akan languages. Jesus' statement underscores the significance of true worship to comprise a true understanding of the essential qualities of God as *honhom* in contrast to the perception by the Samaritan woman of a visible place of worship dedicated to God. The conversation reveals the transition from a theocentric view of a God who dwells in tents and temples to a spiritual experience of God who is spirit. There is no restriction on God by geography or time. The nature of God is spiritual, and this flows directly through the various thought forms and arts which serve as channels of communication to humankind.[95] God is spirit (*honhom*) and human beings should worship God through God's *honhom* in human beings, which is the *ɔkra* – the essence of God in humankind that also relates human beings to God.

---

94 From Ephirim-Donkor's statement, one is tempted to identify God with the wind instead of taking the statement metaphorically. I misunderstood him in my earlier reading of his book *African Personality and Spirituality: The Role of Abosom and Human Essence*, pp. 50, 66, 108. God is *mframa* (wind) is a transliteration of Jn. 4:24, "God is spirit."

95 Andreas Dettwiler does not see the phrase πνεύμα ο θεός "as an essentialist definition of God in Godself, but God is Spirit (and Truth) insofar as God communicates his creative, live-giving power to humankind through the word and the destiny of Jesus, his 'unique Son' – or non-metaphorically speaking, his authentic Revealer" (Dettwiler 2016: 168). Thus, Christ, who bounds us to God, is a reflection of the invisible God (Col. 1:15).

5.6.3. The *Honhom Kronkron* (Holy Spirit)

The book of Acts records the acts of the Holy Spirit in the ministry of the early church. Of great significance to Acts is its contribution to the discussion of pneumatology in the New Testament. First, Jesus predicted the coming of the Spirit as a force for spreading the gospel (Acts 1:8). The entire success of the Christ movement depended on the life support of the Spirit. This is the reason why Luke predicates the apostolic mission with the theophanic alighting of the Spirit (Acts 2; cf. Lk. 24:49). The ecstatic experience of prophetic speaking in new tongues attested to the continuity of the prophetic ministry from the Old Testament times. The expression, "they were all filled with the Holy Spirit" means no one was left out in the room, making Peter refer to the accomplishment of Joel's prophecy in Joel 2:28, "I will pour out my Spirit upon all flesh."

Luke describes the coming of the Spirit "as of a rushing mighty wind" (2:2). He uses the Greek term *pnoes*, which is also synonymous with the Akan term *honhom* (wind or breath). The wind analogy appears here in connection with the presence of the Spirit. Luke is careful in his description of the event. First, he does not see the wind as being synonymous with the Spirit, although the metaphor carries in itself the essence of the Spirit as invisible. Second, the presence of the Spirit filled the room in the same way air or wind occupies a space (2:2). Third, cloven tongues like fire (burning air) signified the manifestation of the charisma of speaking in other languages (2:3). Fourth, they were all filled with the Holy Spirit (2:4).[96] There is no doubt that the Spirit operates as an outside influence; something from without but now within the community of believers as the driving force of the Christian movement.

The metaphor of "rushing wind" that came to fill them with the Holy Spirit (2:4) was an experience of the Spirit as a vital force. The impact of speaking in an unknown tongue shows the effect of the Spirit on people in the same way spirit/breath/*honhom* impacts the body with life (Ja. 2:26). Moltmann uses terms like "vitalizing energy" and "vibration" in this context to illustrate that there is always an ignition of life in the experience of the Spirit. The experience is like breathing air, God's continual breathing upon the soul. Acts 2 significantly represents the breathing in of God's

96 The expression does not look like spirit possession since utterances were that of the disciples and not a foreign agent (2: 4).

Spirit. It is from this experience that the gifts are also described as *dunamis* or *energeia* (Acts 1:8) according to Moltmann (1992: 161, 195).[97] The entitative nature of the Spirit is implicit in Acts 2, even though verse 4 shows that a supernatural agent was at work.

Akan theology designates *honhom* (*ɔkra*) as that which vivifies the body with life. It defines the destiny of individuals and societies, which is vital to allow the power of God to flow freely among them. The *honhom* is singularly an act of God, an essential quality of God that makes the Akan see human beings as children of God. It remains the only spiritual essence of God in human beings that also defines their spiritual part. The *honhom* is the immaterial extension of God, and it comes into origin as life to creation. The Holy Spirit as a vital principle from God is pictured in Luke as the agent of Christ's conception (Lk. 1:35). Luke does not say Christ was the Holy Spirit incarnate because that will disagree with the larger activity of the Spirit in the Lukan corpus. Paul uses the vitality of the Spirit as a metaphor to remind the Christians in Rome that "the Spirit you received brought about your adoption to sonship. And by him we cry, 'Abba, Father'" (Rom. 8:15 NIV). The Spirit is an agent of life, God's breath, which vivifies and unifies all things in God. To call it *Honhom Kronkron* means the Holy Breath or Spirit of God.

5.6.4. The Metaphysical-cosmological *Honhom* of God

I have noted in previous discussions the connection between *sunsum* and the creation. All the created things are inspirited, making the creation powerful. Several conceptions exist hereof which some are discussed in previ-

97 To Moltmann, this energy emanates from the Holy Spirit, that which is seen as a well of life. It is not synonymous with the Holy Spirit. He rejects subordination of pneumatology to Christology by looking at the Spirit as the source of energy for creation (Brackney 2019: 98). Molly Marshall comes to a similar conclusion to designate the energy of the Spirit as cosmological. In her book, *Joining the Dance: A Theology of the Spirit* (2003), Marshall argues that pneumatology must embrace all of creation and recognize the Spirit as a symbol of wholeness, relatedness, energy, creativity, and life. This shift sees the activity of the Spirit as universally necessary. Agyarko sees the activity of the Holy Spirit in a similar sense as the Akan *sunsum* which is the central, unifying vitality that enables a being or object to exercise power and to function in its characteristic manner (Agyarko 2014: 7).

ous chapters. The conclusions were that *sunsum* exists because of the presence of the deities in the Akan universe. *Sunsum* is not the "creative" power or life-giving principle, but the essential innate power exercised by a natural object, including human beings. It can be soundly understood when one thinks of the nonidentical nature of *ɔkra* and *sunsum* in the human being, where *ɔkra* is the life-principle and *sunsum* is the personality. The question, then is, what breathes life in the creation? While I have given several theological reasons why *honhom* addresses the anthropological question of life in the human being, I will now argue that the creative power in creation is the breath or *honhom* of God.

The metaphysical-cosmological dimension of רוּחַ /πνεῦμα makes the "spirit" a creative and vital force from God. The creation names for God among the Akan are Odomankoma, Onyame, and Onyankopɔn; these names are not detached from the created things. The introduction of God as the Creator means that creation itself draws life from God. This is true also for the Jewish accounts of creation. There is no life exclusive of God: "By the word of the Lord the heavens were made, and all their host by the breath [רוּחַ] of his mouth" (Ps 33:6). To read the last statement in Akan as "*sunsum* of his mouth" will account for the veriest tautology, since breath is not identical with *sunsum* as it is with *honhom*. The text here shows the synonymity between the speech of God and the breath of God already at play in the creation accounts of Gen. 1. Jesus brings a similar picture into view: "The words that I have spoken to you are spirit and life" (Jn. 6:63). The synonymity of the "word" and "spirit" is what made Kubat conclude that "the spirit is the mediating force that makes God present" (2016: 301). God is the source of vitality in the whole of creation because God is the inexhaustible source of sustenance for the creation.

How does the creative force from God relate to the Akan concept of *honhom*? For a better understanding of a contextual Akan Christian pneumatology, the notion of animism in the Akan traditional religion needs to be revisited. Rattray had come to the conclusion that the concept of *sunsum* is the basis of the "animistic creed" of the Asantes (1923: 296). In other words, all things are inspirited, making them active and powerful to interact.[98] Several Akan scholars have integrated the notion of animism into their

---

98 George P. u explains the idea of "all things have *sunsum*" as "in conjunction with the belief that in the world there are entities that are both sunsum and also invisible – as well as entities that are not wholly sunsum, but bear sunsum as an aspect of their nature"

overall assessment of Akan religion, even if the term animism does not always or adequately deal with the panentheistic conception of Akan religion.

Granted, however, that the Akan religion is animistic, it will still agree with the Akan notion of *honhom* better than *sunsum*. The classical Latin *anima* or *animus* (cognate with the Greek ἄνεμος (ánemos) "wind") means "air in motion, breath of air," "breath of life; principle of life," "soul that survives death; soul of the dead body," etc. These are also true of the Latin *spiritus* (air or breath) and the Sanskrit *aniti* (breathes) (Vanhove 2008: 195, 196). All these are palpable characteristics of the Akan concept of *honhom*, which is related to breath, wind, air, and the *ɔkra*.

It can, however, be established that the Akan notion of *honhom* shares the same cosmological understanding with other ancient traditions on the concept of animism. Hence, the vital conception of the Spirit in the Bible as the "breath of God" agrees with the traditional conception of *honhom* among the Akan. The creation relies on the breath of God or the *honhom* of God for life (Job 12: 10). The basis for any animistic doctrine among the Akan will be better off if the notion of *honhom* is considered based on the explanation given in this section. Whatever has *honhom* is alive, as the opposite will suggest death (Psalm 150: 6). To reject *sunsum* in this respect also agrees with my conclusion that *sunsum* is only an emanating force, a description of force-beings, and perishable.

The conclusion here is not a denial of the presence of *sunsum* in creation. The innate qualities of creation as *sunsum* have been firmly established; contrary to the notion that *sunsum* is the spirit of life. *Sunsum* as a principle of life is contradictory to what life is dependent upon among the Akan. God is the source of life as the study has rightly pointed out to the *ɔkra,* which proceeds from God and is the principle of life in all living things. The *ɔkra* is the *honhom* (breath of life) from God whose presence means life and absence means death. This idea means the whole creation is united with God and testifies of God's absolute sovereignty on all. The inspirited universe of *sunsum* serves to remind Akan people that the universe is populated with spirit-beings, whose essence and presence are spiritual and fill the universe with power.

(Hagan 1999: 43, 44). The explanation is a summary of the exclusively spiritual and inspirited of Minkus' categories of *sunsum* (Minkus 1980).

5.7. The Implications of *Honhom Kronkron* Pneumatology

The current proposal of *honhom* as the vital principle or breath of God calls for some theological affirmations. First, God is the sole giver of life and the source of every life principle. Without God, there is no life. The Akan honorific name for God, *Ɔboadeɛ* (the Creator), makes God the most singular and supreme Creator of the universe. This theological affirmation underlies the Akan understanding of the reality of vital force which is perceived in the world as a key characteristic of God's workmanship. Ultimately, the creation bears the imprint of the Creator because of the vital force that the Akan have come to find as the animating principle from God. If creation will make sense at all, it is because its primary purpose is affirmed in the vital force. Akan people claim this essential quality of life as the *nkrabea* (destiny) of the vital force (*ɔkra*), which gives purpose to the creation and defines the quality of life. Hence, the concept of God is essential to the Akan livelihood in order to identify the whole essence of life. The affirmation of the Holy Spirit (*Honhom Kronkron*) as the breath of God should help Akan Christians to understand this divine vitality that gives to human beings, the Church, and Christian livelihood its rightful essence. The Church is alive through the mediation of the Holy Spirit (*Honhom Kronkron*), the divine vitality, energy, and life principle from God. This understanding shows that the Church has a destiny to be accomplished.

Second, the presence of God's breath (*Onyame honhom*) in creation points to the immanent aspect of God. The whole creation is bound up together to God in a community. The immaterial dimension of the universe reveals the relationship between the immanent revelation of God in creation, and creation itself. Akan understanding of the substance of "being" as in a relationship is construed or embedded in the theological interpretation of an inspirited universe in which the material and immaterial are a unitary whole. Hence, the conceptual framework of the Spirit of God as a divine vital force unites the spiritual with the physical. Sakupapa comes to the same conclusion by designating vital force as the unifying force where "the whole of reality is understood as inter-related, without any separation between the sacred and the secular" (2012: 426). The Spirit is a unifying force that makes believers see God as active in their lives. In that sense, we can conclude that our shared unity and interconnectedness is a sacred bond that makes all lives – human beings, animals, and plants – to share in equal worth and to be treated in that respect.

Third, a pneumatological proposal based on *honhom* as breath or vital principle gives us the possibility to see in the universe that which transcends the created order, i.e., both natural and spiritual forces, and which constitutes the most compelling rationale for the worship of one God. That is to say, if all things, including the pantheon gods and the spiritual forces, rely on God's vitality, then there is none but one Great Spirit who is directly connected to all, and is therefore to be worshiped directly. Rattray, perceiving what Akan religion would one day look like without the intermediaries (pantheon deities), acknowledged the Akan God as "one Great Spirit, Who, being one, nevertheless manifested Himself in everything around them [the Akan], and taught men to hear His voice in the flow of His waters and in the sound of His winds among the trees" (1959: 24). To underscore the essence of the Holy Spirit as *honhom* signals the awareness that worship experience is to emphasize God as Spirit, and to approach God in that sense. The Holy Spirit, therefore, leads believers into this worship experience (cf. John 4: 24). As the vital principle leads to God, so the Holy Spirit leads humanity to see God.

Fourth, I have likened the Spirit to the work of the *ɔkra*, the vital principle that vivifies the whole creation. Besides the giving of life and pulsation, the *ɔkra* vibrates perceptions that are closely linked to the revelation of God and the will of God for each individual. These are summed up in the Akan expression of the predetermined *nkrabea* (destiny) to be lived in the world. The Akan explain *nkrabea* as the "message" God gave to the *ɔkra* at the moment of departure from God to the mundane life to determine the course of the individual's life on earth (Gyekye 1978: 104, 108). The *nkrabea* is God's "will" in the *ɔkra* for the individual. Danquah thinks the *nkrabea*, which is the "message," is the *intelligence* to be lived (1944: 28, 82, 86, 113, 152). That means, all things being equal, each person is born intelligent to achieve the full measure of their predetermined purpose in life. Danquah further explains that *intelligence* makes each person to be "in direct touch with the Source, and only needs, on this earth, an examplar or intermedium who will take him nearer to the Source or make the Source better understood" (1944: 82). A person's destiny, therefore, depends on the ability to live the *intelligence* (*nkrabea*), which permits a proper cosmological perception and transcendent possibilities in the fulfillment of one's duty and spiritual evolutions. There is a strong connection between the *nkrabea* and *sunsum*. It is the *sunsum* that prepares the way for destiny to take place by fighting the evils that seek to harm the individual. However, since the *sunsum* is susceptible to evil, it fails most of the time, exposing the individual to danger.[99] The Holy Spirit, as Onyame *Honhom*, empowers believers in their quest to return to God by making way for God's predetermined will (*nkrabea*) to save the world through Christ to be fulfilled. The Spirit's prophetic impact, endowment of spiritual gifts, and continual fellowship with believers, endows the Church with transcendent responsibilities for the accomplishment of God's will for the entire world.

Fifth, how does the proposal of *Honhom Kronkron* pneumatology relate to Christology?[100] A number of Christological proposals exist within the Akan context: Ancestral Christology (Pobee 1979; Bediako 1995), divine conqueror Christology (Appiah-Kubi 1977), and *Nyamesofopreko* Christology (Agyarko 2009). Ancestral Christology permits Akan people to see Christ in their spiritual and social needs. Divine conqueror Christology presents Christ as the deliverer from the powers of African evil forces. *Nyamesofopreko* Christology seeks to respond to the problem of alienation that exists between God and humanity. So, Christ is seen as God's unique priest who mediates between God and humanity because he is Nyamekrateasefo (The *ɔkra* incarnate of God). Each proposal presents Christ in a unique way out of the Akan social and spiritual experience.

Nevertheless, it seems to me that Akan theologians have ignored theologization of the concept of the Abosom as a Christological model. The Abosom are mediating spiritual agents who manage the ecology, including humanity. Their involvement in humanity is both ontological and historical; ontological in the sense that the Abosom transmit or incarnate their essence, known to the Akan as *ntorɔ* and *sunsum,* in creating human beings.[101] Hence, human beings are by nature Abosom in human flesh (Ephirim-Donkor 2016). Historically, the Abosom have always been part of the Akan

---

99 The Akan notion of *sunsum* is like a bodyguard who protects the *ɔkra* from the evils that seek to harm the individual. However, the *sunsum* is not always reliable as it can be knocked about or can be contaminated with evil (Danquah 1944: 83, 87).

100 More details can be found in Agyarko (2009).

101 An Akan proverb goes, *Ɔbosom a ɔma mma no, na ɔfa mma*, literally, "The god who gives children, also takes children."

through the religious expression of the roles they play as intermediaries between God and the Akan, which has also been the source of moral and ethical expressions. Therefore, the place of the Abosom in human life and wellbeing, as well as the entire creation, seems to have messianic motifs embedded in the immanence and incarnation of Jesus Christ, the Son of God. Should the Akan see Jesus as the anointed Ɔbosom?[102]

The development of a contextual Christology based on the Abosom is not supposed to be a subject of discussion here. Nonetheless, the current proposal for a *honhom* pneumatology agrees with the existing Christologies, namely: ancestral, divine conqueror, and *Nyamekrateasefo* Christologies. All these Christologies help us to understand the different models of Akan Christology which are directly connected to *honhom* pneumatology. *Honhom*, the preexistent breath of God or *ɔkra*, creates all things and dwells in all things. Activities like animation and inspiration are all essential roles of *honhom* in Akan worldviews. Whatever becomes a human being needs this divine life entity else life is impossible. If we take Ancestral Christology and *Nyamesofopreko* Christology as examples, ancestors exist because they were once human beings or *akrateasefoɔ* (living souls). The survival of *ɔkra* after death and its posthumous spirituality as an ancestor makes both Ancestral and *Nyamesofopreko* Christologies pneumatological Christologies. Thus, the vital role of *honhom* in Akan cosmology shapes our view of reality in the relationship between the Spirit and Christology. The Spirit's creative activity in the birth of Christ and its indwelling presence in Christ affirms how pneumatology is directly related to Christology.

In summary, the New Testament writers have grounded the manifestation of the Spirit in the Christ-event in relation to the movement of the Church as crucial to understanding the person and ministry of Christ. The role of the Holy Spirit, as an agent in the conception and ministry of Jesus Christ, brings to mind how biblical pneumatology legitimates the Lordship of Jesus Christ (Matt 3: 16; Mk. 1:10; Lu. 3:22; 4:18; Acts 10:38). The Holy Spirit brings to our understanding the enlightenment of the teachings of Christ (Jn. 14:26; 16:13, 14). This is an epistemological function of the Spirit in relation to the Church and the world at large. The notion of *honhom*

102 Danquah had already raised a question on such a Christology. He thinks the gods are many and of uneven propensities, hence, a future messiah for the Akan would come as a "Nana or elder, a father 'Nyame' of the people" (1944: 8). Danquah's statement and his exposition on Akan ancestral cult laid the foundation for Ancestral Christology.

as the reality of the vital force, through which also all things (visible or invisible) have their reality of being, helps to unravel the mysteries of biblical Christology. The Spirit (*Honhom*) incarnates Christ in the believer as his vital force. As a person's whole existence and capacities are dependent upon the vital force (*ɔkra*), so the body of Christ, the Church, is alive and active through the *Honhom Kronkron*, who enlivens the Church, the body of Christ, by its charismatic force.

5.8. Summary

The identification of the spirit with "breath" or "wind" or as "the principle of life" has been the theological justification for *honhom* as the basis for contextual Akan Christian pneumatology. I have shown that the word *sunsum* is not the only term Akan people use to describe spiritual realities. Among other things discussed in this chapter is the nature of the Spirit according to the Bible and how that understanding affects the designation, translation and understanding of the Holy Spirit in Akan languages. Given the various dimensions of the Spirit in both the Old and New Testament, the question of the nature of the Spirit arises for the Akan reading of the Bible. It has become apparent that the nature of *sunsum* is not outrightly a "spirit," i.e., a spiritual entity. The implications of that undertaking underly the central thesis of my study that has challenged the already established notion of the *sunsum* as a "spirit" instead of an emanating spiritual force. As a spiritual force, it can act in spiritual activities and has the ability to interact with other spiritual beings. All these characteristics and many others define the *sunsum* as a spiritual element. However, the concept of *sunsum* does not suffice for the development of a contextual Akan Christian pneumatology. The ethereality of the nature of the spirit as air, wind, and principle of life agrees with the Akan notion of *honhom* better than *sunsum*. *Honhom* provides the basis for appropriately redefining the spiritual worldviews of Akan people for the development of a contextual Christian theology and practice and, broadly, for academic learning.

6. General Conclusion

In the general introduction, I mentioned the rigorous theological discussions surrounding the study of the concept of *sunsum*. Agyarko's theological works in Akan pneumatology highlight the significance of *sunsum* in the spiritual formation of the Akan people. The strength of the *sunsum* pneumatology lies in its focus on God as *Sunsum* and the ways the One (Onyame) and the many (all life forms) interconnect through God's *Sunsum*. In other words, *sunsum* is simultaneously immanent, transcendent, and an archetype of "Godliness" that shapes the ethical and moral lives of human beings in relation to God and the rest of creation.

Further, Agyarko's contextualization of the Holy Spirit as Onyame *Sunsum* emphasizes the crucial role of the Spirit in effecting a renewal of the heart in humans, and consequently, the entire creation. The theological framework of *sunsum* pneumatology, along with other theological works concerning Akan realities, is helping to demonstrate that Akan traditional religions indeed possess elements of revelation that remain relevant for providing spiritual guidance.

My proposal has revolved around the introduction of the Akan concept of *honhom*, which I have advocated as a better alternative for discussing contextual Akan pneumatology. *Honhom* has been demonstrated to possess a polysemic value in describing both meta-empirical and unseen realities such as breath, wind, air, soul, and spirit. These characteristics align with the biblical רוּחַ and πνεῦμα and directly connect to the Akan people's understanding of life as a whole. Life is interconnected by a single animating principle, which is Godself, referred to as *honhom*. Through *honhom*, God, the source of life and creator of all things, becomes immanent within and throughout creation. I argue that the nature and operation of the Spirit better align with the concept of *honhom* and should thus form the basis for contextual Akan Christian pneumatology. This new proposal serves as my contribution to Christian theology, focusing on essential areas such as Akan spirituality and religious constructs.

The study has also shown that my critique of the pneumatic nature of *sunsum* is sustainable because *sunsum* is not adequate to articulate a contextual Christian pneumatology, and by introducing *honhom* pneumatology, I have shown that *sunsum* is not the ultimate vehicle (neither is *honhom*) with which to articulate contextual Akan pneumatology. For the new proposal, I am very much aware that *honhom* pneumatology is not without some limitations. An example is how the two terms, *honhom* and *sunsum*, relate with each other. Is *sunsum* an aspect of *honhom*, or vice versa? My research has offered very little details to answer this question. Therefore, future research should raise this and many other questions to deal with it accordingly.

In closing, it is important for theologians and Christians to continuously seek a deeper understanding of indigenous spiritual constructs and their potential contributions to Christian theology. By engaging with these rich traditions, we can foster more inclusive and contextualized interpretations of faith that resonate with local cultures and spiritualities. Let us remember that Christianity is a living faith that thrives in dialogue with diverse perspectives, always striving to broaden its understanding and embody the universal love of God. I pray that this work will inspire further exploration and appreciation of the unique insights that can be found within the Akan spiritual traditions and beyond, as we continue to seek the divine presence in all aspects of human life.

It is again essential for us to embrace the diverse expressions of spirituality and faith found across the world, as they hold the potential to enrich our collective understanding of the divine. By appreciating and integrating these different perspectives, we not only strengthen our theological frameworks but also cultivate empathy and unity among people of various cultural and religious backgrounds.

Again and again, as we continue on our spiritual journey, let us be open to the wisdom and insights that can be gleaned from the traditions of others. This is what my research into Akan pneumatology and its interaction with the Christian faith seeks to achieve. It is my ardent desire that the exploration of the Akan spiritual constructs and their relationship with Christian theology will serve as a reminder that the divine can be found in unexpected places, and that it is through sincere dialogue and mutual respect that our faith can truly grow.

In a world that is increasingly interconnected, it is more important than ever to foster open-mindedness and embrace the diversity of spiritual practices and beliefs. As theologians, believers, and spiritual seekers, we can strive to create a community that is enriched by our differences and united in our shared pursuit of understanding and wisdom.

However, as we embark on this exploration and integration of diverse spiritual perspectives, it is important to approach these endeavors with caution and discernment. Here are a few considerations to keep in mind:

First, respect cultural boundaries. While engaging with other spiritual traditions, be mindful not to appropriate their practices or beliefs in a way that undermines or disrespects their cultural heritage. Approach these traditions with humility, recognizing that they have their own unique contexts and histories.

Second, maintain theological integrity. When incorporating insights from other spiritual perspectives, ensure that they align with the core tenets of your own faith. It is crucial to preserve the essential beliefs and doctrines of Christianity while allowing for a more inclusive understanding of the divine.

Third, acknowledge limitations. Recognize that no single tradition or perspective holds all the answers. Be open to the idea that your understanding may be incomplete, and that others may have valuable insights to contribute.

Fourth, encourage dialogue and collaboration. As you explore different spiritual traditions, foster an atmosphere of open-mindedness and mutual respect. Engage in meaningful conversations with believers from diverse backgrounds, and work together towards a greater understanding of the divine.

Fifth, practice discernment. Not all beliefs or practices from other spiritual traditions may be compatible with Christian theology. Exercise discernment in determining which insights can enrich your faith while maintaining its core principles.

May this book serve as a catalyst for further studies in Christian pneumatology and collaboration, inspiring both scholars and individuals alike to delve into the rich trajectories of human spirituality. Together, we can learn from one another, grow in our faith, and work towards a more compassionate and inclusive world that truly reflects the boundless love of the divine. May the grace of our Lord Jesus Christ, the love of God, and the abiding sweet fellowship of the Holy Spirit, be with all of you, Amen!

AFTERWORD

TOWARD AN AKAN CHRISTIAN THEOLOGICAL ANTHROPOLOGY

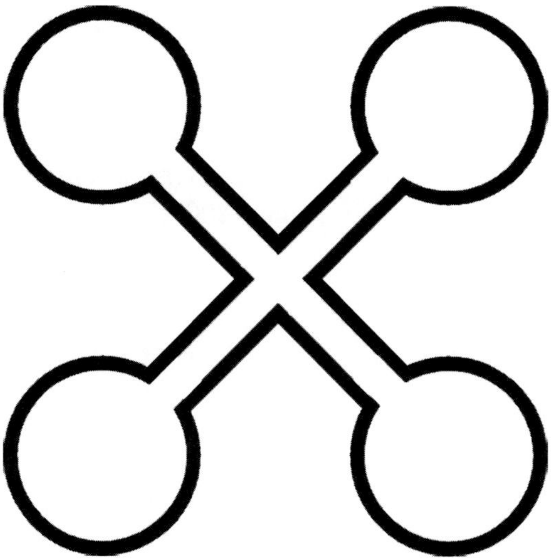

NYAME BEWU ANSA NA M'AWU
"God Will Die Before I Die"
Adinkra symbol of God's immortality and protection of human life

7. WHO AM I?

"Out of an experience of great inquietude over the past 500 years, Africans have now put into place, with great resistance as we shall see, the elements necessary for a truly African renaissance founded on African principles and the centrality of African interests. What is at stake is clear. Either the African people will escape the intellectual plantation that has paraded as universal or will be stifled in every attempt to express their own sense of culture" – Molefi Kete Asante (2007:7).

7.1. Introduction

The proposal towards the development of Akan theological anthropology forms part of the theological quest into the Akan pre-Christian socio-religious conceptual narratives. In this postscript, I intend to formulate a theological anthropology from the religious elements of the Akan people. This formulation takes a step towards a theological framework for the practice of Christian faith, theology, and appreciation of the surviving values of Akan traditional religions.

"Who am I?" is the question asked in the Akan theological anthropology. This question, without any doubt, has had many profound philosophical and theological reflection since the European Enlightenment, and an enigma that continues to today. Some notable thinkers who have grappled with this question include René Descartes (1596-1650), who contributed to the field of philosophy by his understanding of body and mind, and perceived human identity from the distinctiveness of the human thought: "I think therefore I am." To Descartes, the consciousness of the body or existence stems from the thought, which is independent of the body.

Immanuel Kant (1724-1804) propounded theories about self and identity found in his *Critique of Pure Reason*. He explored the nature of the self and its relationship to experience and knowledge. Jean-Jacques Rousseau (1712-1778), a key figure in both the Enlightenment and Romanticism, dealt with the question of selfhood in his works, including *The Social Contract* and *Emile*. He emphasized the importance of the individual and the role of society in shaping personal identity. Søren Kierkegaard (1813-1855), a philosopher and theologian, explored existentialism and the nature of the self in works such as *The Sickness Unto Death*. He highlighted the individual's subjective experience and the importance of personal choice in defining oneself. Friedrich Nietzsche (1844-1900) delved into questions of anthropology encompassing identity and societal constructs in his *Thus Spoke Zarathustra* and *Beyond Good and Evil*. Nietzsche questioned the nature of the self and the influences of culture and society on individual identity. Martin Heidegger (1889-1976) was a German philosopher who tackled the question of personal identity and existence in his magnum opus, *Being and Time*. He focused on the concept of *Dasein*, the unique mode of human existence, as a way to understand the self. Jean-Paul Sartre (1905-1980), another prominent existentialist philosopher and theologian, addressed the question of selfhood in works like *Being and Nothingness* and *Existentialism and Humanism*. He maintained that the individual is responsible for defining their own identity through choice and action. Likewise, Dietrich Bonhoeffer (1906-1945), a German theologian, had to confront the question of identity crisis. In a poem written from prison, shortly before his death, in April 1945 reveals his ruminations over this same question. The poem captioned "Who am I?", tells Bonhoeffer struggling between public perception of himself and his inner conviction of self. Being unable to resolve this enigma, he finally settled the essence of his identity in God.

The perplexity of this issue extends beyond these philosophers. It is an anthropological problem as people everywhere seek to understand their origins, selves, and place in the universe. The Akan people also grapple with this question. However, Akan thought on identity encompasses both social and spiritual dimensions, leading them to view personhood as rooted in relationships.

This relational perspective begins with God, as expressed in the Akan maxim: "All human beings are the children of God." This concept establishes an ontological connection in which God is considered the supreme ancestor, and all people form a single family, responsible and accountable to one another. Consequently, individuals are inherently social, meant to engage with their communities and the world around them.

At this point, it is important to examine how the Akan people arrived at an understanding of these fundamental questions concerning human existence. Additionally, what are the underlying concepts that contribute to reshaping their understanding of humanity and the global challenges humans face? The Akan people's conception of a universal essence or animating force, referred to as *sunsum*, functions to bring harmony among the elements of creation and enhances our understanding of humanity's place within the grand scheme of history.

7.2. Toward A Theological Anthropology

Theological anthropology is the branch of systematic theology that explores and seeks to understand the nature of human beings and their existence in relation to God. This field delves into the history of humanity, as well as the essence of what it means to be human in a theological context. The study adopts a dual approach, incorporating both the anthropological dimension of humanity and the theological dimension addressing God's role in human history. This synchronic, interdisciplinary study positions theological anthropology as a theocentric discipline. Key aspects include the creation of human beings, the origin of evil, questions of human will and morality, global challenges, and the salvation of humankind in relation to God. As the current study is focused on developing an Akan theological anthropology, it will place a particular emphasis on some of these aspects and bring forth the Akan's cosmic understanding of human beings. The objectives shall include to:

1. understand the nature of being human in the image of God from the Akan perspective.
2. understand the intervention of God in the history of mankind through Christ and its relation to the *sunsum*.
3. understand the human nature with its spiritual, ethical, and contemporary global challenges.
4. emphasize the conscious realization of love, justice, peace, and creation of beauty for a dignified society.

5. understand the destiny of human beings and salvation.

In this comprehensive study, my aim is to accomplish the following objectives with an Akan theological anthropology:

First, I seek to impact academic learning, an environment where theories and methodologies can be optimally developed. To ensure effective communication of this theological anthropology, it is essential to foster a conducive academic atmosphere that facilitates in-depth scientific research into its content, structure, and potential reconstructions of its various theories. This will lead to a more profound understanding of the subject and stimulate interest in African studies, both in Ghana and beyond.

Second, this study underscores the inherent values of pre-Christian Akan traditional religions, which have consistently been an integral part of Akan culture. Theological anthropology will explain the principles pertaining to God's mediation in human history and the divine plan for humanity's salvation through Jesus Christ, to which Africans are not excluded. Consequently, the Akan theological anthropology will emphasize Christology from an African standpoint.

Lastly, this research raises the issue of integrating Akan religious anthropology into societal life, emphasizing that theory and practice should not be contradictory. The study addresses concerns related to social, civil, and political administration. Public officials are expected to operate with dignity within the context of the anthropological identity outlined by this research, promoting justice and equity, and the well-being of the people they serve. Citizens, in turn, should acknowledge their responsibilities within the larger community by maintaining the integrity of fundamental human values.

The methodology for developing the Akan theological anthropology is rooted in inculturation, focusing on the principles of substance ontology, relational ontology, and functional ontology within the Akan conception of the human being.

7.3. Models of Contextual Christian Theology

It is crucial that before entering into any further discussion on Akan theological anthropology, the understanding of some various models underlining African contextual Christian theology be given attention.

There are so many approaches in African contextual theolgy (*See* chapter two). These approaches are used to articulate the process of interpreting and applying Christian theology within the unique cultural, social, political, and historical contexts of Africa. In this chapter, I will discuss models of African contextual Christian theologies. African theologians use models to refer to the actual theological systems or structures that have been developed using one or more approaches to contextual theology. Models represent concrete examples of how theologians have applied the broader approaches to specific contexts, resulting in particular theological expressions or constructions that address the unique concerns and issues within that context. The purpose of this is to bring out to bear the various philosophical layers underlining the development of a contextual theological anthropology.

Stephen B. Bevans, a renowned theologian, has identified six dominant models of contextual theology in his book *Models of Contextual Theology*. These models provide different approaches to understanding and interpreting Christianity in various cultural, social, and historical contexts. The six models are:

1. *Translation Model*: This model emphasizes the importance of translating the core message of Christianity into the language and thought patterns of a particular cultural context, making the gospel relevant and accessible to diverse communities.
2. *Anthropological Model*: This model focuses on the cultural richness of a particular context and seeks to incorporate its values, symbols, and practices into Christianity. It emphasizes the importance of respecting and celebrating the unique cultural expressions of faith in each context.
3. *Praxis Model*: Grounded in liberation theology, this model is centered on the idea of action and reflection. It emphasizes the importance of engaging in social, political, and economic struggles

for justice and human dignity while continually reflecting on the implications of these actions in light of the gospel.

4. *Synthetic Model*: This model encourages dialogue between various theological perspectives, cultures, and traditions. It seeks to create a synthesis that is mutually enriching and transformative, allowing for the development of a more comprehensive and inclusive understanding of the Christian faith.
5. *Transcendental Model*: This model emphasizes personal experience and the role of the individual in the process of contextualization. It encourages believers to reflect on their own faith journey and engage in ongoing theological reflection based on their unique experiences and insights.
6. *Countercultural Model*: This model challenges the dominant cultural values and assumptions that may be in conflict with the gospel message.

These models explain the startups of a distinct theological discipline. It also takes a particular context very seriously and with its distinct theological presuppositions (Bevans 1992: 27).

Bevans' models are so important in constructing a particular contextual theology. For the purpose of this study, I will be discussing the most prominent and radical model that has significantly influenced contextual theology, particularly in Africa's post-colonial era. This model, known as the anthropological model, resonates profoundly with the current work and is the primary focus of this chapter. It emphasizes "cultural identity and its relevance for theology more than scripture or tradition" (Bevans 1992: 27). Bevans expounds the *telos* of the anthropological model of contextual theology as that part of theology that seeks to preserve cultural identity by the person of the Christian faith (Bevans 1992: 47). Its primary concern is about the person's fulfillment in the Christian faith (Bevans 1992: 47).

7.3.1. Anthropological Model of Contextual Christian Theology

Two aspects of the anthropological model are identified by Bevans. First, the model is centered on the value and goodness of *anthropos,* the human person who is the criterion of judgment within a particular social experience or geographical circumstances (Bevans 1992: 47, 48). The second aspect lends itself to acquiring insights into the social science of anthropology, i.e., an exploration of the social context of some particular people. Bevans explains further that the primary purpose of this particular approach is related to culture: "For this model, it is in a study of and sympathetic identity with a people's culture that one finds the symbols and concepts with which to construct an adequate articulation of that people's faith" (Bevans 1992: 48).

The anthropological model has not only been hailed as compelling and rich in doing contextual theology but it has been tested and found particularly useful at addressing and meeting people at the very point of their needs "rather than by imposing questions from other contexts" (Bevans 1992: 53). The western missionary and theologian, James Edward Lesslie Newbigin has strongly emphasized the necessity to begin the proclamation of the gospel with the people in context.[103] Newbigin had critical concerns for cultural dimensions:

> The idea that one can or could at any time separate out by some process of distillation a pure gospel unadulterated by any cultural accretion is an illusion. It is, in fact, an abandonment of the gospel, for the gospel is about the word made flesh. Every statement of the gospel in words is conditioned by the culture of which those words are a part, and every style of life that claims to embody the truth of the gospel is a culturally conditioned form of life (Newbigin 1986: 4).

It is because of the gospel's "culturally conditioned form of life" that one must find it fitting to take into consideration certain aspects of the immediate culture, such as the language of the recipients to begin missionary work. Newbigin, who hailed from a European cultural background that has profoundly influenced Christianity, posited that theologians

[103] Lesslie Newbigin spent a considerable time (about forty years) in India as a missionary worker. His missionary experience with the indigenes of India shaped his theological career to write more about doing theology in context. He's considered as one of the successful and leading missionaries in the twentieth century.

would provide a more genuine representation of the gospel by actively engaging with and listening to others. To him, when culture shapes the minds of Bible students, it leads to an enriching mission of doing contextual theology and mission (Newbigin 1989: 152).

Apparently, one cannot listen or understand another if one does not understand the other's language. Hence, the indigenous language helps a person to understand deeply the essential elements embodied in that culture (Newbigin 1986: 5, 6). Through this immersion into the culture, one becomes prepared to initiate a dialogue between the Gospel and the prevailing customs and traditions of the people. For this discourse to effectively convey the message of the gospel of the kingdom and encourage individuals to seek repentance, it is imperative to maintain mutual respect in the exchange. Newbigin asserts, "if it is truly the communication of the gospel, it will call radically into question that way of understanding embodied in the language it uses. If it is truly revelation, it will involve contradiction, and call for conversion, for a radical *metanoia*, a U-turn of the mind" (Newbigin 1986: 6). Newbigin's thought in communicating the gospel across cultural frontiers can be summed up in three main methods: (1) Communicating in the indigenous language leads to understanding; (2) if there exists a revelation, it will lead to a radical *metanoia* that (3) can only be a work of God, a kind of miracle–not natural but supernatural (Newbigin 1986: 6).

From this background, Africa's contextual Christian theology should not be viewed as wayward. Like any other contextual Christian theology, it is in the process of formulating theological thought forms for the people of Africa, enabling Christianity to be understood in the languages and ways that African Christians can easily relate to and comprehend. For this purpose, contextual Christian theology has dominated African theological circles since the mid-twentieth century. African theologians have sought to pursue a rebirth, which, in a way, can also be seen as a quest for Africanness. The "African" becomes the object and end of theology. This is why the anthropological model of contextual Christian theology is significant in African theology.

The next point to address is how this model has taken shape in the African theological discipline. The anthropological model in African contextual theology has taken two main forms, namely: inculturation and liberation theologies (these have been treated in chapter two). Both of these aspects of African theology are focused on the African individual and one's identity with the Christian message.

Notable theologians and scholars who have employed the anthropological model include Charles Nyamiti (born December 9, 1931) from Tanzania. He was trained in philosophy and theology at the Catholic University of Louvain in Belgium and the University of Vienna. Nyamiti is known for his appreciation of Thomistic theology, and his approaches to African theology have primarily focused on Africa's worldviews and Christianity. He is considered one of the important pioneers of African inculturation theology.

As a professor of theology, Nyamiti influenced many young people to theologize, theorize, and philosophize the African *Sitz im Leben* and orientation (Wachege 2006). One of his major works is *Christ as Our Ancestor: Christology from an African Perspective* (1984). In this book, he articulated and correlated the African concept of kinship with that of the Trinity, presenting Jesus as a descendant of the Father and the Father as the Ancestor of the Son. This radical interpretation of the Trinity gives a sense of the overall theological approach of Nyamiti.

Another important theologian to mention is John Mbiti. He remains one of the most prolific and influential African theologians in the twentieth and twenty-first centuries (Hesselgrave & Rommen 1989: 98). His theological works have placed great importance on the gospel and culture. To Mbiti, being an African is not just being black or having indigenous Africanness. Being an African is to rediscover one's sense of humanness through the traditional values. These foundational ideas shaped his theological work to concentrate mainly on the existential dimensions of African values. While some might perceive Mbiti's integration of African cultures in his theological methodology as syncretism, his primary concern was to give meaning to the gospel and to understand his African identity within the context of Christianity in Africa. Augustine Musopole (August 12, 1948 – to present), in a review of Mbiti's theology, noted that "Mbiti's Africanness is manifested in his dogged insistence that African culture is a fundamental element in the doing of African theology. He is primarily interested in local theological creativity. He wants a theology that bears the mark, MADE IN AFRICA BY AFRICANS" (Musopole 1994: 23).

Again, the Ghanaian theologian Kwame Bediako has articulated in his book, *Theology and Identity: The Impact of Culture upon Christian*

Thought in the Second Century and in Modern Africa that human cultural settings have never been taken for granted in the transmission of the gospel (Bediako 1995). Bediako's theological tasks have centered on the need to retrieve from the African Traditional Religion (ATR) those revelations that speak profoundly to his identity as an African. Bediako observed that early Christians were significantly influenced by the Greco-Roman cultural context in which they lived. By examining the works of Justin Martyr and Clement of Alexandria, he posited that their approach to engaging with culture and the gospel should serve as a blueprint for developing Africa's contextual theology, ultimately shaping a distinct African Christian identity. Bediako's contribution to African theology serves as a rich repository of knowledge, as he demonstrated a profound understanding of the intricate relationship between the gospel and culture. The methodology employed in his contextualization asserts that the establishment of a distinctly African Christian identity relies significantly on a constructive reassessment and revitalization of the traditional African religious heritage, which served as the foundation for the emergence of Christianity (Ferdinando 2007: 123). Bediako was an outstanding theologian who possessed an in-depth understanding of the African Traditional Religions.

African theologians who have made attempts to do theology following the anthropological model have proven successful over the years. It has fostered a far-reaching appreciation of Africa's cultural values in the last six to seven decades. As Bevans noted, the anthropological model, "more than any other, focuses on the validity of the human as the place of divine revelation and as a source (locus) for theology that is equal to scripture and tradition" (Bevans 1992: 48). Bevans' statement emphasizes the anthropological model's focus on the human experience as a valid and significant source of divine revelation and theological understanding. This idea highlights the importance of considering cultural, social, and historical contexts when engaging in theological discussions, as it seeks to recognize and respect the diversity of human experiences in relation to the divine.

7.4. Toward an African Theological Anthropology

At this point, I will discuss the development of Africa's theological anthropology as one branch of Africa's theological discipline. Theological anthropology in general deals with the connection between God and the human person. Christian theological anthropology therefore is the study of the history of humanity, taking into consideration the creation of human beings, the fall, death, redemption, Christology, and various aspects of human existence and its relation with God. The image that emerges for African theologians is the creation of a meaningful African existentiality for Africans.

7.4.1. Christian Theology in Africa

African Christian theology boasts a history as old as Christianity itself. Early Church Fathers, such as Clement of Alexandria, Tertullian, Origen, and Augustine of Hippo, all hailing from this region, have significantly impacted the trajectory of theology and the development of church traditions within the Christian world. Today, African theologians continue in shaping theology by cultivating diverse theological perspectives and approaches.

One branch that has not garnered substantial attention within African theology, yet has been the subject of rigorous discussion in the field of African philosophical studies, is theological anthropology. This branch is viewed as imperative for humanizing African people from a Christian standpoint. As I examine the works of Augustine Musopole, I wish to express my appreciation for the interest he shows in "the relevance of the concept of humanness to the Christian gospel for the construction of a culturally relevant doctrine of the human person," and, consequently, for the African person (Musopole 1994: 1).

African traditional worldviews have consistently exhibited anthropocentric and theocentric characteristics, which form the foundation of African Traditional Religions. This ontology, to a certain extent, shares commonalities across various African traditions. Therefore, theological anthropology is not a remote discipline from these traditions, and embracing it represents a redemptive endeavor to reshape and impact the socio-economic, socio-political, and socio-religious experiences of the African people.

7.4.2. Being Human in Africa

Augustine C. Musopole was a Malawian, born on August 12, 1948, in Chinongo Village, in the Misuku Hills of Chitipa District in northern Malawi.[104] He served as an associate professor in the philosophy of religion and theology at Chang Jung Christian University in China. As the director of the Conflict Study and Research Center, he trained individuals in conflict resolution methodologies, uncovering hidden causes of conflict, researching best practices in traditional communal mediation, and networking with related organizations worldwide. Musopole, who passed away on December 29, 2021, was also an ordained minister of the Presbyterian Church and a church leader. His research areas focused on the transformation of African societies, with a particular emphasis on African humanness as the key to development, as taught in the *Umunthu* philosophy for African reawakening.[105]

Musopole's groundbreaking work, *Being Human in Africa: Toward an African Christian Anthropology*, stands as a highly significant contribution to African theology today.[106] Its importance lies in its transition from theoretical considerations to practical approaches addressing factors that impact and shape human existence in Africa. Over the past five decades, African theology has often been characterized by apologetic, reactionary, or descriptive perspectives, rather than practical ones. Musopole's work, however, ventures beyond these limitations to develop a pragmatic formulation of African theological discipline, aimed at establishing an African Christian anthropology.

Furthermore, Musopole's work is notable for its practicality, as it investigates the essential components required for social change, renewal, and

---

104 "Musopole Augustine Chingwala," *Dictionary of African Christian Biography*, https://dacb.org/stories/malawi/musopole-augustine/. Last visited April 25, 2023.

105 *Umunthu* encapsulates the dictum, "I am because we are, and since we are, therefore, I am". It is a solidarity concept which captures the essence of being human. "Umunthu" should not be confused with "ubuntu" of South Africa, which is the concept that a return to traditional values is essential to liberate the society. See more discussion from (Englund 2002: 173).

106 The author published the book *uMunthu Theology: An Introduction* shortly before his passing. Unfortunately, the current researcher does not have access to this work. Readers interested in deepening their knowledge of the *uMunthu* concept as articulated by Augustine C. Musopole are encouraged to seek out this book.

the navigation of human experience in Africa. He accomplishes this by examining African traditional values and scripture through the lens of Jesus, placing particular emphasis on His teachings. At the heart of the book, Musopole engages in a profound dialogue with John Mbiti, exploring the various African perspectives on humanity and the concept of *umunthu*, which encapsulates Africa's unique understanding of humanness.

Musopole takes much inspiration from the *umunthu* theological thoughts and thus formulated his theological anthropology to point to the fact that "JESUS CHRIST, THE AUTHENTIC MUNTHU IN AND ABOVE AFRICAN CULTURE IS THE ULTIMATE IDENTITY FOR AFRICAN PEOPLES" (Musopole 1994: 1).[107] Reaching the end of his book, the author emphasizes his Christocentric stance on African Christian anthropology, advocating for a new life in Jesus Christ. He states, "I contend that authentic humanity, as exemplified in Jesus, is also divinity. To be divinized in Christ is to be authentically humanized; this is the meaning of salvation and/or 'inheriting the reign of God'" (Musopole 1994: 172).[108] He highlights the significance of Jesus Christ as the central figure for achieving a sense of genuine humanity. Embracing divinity through Him allows individuals to become their most authentic selves. This approach reconciles both the spiritual and human aspects of existence, emphasizing the interconnectedness of these two dimensions.

Within the framework of African Christian anthropology, this perspective advocates for the incorporation of cultural and religious aspects alongside the teachings of Jesus Christ. In doing so, a more holistic understanding of humanity is fostered, transcending cultural barriers, and resonating with individuals from diverse backgrounds.

The notion of salvation and inheriting the reign of God is posited as the paramount objective of human existence, attainable through the harmonious integration of divine and human elements. This idea of spiritual development and self-actualization aligns with multiple spiritual traditions and philosophies, further accentuating the universal appeal of Musopole's argument.

---

[107] Emphasis is not mine.

[108] In his introduction of *Being Human*, Musolpole stated that "This book is about an encounter between an African view of humanity and the gospel of Jesus Christ understood as re-humanization" (Musopole 1994: 1).

7.4.2.1. Ontological/Life Relationality

Musopole's theologizing of the *umunthu* philosophy toward an African Christian anthropology is found in the last chapter of his book. Musopole initially acknowledges Mbiti's contribution to the *uMunthu* concept. However, he contends that Mbiti limited the concept solely to the explanaiton of kinship and the African communitarian ethos (Musopole 1994: 173). Nonetheless, Musopole's work endeavors to broaden this perspective beyond the African context to a more universal understanding of the interrelationships that exist among humans. This, he calls *Ontological or Life Relationality.* To him, it is "foundational to the personal, communal, historical and cosmic consciousness of African peoples" (Musopole 1994: 173). Human relationship is a factor to humanization in the theological thoughts of Musopole.

In an attempt to explain the life relationality concept, Musopole designates its expression in what he calls life cognition; thus, the process by which one comes to acknowledge the consciousness of perception, intuition, and reasoning. Further explanation of its various components includes "rationality, feelings, faith, doubt, imagination, consciousness, wisdom, and all experience, and it aims at totality of impression and expression" (Musopole 1994: 173). For life cognition to function effectively, it is necessary to have a comprehensive integration of the entire "conscious self, along with its depths of unconsciousness." This foundation gives rise to multiple logics due to "our human consciousness situated within a cultural context" (Musopole 1994: 174). It is within this logical framework made possible by the conscious self and cultural context that each "individual person becomes a center of integration and communication of all that experience and the concomitant knowledge" (Musopole 1994: 174). By this theory, Musopole establishes the fact that each person is made to experience a humanization network of interrelationship and communication which is a "conscious appropriation and objectification" of the cognitive experience (Musopole 1994: 174).[109] He made it clear that the "cognitive experience fits well into an understanding of humanity in which humanization is an ongoing process throughout a person's life rooted in a multi-dimensional network of relationships" (Musopole 1994: 174). The humanization process of

[109] Humanization according to Musopole is being human by always becoming human (Musopole 1994: 174).

the individual is that which enhances the larger community towards a "Good Village or Community" since that process is not independent but relational, i.e., dependent on each other.

By way of justifying his ontological interrelationship theory, Musopole does recognize the life cognition as the cognitive experience of the conscious self that operates in multiple logics towards the humanization of self and finally the community. The objective of the ontological relationality is to help the individual to be morally actualized in character and be capable of contributing economically. Musopole believes that "[c]haracter and economic productivity are the indices of human integrity and authenticity" and also "only through mutuality can a responsible human community emerge" (Musopole 1994: 174, 175). He does not however imply that non-productivity or people without economic progress have less integrity or without authentic humanness. His argument is on political grounds. A nation that strives towards economic productivity needs citizens and leaders with character and authentic integrity of which without a nation stands to fall.

Musopole gears his argument towards the meaning of being human and its effects on the larger community, in which God finds His ultimate preference. He sums up thus, "[o]nly this kind of individual can truly be a cosmic priest to God and a member of a community that becomes a Good Village (holy nation) by striving towards being truly human" (Musopole 1994: 175). It is not a mistake for one to consider Musopole as a moralist.

7.4.2.2. A Case for Redefinition and Refining

Musopole, just like many other contemporary African theologians, believes that the doctrine of anthropology that was imported to Africa by the European missionaries lacked any contextual African substance and also was not practically congruent with the missionaries' view of Africans. In a sharp criticism of the missionaries, he claims that "the imported doctrine on humanity—based on the truth that all people are made in the image of God and are loved by God for redemption in spite of themselves—was not matched by the messengers' practice especially in their view and treatment of the African people" (Musopole 1994: 175).[110] Such a conclusion leads Musopole to claim that "African theology has been searching for theological method(s) as it attempts to define itself and its agenda" (Musopole 1994: 176). For this matter, I share the same concern with him that African theological anthropology must become both a redefinition and refining agenda towards an African humanness.

7.4.2.3. Toward a Pragmatic and Programmatic Theology

To imbue existential significance, as previously noted, African theological anthropology should transition from abstract concepts to a more substantively relevant approach. This entails addressing "the cultural, socio-economic, political, and historical understanding of humanity" within the African context (Musopole 1994: 176). Musopole emphasizes that doctrines concerning African humanness should be both "pragmatic and programmatic" (Musopole 1994: 176).

Musopole delves into this institutionalization model of theological anthropology in Africa, explaining that a pragmatic approach must "deal with our historical and cultural existence as the concrete expression of our essential Africanness" (Musopole 1994: 176). Maintaining its essence and essentiality, Musopole argues that African theological anthropology must be programmatic "in order to establish a lifestyle that prioritizes human well-being (salvation/liberation) as its primary concern" (Musopole 1994: 176). To be effectively communicated, this type of theological framework must form the foundation of African theological anthropology.

7.4.2.4. Humanness As a Reflection of the Image of God

From an African perspective, humanity is a creation of God and, therefore human beings are children of God (Musopole 1994: 177). These African traditional worldviews are related to the biblical accounts of the creation of human beings in the image of God. Human beings do not only bear the

---

[110] Kwame Bediako has provided an in-depth analysis of the early missionaries and the African condition before their arrival. His discussion, titled "Christianity as 'Civilization': The Legacy of 'The Third Opportunity' and the Making of a Modern Identity Problem," can be found in his *Theology and Identity* (Bediako 1992: 225-266).

imprints of God's special creation, but also, they share an ontological filiation which Musopole has called *ontological relationality*.[111] This double relationship to God defines the sacredness of humanity above all creation, and this effect, according to Musopole, is a "consciousness of a dignity and an integrity (humanness) that is exclusively human" (Musopole 1994: 177). When individuals come to be conscious of their inherent self-worth as human beings, they begin to embrace the divine likeness within them. This realization of humanity's intrinsic value reflects the ultimate expression of God's image and constitutes the true essence of human glory. Musopole's reference to the fall of Adam and Eve states that "...when Adam and Eve realized their nakedness, they had lost their dignity. They found themselves in a state of utter humiliation brought on by their actions. This loss of dignity and integrity marked the condition of our fallen humanity: a life of contradiction and a divided existence" (Musopole 1994: 178).

There is nothing so superior to designate a human being as both sacred and human than the glory that is shared in the ontological relationality with God. A conscious effect of this notion is the awareness of one's humaneness that affects and enhances the humanness of all other human beings. Life becomes a community other than individual species. Musopole expresses that "[h]umanness as the expression of the image of God in us translates itself into relationships characterized by integrity and wisdom" (Musopole 1994: 178).

7.4.2.5. Reconciliation in Community and Communion

Life does not exist without community and communion. Musopole's concept of reconciliation follows that of his interlocutor Mbiti. Both have suggested that one does not exist because one lives. Existence is corporate. Mbiti makes it clear that "... the individual does not and cannot exist alone except corporately. He owes his existence to other people... The community must therefore make, create or produce the individual... Only in terms of other people does the individual becomes conscious of his own

---

[111] The Akan proverbs that "*nnipa nyinaa y3 nyame mma*," meaning, "All human beings are children of God". Or "nipa ny3 aboa" meaning "*The human being is not animal*" express in them exclusiveness of human integrity and worthiness. So, humanity has never been a distant figure from God and therefore it exists in the core of the African Traditional Religion each person's allegiance to the supreme deity.

being, his own duties, his privileges and responsibilities towards himself and towards other people" (Mbiti 1969: 108). Community, then becomes a place where the individual is reconciled to other members to define one's identity and uniqueness as a human being. Musopole stresses this reconciliation between the individual and community as the ideal way to achieve a harmonious society. He says, "[t]o be human in Africa is to be a reconciled person-in-community-and-communion responsibly living out the integrity of one's humanness in all spheres of life and thus contributing to the development and realization of what we have called the Good Village or Community and harmony in the cosmos" (Musopole 1994: 179). African individuality, therefore, becomes "I am because we are, and since we are, therefore, I am."

From this conception, African individuality is without alienation. Alienation from community and communion is "a feeling of not being at home, a condition of wandering about because one is lost and perpetually searching for a life that lasts" (Musopole 1994: 179). A condition of alienation is a condition of "destitution" and such "a state might be partly self-inflicted and partly due to other people within or without one's community" (Musopole 1994: 179). In the traditional sense, alienation will equal a fall away. Since separation constitutes in itself a disharmony of the African community and seems to be an irrevocable apostasy, the event of reconciliation, therefore, becomes imperative through the intervention of God which leads humanity into a *koinonia*.[112] This *koinonia* is already understood by Africans as the "sharing in the flow of a common life and common spirit of goodwill in the community" (Musopole 1994: 180). The church, according to Musopole, embodies in herself this "organic rationality" in accordance with the African way of life. He writes: "The church as the community of redeemed humanness is the new society; it is the new being made manifest and becomes in turn an agent of humanization (or redemption)" (Musopole 1994: 180). Musopole seems to solve the problem of division, a prime challenge to the harmony of every human community by emphasizing the core values that sustain human freedom and dignity in the image of God (Musopole 1994: 181-183).

---

112 Musopole's discussion with Mbiti reveals that African myths do not even provide an escape from alienation. The one who suffers alienation therefore becomes lost. Hence God's intervention in mankind provides a way of escape which effects a radical turn around into *koinonia* (community-in-communion) (Musopole 1994: 179).

7.4.2.6. From Bondage to Freedom for All

Musopole's thesis now moves towards the ethics of freedom. Each person is created to have the freedom of individuality which is not supposed to be altered by any political forces or repressive institutions. This form of individual's freedom does not translate itself into individualism, rather, it must enrich the community and enhance communion (Musopole 1994: 184).

Another important aspect raised by Musopole is the challenge of political dictatorship to individual freedom in Africa. He writes: "Political challenges to humanness in Africa take the form not only of apartheid South Africa, but also of single party dictatorship which rule by fear generated by a few privileged people supported by capitalist weapons and money at the expense of the ordinary rural and working class people" (Musopole 1994: 185). Emerging from the chaotic effects of colonial regime, most African leaders subsequently transitioned into becoming the key agents undermining the well-being of Africa's political landscape. Excessive power struggles, corruption, and manipulation of national constitutions to establish party dictatorships have ultimately led to the subjugation of citizens. Political structures are meant to be the vehicles for national progress. However, when these structures become tools against economic advancement and individual freedom, the government devolves into a morally bankrupt tyranny.

African leaders can only achieve lasting progress if they commit to upholding values that foster human potential and prioritize individual freedom. An accountable government does not exploit its citizens but seeks to improve their living conditions. By cultivating authenticity in governance, individual freedom is reinforced. Conversely, neglecting these principles undermines both freedom and the essence of humanity (Musopole 1994: 185-186).

The other challenge comes in the form of some misconstrued schemes against the freedom of children and women. Though Musopole did not pinpoint some of these schemes, one can still find references to some of these unfortunate phenomena on the continent of Africa. These may include deprivation of education, child labor, girl-child marriage, female genital mutilation, etc. Musopole sees these challenges as bondage. He remarks that "[a] community with more than half of its members under cultural servitude is itself in bondage and ignorant of humanness; such a community is impoverished by such bondage" (Musopole 1994: 186). Consequently, the rise of Feminist theology in Africa serves the purpose of articulating the emancipation of women and children under oppression.[113] Musopole therefore recognizes that the liberation of women is essential to Africa's cultural freedom and as he stated later, liberation "must be liberation for all, leading to servanthood by all under the lordship of Jesus, the true servant" (Musopole 1994: 186-187).

7.4.2.7. Humanness Must Affect Institutions

African humanness cannot be achieved without the strength of institutions. Such involves, according to Musopole, "[t]he creation of just socio-economic and political structures locally, nationally, and internationally… towards the realization of authentic humanity" (Musopole 1994: 188). It was, therefore, a matter of urgency when the US President Barack Obama advised African leaders to build strong institutions. The president on July 11, 2009 challenged African leaders that "[i]n the 21st century, capable, reliable and transparent institutions are the key to success - strong parliaments and honest police forces; independent judges and journalists; a vibrant private sector and civil society. Those are the things that give life to democracy, because that is what matters in peoples' lives."[114] African authentic humanity relies upon its numerous social and political institutions. The strength of these institutions must be seen as indispensable for the health of Africans' integrity.

Finally, Musopole submits that religion must not be only focused on just rituals. It must be existential if African humanness is to be realized. It must be the practice of good religion. The right elements in religion must be internalized in daily life in order to collapse every evil practice that dehumanizes (Musopole 1994: 189). Christ becomes the ultimate channel to these

---

[113] African Feminist theology arose as the concerns and experiences of women became an object of theology. African feminists began to investigate the oppression of women under both social and political context. Christian women began to express concerns about gender discrimination and raised many questions over Western Christianity and other religio-cultural traditions that seem to suppress women's legitimacy in many things. Read more from (Phiri 2004: 137-162).

[114] Barack Obama, *A New Moment of Promise in Africa*. Speech delivered on Saturday July 11, 2009 at the Ghana Parliament. https://obamawhitehouse.archives.gov/the-press-office/remarks-president-ghanaian-parliament. Last visited: March 29, 2023.

realizations. African humanness must be identified through him. Since Jesus Christ, "who is the image of the invisible God, has manifested authentic humanity in an ultimate way, it is only in relationship with him that good religion is possible, because through him we attain to authentic humanness ontologically and existentially" (Musopole 1994: 189). This is the whole centrality of Musopole's Christian theological anthropology: "JESUS CHRIST, THE AUTHENTIC MUNTHU IN AND ABOVE AFRICAN CULTURE IS THE ULTIMATE IDENTITY FOR AFRICAN PEOPLES" (Musopole 1994: 11).

7.5. Summary

The encounter between Christianity and African people also represented an encounter with societies deeply rooted in complex cultural traditions. To effectively articulate Christianity in the African context, Africans must understand how the Christian message can liberate them from the clutches of their problems and bring them freedom. This was a task that Western missionaries failed to accomplish, ultimately leading to theological imperialism and a Western-branded version of Christianity.

As a response to these pitfalls, African theology emerged, aiming to reconstruct theology to better suit the African context. Consequently, African theology adopted an anthropological model, which has proven highly successful in promoting African humanness. Despite these successes, African theologians face various challenges. Among them is the role of scripture in Africa's contextual theology, which, in my opinion, requires careful reflection.

8. ASPECTS OF AKAN ANTHROPOLOGY

> *"The old primitive belief that a soul has the personality of its owner, but can be separated from the body (as experienced in a dream), and that it is indestructible and survives and lives on forever when the organs of the body no longer function, is still a view widely, if not universally, held"* – Sam K. Akesson (1965: 280).

8.1. Introduction

The concept of an existential numinous being, known in Akan terminology as *Onipa* (*nipa* is singular, and *nnipa* is plural), provides the basic framework upon which Akan socio-religious and political structure is constructed. *Onipa* is the generic Akan term for the human being. The Akan philosophical notion that "all human beings are the children of God and none is a child of the earth" establishes three basic ontological realities for understanding Akan anthropology. First, the human being has a numinous substance and not only natural. Second, the human being does not live in isolation but has a relational ontology. And third, the human being has a functional ontology after the ways of God. This chapter gives a considerable amount of space to discuss these aspects of the human being and how they form the basis for the development of Akan theological anthropology.

8.2. The Origin of Human Beings

Life as a whole comes with some ontological questions such as: "Where did I come from?", "Who am I?", and "Where am I going?" These represent the existential questions that a person belonging to the Akan ethnic group might pose. The first question deals with human origins. The second question deals with ontology. And the third question deals with destiny with death playing a significant role. All these issues will be treated in the light of the Akan anthropology. How do the Akan trace the origin of human beings? What makes up a human being? And for what purpose does a human being exist?

Many ancient traditions across space and time have stories pertaining to the origin of human beings. Notable in the academic literature are the monotheistic Abrahamic religion of the Jews, the Popol Vuh for the Quiché people (a Guatemalan Mayan community), and the famous Gilgamesh tablet. The Jewish Bible is better known for its sequential narration of the creation accounts and the origin of humanity. In the Jewish Bible, the story of human beings begins with God forming man out of the dust of the earth (Genesis 1, 26-30; 2, 7). In the tablets of the *Gilgamesh Epic* and the *Popol Vuh*, accounts of the origin of human beings are recorded. Though the *Gilgamesh Epic* does not offer details about the creation of humankind, the tablet narrates how the god Aruru created Enkidu with clay and saliva (George 2003). The *Popol Vuh,* on the other hand, records how the creation of human beings by the gods was first experimented with wood and mud. After their first attempt had failed, they finally succeeded with corn (Tedlock 1996). Similar stories can be found in other Sumerian tablets. The Akan tradition lacks such a fundamental creation story of the origins of humanity. The myths do not provide a coherent standpoint.[115] Ephirim-Donkor has noted that the first Akan ancestor was *abrewa* (the old lady). She is the spring of the Akan people and for that matter every Akan bears a physio-material of the *abrewa* called blood which is the *abusua* (clan). However, Ephirim-Donkor does not provide how this old lady came into existence (Ephirim-Donkor 2010: 12, 30-32). The tradition presents only an explanation of the metaphysical origins and the biological composition of a human being, and one's destiny that predates the individual's conception. This gap does not negate the fact that the Akan people possess valid reasons for believing in a specific origin for human beings.

Akan conception of the origin of humanity begins as a theistic connection. Onyankopɔn or 'Nyankopɔn, the name of the Akan God, is a suprasensible deity transcending all in His absolute reality. The derivation of the name from Nyame (God) kro (Only), pɔn (Great or Supreme), thus "The Only Supreme God," asserts the supreme importance attached to 'Nyankopɔn. God is self-evident, self-announced, and is part of the cognitive

---

[115] There are many creation myths existing among Akan people that explain how humanity arrived on the earth (Wilks 2005: 19-75).

awareness of the Akan epistemological experience (Pobee 1979: 46). The Akan maxim supports this fact: *Obi nkyerɛ abɔfra Nyame*, literally, “No one teaches a child to know God.” These honorific attributes of God make the Akan come to discover the value of independent awareness or discovery of God and how the depths of those revelations inspire their communal spirituality (Danquah 1968: 1).

‘Nyankopɔn as the creator of all human beings is encapsulated in the adage, “All human beings are the children of God,” thus establishing God as the ultimate progenitor (ancestor) of humanity. Children as not in the biological sense, rather, in a metaphoric filiation, because God is the source and sustainer of all life. What makes this connection with God possible?

Gyekye tries to trace the origin of this notion of “children of God” by linking it with the Akan conception of the *ɔkra* (translated as soul in Gyekye’s understanding) which preexisted with the Supreme Being (Gyekye 1987: 85, 94-98). Humanity’s existence thus transcends naturalism. This perspective does not create allowance in the Akan tradition to sustain any evolutionary theory that disconnects the origin of humankind from God. Neither will the Akan conception embrace the concept of the phylogeny of humanity.[116] Human beings were created on purpose for a higher purpose than animals. This core belief among the Akan affirms the value of human existence.

The Akan belief that humans are the children of God establishes a social ontology in which individuals are perceived as interrelated siblings rather than adversaries. This social ontology underscores the Akan conception of personhood and community, making the Akan term for a human being, *onipa*, the foundation of Akan social structure.

Gyekye and Wiredu (1992) have recognized the term onipa as ambiguous, as it expresses both the notion of a human as a “being” and the idea of a person as a degree of quality. These aspects can be expressed in descriptive and normative contexts. In a descriptive context, *onipa* differentiates a “human being” from an animal or an object (Gyekye 2011). Akan phrases such as “ɔyɛ nipa” (she is a human being) and “ɔnnyɛ nipa” (she is not a human being) serve to distinguish human beings from non-human objects.

---

[116] Phylogeny is an evolutionary term which means the science of the relationship between species. The concept classifieds human beings among other animals such as chimpanzees and gorillas as one family group belonging to a common ancestor.

The second category presents the human being as a "person," the criterion for moral judgment. Normative judgments like "ɔyɛ nipa" (she is a person), suggest the person represents commendable social norms and standards such as kindness, generosity, and sympathy (Gyekye 2011). The opposite, "ɔnnyɛ nipa" (she is inhuman), denotes the individual falls short of socially commendable norms and standards. It may suggest the person is unkind, corrupt, unloving, unfaithful, etc. These expressions of the human being provide the basic framework to construct Akan socio-religious and political structures.

8.3. Onipa: The subject of experience in Akan Anthropology

Broadly, the Akan do not define a human being with physical components such as flesh and blood. The Akan indigenes perceive a human being as possessing immaterial, material, and social elements.[117] These are *ɔkra* (aw-krah') "life-force," *mogya* (mo-ja) "blood," *ntorɔ* (n-to-ro) "fatherhood," *nipadua* (ni-pa-du-a) "body," and *sunsum* (sun-sum) "spirit." *Ɔkra* and *sunsum* are immaterial whereas *ntorɔ* and *mogya* are biogenetics responsible for the social affiliations of the child. The *nipadua* is only a physical material and the subject of perceptible experience of the whole person. These are the basic substances of the human being.

Ɔkra and *sunsum* are immaterial in the sense that their origin comes both/either directly or indirectly from God. The *ɔkra* is the life principle, "the innermost self, the essence, of the individual person," "the embodiment and transmitter of the individual's destiny (fate: nkrabea)," "a spark of the Supreme Being," "the divine essence" and "having an antemundane existence" with God (Gyekye 1987: 85). A separation of the *ɔkra* and the body is death. The *sunsum*, on the other hand, is a dynamic spiritual substance, an "activating principle" of all-natural objects (Gyekye 1987:73, 75, 88, 98). It is believed to be the operational force for human morality and that which is responsible for *suban* (character), genius, temper, and quality (Asante & Abarry 1996: 453). Akan people believe individuals receive their *sunsum* from the father.

[117] The term immaterial is used in this sense to denote nonphysical and nonperceivable objects.

Besides the spiritual essences of the person, the Akan believe the human being is composed of social biogenetics. This biogenetics is the basis for the social experience of the individual. They are *ntorɔ* (fatherhood), *mogya* (blood), *abusua* (clan) and *nipadua* or *honam* (body). The *ntorɔ* and *mogya* are biogenetics that gives social affiliation to the Akan child. These genetic components are emitted during sexual intercourse between a man and a woman. The *mogya* is understood to come from the mother and the *ntorɔ*, which is understood as the semen, from the father (Gyekye 1987: 94). The *ntorɔ* is a biological input believed to be a tutelary spirit from a river god (Denteh 1967: 91, 92). Akan do recognize twelve river gods responsible for the transmission of the *ntorɔ*.[118] It is worth noting the fact that the *ntorɔ* is a proto-psychological character from the father or members of the patrilineage (Denteh 1967: 96). The *ntorɔ* does not give a physical resemblance to the child (Gyekye 1987: 226). It is only "responsible for the degree of personal presence that each individual develops at the appropriate stage" (Gyekye & Wiredu 1992: 196, 197). Akan thinkers also believe that the biological input from the father is responsible for the formation of the child's degree of charisma (Gyekye & Wiredu 1992: 196, 197). The *mogya*, on the other hand, "represents a physiological bond to one's mother and an independent membership into her clan (*abusua*), or maternal lineage" (Neville et al: 2009: 51). The Akan matrilineal system is based upon the *mogya* that legitimate a person's citizenship in Akan society as well as one's ancestry in the postmortem life.

The *nipadua* in the Akan anthropology is the physical part of the person which can be seen and felt. The Akan see the figure of a person like the shape of a tree, with branches as hands and fingers, the leaves shaped like the human head, the trunk standing like the body, and roots as legs and toes. Hence, the compound *onipa* (human being) and *dua* (tree) (Gyekye & Wiredu 1992: 156). In a more scientific terms, the *nipadua* will be seen as the biological identity of the person comprised of cells, tissues, muscles,

---

[118] These are : 1) Bosompra (Tough/Strong/Firm), 2) Bosomtwe (Human/Kind/Empathetic), 3) Bosompo/Bosomnkóteaa (Proud/Audacious), 4) Bosomafram (Liberal/Kind/Empathetic), 5) Bosommuru (Respectable/ Distinguished), 6) Bosomkonsi (The Virtuous), 7) Bosomdweróbe (Eccentric/Jittery), 8) Bosomayensu (Truculent), 9) Bosomsika (Fastidious), 10) Bosomkrete (Chivalrous), 11) Bosomakim (Fanatic), 12) Bosomafi (Chaste) (Denteh 1967: 96).

and organs. The *nipadua* is the flesh, as opposed to the other spiritual components of a human being such as the *sunsum* and *ɔkra*. Some vital assemblies of the *nipadua* include the heart (*akoma*), brain (*adwene*), and blood (*mogya*) (Neville et al 2009: 51). The formation of the *nipadua* begins from the womb when the immaterial and the biogenetics combine to form a fetus. It is the *nipadua* that suffers death and corruption.

8.4. The Social Experience of the Human Being

Another aspect of the Akan concept of personhood is the social experience. According to Akan, the unborn child is already a member of the social groups (Pobee 1979: 49). Each Akan child is born with an affiliation to a social unit already mentioned as *abusua* (clan/extended family). This is the social unit where the child shares strong ties of kinship to affirm the Akan worldviews of the individual as a social being. As Pobee pointed it out, the Akan child's existentiality is based on the blood relation (Pobee 1979: 49). The *mogya* from the mother establishes the physiological bond to the matrilineal family system (*abusua*) (Neville et al 2009: 51). The matrilineal system claims the child as belonging to the mother's bloodline, and they offer support and protection. This social theory confers on the child the power to inheritance such as in the kingship. The child's right to ancestry is established in the extended family of the maternal lineage.

Akan children also have a paternal group affiliation. The father's *ntorɔ* is believed to be a transfer of the father's lineage charisma to the child, which gives the child the right of affiliation to the father's clan. As Wiredu noted, "[t]he biological input from the father is responsible for the degree of personal presence that each individual develops at the appropriate stage" (Gyekye & Wiredu 1992: 196, 197). Each Akan child bears this spiritual image of the father, often referred to as charisma. This affinity does not make the child a member of the father's clan. However, the child is greatly esteemed as near kin because of the *ntorɔ*. This affiliation is "the framework of a lot of goodwill" such as economic protection after the death of the father from his brothers and sisters (Gyekye & Wiredu 1992: 196, 197). The Akan proverb, *Agya bi wu a, agya bi te ase*, literally, "When a father dies, another father lives," captures the *ntorɔ* social affiliation of the child to the brothers of the father, or in a larger sense, fatherhood extends beyond one's biological father. This notion provides the understanding of why the Akan child addresses the brothers of the father with the title "father." The *ntorɔ* social affiliation gives the father the right to name his offspring as a symbol of authority of the father over the child.

Given the above analysis, a person is social in the sense that the social fiber of the community confers a social identity on the child. The expression of the individual's existence stems from the social system and construction. Gyekye rightly pointed it out that "[i]f one is by nature a social being, and not merely an atomized entity, then the development of one's full personality and identity can best be achieved only within a communal social system" (Gyekye 1987: 161). Such a social framework of the Akan existentiality promotes a community in communion with each other. A person's individuality becomes a means of achieving social ideals. This background leads to the discussion of the individual's functionality in the broader community.

8.5. Akan Social Setup

The intricate relationship between individuality and community plays a pivotal role in shaping social dynamics. This interplay cultivates a distinctive sense of mutuality and reciprocity, which subsequently propels the community toward the achievement of common objectives. The integration of both communal and individual values serves as the driving force behind the social structure, fostering personal worth and contributing to the overall well-being of society. This integrated social network makes Akan anthropology to define itself in terms of the interconnectedness and interdependence of individuals and communities. Through this perspective, Akan anthropology highlights the significance of both individual and communal contributions to the development and perpetuation of cultural values, traditions, and socio-economic structures.

The Akan worldviews of community are the participation of each person. Gyekye has seen this as "amphibious," that is to say the social composition is characterized by "both communality and individuality" rather than being strictly communalism (Gyekye 1987: 154). The vital element towards achieving an ideal societal system is by the collective participation of each individual. Hence, both the community and the individual share a common level of mutuality. So, in this conception, individualism is a negation in the Akan social construction. Gyekye writes: "The reasons for this statement are that the communal social order is participatory, and that it is characterized by such social and ethical values as social well-being, solidarity, interdependence, cooperation, and reciprocal obligation – all of which conduce to equitable distribution of the resources and benefits of the society" (Gyekye 1987: 157). The social network confers worthiness on the individual, "making it almost impossible for an individual to feel socially insignificant" (Gyekye 1987: 157).

The social scheme forms the bedrock for each individual to realize certain goals in life. And by virtue of the communal cooperation, the community supports, encourages, and inspires worthy cause of individuals. Since one's socio-economic welfare contributes to the larger good of the community, the concept of pushing individuals to reach higher standards is essential. Many phrases and proverbs encourage this. One phrase is *Sɔ n'asene,* literally meaning, "To hold the waist of someone," thus, giving an idea of pushing or holding someone firmly. There is also the proverb, *Sɛ wo foro dua pa a na yɛpia wo,* literally, "It is when you climb a good tree that we push you." Implicitly, the society is apt to support any worthy cause of its individuals, and the individual is assured of receiving the necessary support.

Because of the strong ties in human relations among the Akan, any attempt to fall away from the social network has grave consequences on the social welfare of the individual and is a threat to the social fraternity of the community. Since the Akan existentiality is social, and personhood is defined in that sense, an individual's security is measured by the individual's level of intimacy within the social network. Hence, individualism (unlike individuality) and egocentrism are classified as immoral states of being (Gyekye 1996: 58-62). The Akan expresses these in the following phrases, *Ɔmpɛ nipa* (He dislikes people) or *Ɔyɛ pɛsɛ-me-nko-nya*, (He is selfish). Other proverbs capture the same idea, *Nipa nua ne nipa*, literally, "A human being is a human being's neighbor," and *Onipa hia mmoa*, meaning, "A human being needs help." The mutual solidarity is quite imperative as Akan see it as a blessed ontology for human survival.

8.6. Morality and Virtues

This section delves into the importance of moral virtues and character in shaping communal solidarity and fostering a just society. While acknowledging that religion may have some influence on morality, Gyekye emphasizes the role of the individual in upholding ethical standards and perpetuating moral values. This discussion explores the significance of moral virtues in the Akan community, the impact of character on society, and the importance of maintaining communal ideals.

On the grounds of Akan conception of moral issues, Gyekye rejects the idea that Akan morality was derived from religion (Gyekye 1996: 129, 130). Scholars, including J. B. Danquah, Peter K. Sarpong, and Kofi Asare Opoku, have asserted that the origin of morality stems from religious experiences (Danquah 1944: 3; Sarpong 1972: 41; Asare Opoku 1978: 152).

Gyekye argues that African traditional religion "is not a revealed religion" and, however, has no "access to the commandments of God to use as the basis of their moral system" (Gyekye 1996: 56). In order not to undermine his radical stance, Gyekye accepts somewhere that certain aspects of morality could have some supposed religious biases. He writes: "The messages purported to be received occasionally by priests from the deities they serve may have some moral import and relevance for the people of a community, but because these messages are sporadic, they can hardly constitute an elaborate and coherent basis, of the moral values of the people" (Gyekye 1996: 56). He does it well to justify it further that "religion cannot be completely banished from the domain of moral practice, notwithstanding the fact that the moral values of the African society did not derive directly from religion" (Gyekye 1996: 57).[119]

The communal solidarity becomes a catalyst for all morality. Since a community is a cluster of individuals, moral stability depends on the level of an individual's ethical standards. A person's morality finds expression in character. Akan may define the character (*suban*) as the nature of a person's *sunsum* as discussed above. A person's character defines one's personality. Hence, moral virtues underline almost all of the Akan' pedagogy in the proverbs and folklore. Moral virtues form a greater portion of the

[119] See (Sekyere 2016) for further discussion on Akan morality and ethics.

telos of the larger Akan epistemology. Every Akan child is therefore inculcated with principles of faithfulness, probity, responsibility, justice, honesty, moderation, patience, generosity, kindness, respect for human life, respect for aged persons, faithfulness in marriage, submissiveness, humility, hospitality, and so on (Gyekye 1996: 58). These virtues are woven into the fabric of folklore and proverbs as a means of educating individuals, due to their profound social impact and enduring influence on one's identity.

A person's moral aptitude is pervasive in the sense that Akan people relate character to posterity. There is the Akan proverb that says, *Sɛ wo rekɔ awadeɛ a bisa* (Make inquiries before you marry). This proverb points out to the priority of the worthiness of the suitor and the bride-to-be, and how the two lineage groups are satisfied with the marriage.[120] There is a strong belief among the Akan that a person's character can have effects on their progeny. We know this because of the proverbs *Ɔkɔtɔ nwo anoma* (A crab does not give birth to a bird) and *Sedeɛ sekan teɛ no, saa ara na bɔha teɛ*, (Like the cutlass, like the knife). These expressions are similar to the English maxim, "Like father, like son." Hence, Akan people are sensitive to the moral goodwill of the particular family from which their children seek to affiliate in conjugality. This and many other social structures put a responsibility on the individual to fulfill and promote the required communal moral virtues.

A person's character is very crucial in Akan communities, and it is the work of the *sunsum* (Gyekye 1996: 66, 67). Hence, moral virtues become the most significant segment in Akan's traditional pedagogy and that which "leads people to pursue the kinds of morally commendable actions and behavior expected in the context of a social morality" (Gyekye 1996: 67).

---

[120] It has been recognized among Akan—and many other African societies—that marriage is not only a union between the individuals willing to be joined together. The marriage ceremony is also a union of the two clans who are giving their "royal" children to the marriage. Gyekye writes: "A marriage might seem to be between two families. The man and the woman are both warned straightaway that they are not being married to an individual but to a family. In many societies in Africa, then, marriage is said to be a union of families rather than of just two individuals" (Gyekye 1996: 78, 79). This union is also witnessed by the ancestors of the two clans uniting in this respect, as they are invoked as witnesses and guardians of the marital posterity by the pouring of libation. The union also has a lasting effect on the yet-to-be-born Akan child in both clans as now their children would have their social group membership in both clans. The child will belong to the *abusua* of the mother and will share in the father's *ntorɔ*. This communal ethos characterize marriage with the most importance and sacred ceremony.

Some of these moral virtues may include "probity, patience, kindness, fairness, humility, gratitude, moderation, temperance, generosity, contentment, hospitality, perseverance, trust-worthiness, truthfulness and honesty, respect for older people, chastity before marriage, and faithfulness in marriage" (Gyekye 1996: 68). These virtues set out the spirituality of the individual towards many interventions in society.

It is within the enhancement of these attributes that the person comes to appreciate and to internalize those virtues for an excellent character and towards a just society. In commenting on the Akan maxim "When virtue founds a town, the town thrives and abides," Gyekye writes: "That is to say, when virtue forms or is made the foundation of a society or state, that society (or state) becomes strong, flourishes, and continues to grow" (Gyekye 1996: 67). He further explains that "constant attempts are made in the process of socialization to inculcate those excellences of character in the growing children and young adults of African societies, to make them appreciate, internalize, and practically display those virtues in their moral lives" (Gyekye 1996: 67).

How do an individual's moral virtues influence society? Given that the Akan conception of humanity is inherently social, as previously discussed, the moral system is inherently situated within the social framework, aimed at ensuring the well-being of all members of society. Consequently, the realization of morality is deeply rooted in communal solidarity, effectively countering individualism, and egocentrism within the Akan social setup.

8.7. Justice and Equity

Community development lends itself on social norms and laws. Though they may form part of the fabrics of society, they need to be protected and promoted. The Akan political theory of traditional kingship aims at achieving these ends. This in its totality is enshrined in the chieftaincy (ahenesɛm).[121]

[121] The English translation "kingship" and "chieftaincy" for *ahenesɛm* is quite masculine. In the Akan language *ahenesɛm* has to do with both the "*Ɔhene*" (chief) and "*Ɔhenemaa*", literally, "*Ɔhene maame*" (the mother of the chief). Contrary to other cultures, the queen mother, among Akan, is not the wife of the chief.

Traditional Akan politics is enshrined in the kingship or chieftaincy. Kings and queens rule Akan communities. The role the king plays is among other things a sacred role as he maintains the religion and social order of the community (Pobee 1979: 44, 45).[122] The queen mother represents the traditional feminist's voice. It is part of her duties to protect and ensure women's equity and justice.

When a king swears to the throne, it is part of his duties to promote the security of the entire community. These require strict enforcement of the laws and customs of the society. Since the chief is to enforce these values and to promote them, every Akan chief, before the ascension to power, is vilified of his level of integrity (Gyekye 1996: 113). A chief's integrity is essential to his governance responsibilities. The king must lead the way to ensure peace, justice, and equity in the community. Because the king's role provides the maintenance of both the religious and social system, he becomes accountable to both God and the people he serves. For further reading on Akan chieftaincy, consult (Muller 2013).

8.8. Evil

The origin of evil is obscure among the Akan. Not even does the African traditional religions give all the answers to evil. Gyekye has already probed the complexity of the origin of evil in the Akan traditions as more difficult than the West (Gyekye 1987: 123). Nevertheless, the Akan do recognize the reality of evil as both anthropological and metaphysical.

The Akan worldviews on evil are cosmic in scope, with its potential to impact natural objects. A key aspect of Akan universalism is the recognition of the presence of evil in the world. The Akan metaphor, *Wiase yɜ sum*, which translates to "the world is full of darkness" or, "the world is mystic,"

---

[122] Religion and politics in the Akan ethnic group are indispensable. The chief who is the political leader also represents the people in their religious experience and maintenance in various intricate ceremonies such as festivals, pouring of libation and various pacifications. The stool (reserved stools from previous chiefs venerated as pioneer ancestors) upon which the chief is enthroned and crowned is considered to contain ancestral spirits who are venerated as living spirits. It is also important to remark that most of the relics around the chief are considered to be containing *sunsum* (*tumi*/power). So, the office of the chief is both political and sacerdotal. For more information on Akan' chieftaincy, read (Gyekye 1996: 109-121 & Muller 2013).

signifies that evil is an inherent part of the world. Moreover, the proverb *Suro nipa na gyae osaman*, meaning, "Fear a human being more than a ghost," highlights the potential for human beings to be malevolent or to serve as instruments for evil purposes.[123]

J. B. Danquah has designated *sunsum* as the depository of evil in humanity. He wrote: "Evil, therefore, exists but only in the *sunsum* side; the world of the *sunsum* not the world of *okara*" (Danquah 1968: 87). He interpreted the contamination of the *sunsum* with the existence of sin in the world by which through neglect and submission of the *sunsum,* perpetuates evil in the individual. In other words, Danquah postulates that no one is born evil because there is no evil in the *'kra* (Danquah 1968: 87). Evil is an inclination of the *sunsum* due to societal influence. But who is responsible for evil and from where did it come?

The two primary sources of evil identified by Gyekye are first, the lesser deities, who are held to be either good or bad, and the second is the human freewill which makes individuals and communities architects of their moral standards.[124] God is never the source of evil and evil is not associated with him (Gyekye 1996: 9, 12).[125]

The lesser deities, or the lesser spirits, according to Gyekye, "are held either to be good and evil or to have powers of good and evil." Such potency to cause evil stems from their very nature that is partly evil (Gyekye 1996:

[123] The origin of their evil nature is unknown by Akan. The most possible reason may be attributed to Akan' understanding of the essence of evil as a phenomenon that corrupts one's thoughts and communal health. It is the moral act that is judged mostly as either wanted or unwanted, or whether it promotes comfort or discomfort. The ontology of these evils is quite complicated to ascertain. But Akan have a clear knowledge about the evil nature of these entities.

[124] Gyekye names lesser spirits, supernatural forces such as magical powers (probably dwarfs) and witches as part of the deities. To classify these entities under deities is questionable in so many respects according to the Akan religion. The deities as understood by Akan comprise of *Onyame* or *Onyankopɔn* and the lesser gods. These entities protect human beings and seek to promote humanity's well-being. Even though the lesser deities can trigger calamities on humanity, these are retributive justice meant to course a communal repentance after the gods have been desecrated (*efi*) by human evil deeds. Aside God and the *Abosom* (gods), all other supernatural forces or dwarfs or witches are not considered as deities among the Akan.

[125] Akan people also consider God as just. God's justice is captioned in proverbs such as *Aboa ɔnni dua no Onyame na ɛpra ne ho*, literally, "God helps to drive away flies from the animal without a tale", and "*Onni bi agya ne Nyame*," literally, "God fathers the needy." Thus, God's distributive justice is fundamentally part of His nature.

12). These lesser deities have the power to cause sickness, natural disasters, and even to facilitate a person's death if the individual offends them. Gyekye notes that "though the deities were created by God, they are believed to operate independently of God and in accordance with their own wills: they can, and do, use their independent wills to pursue evil" (Gyekye 1996: 12).

The second source of evil, which is the freewill, is considered to stem "from human character, conscience, thoughts and desires" (Gyekye 1996: 9, 12). The freewill makes human beings to be architects of their moral standards. A person has the capability to choose to practice what is good as well as evil. However, since the practice of evil is an unacceptable norm, the freewill becomes a means by which persons exercise it for the good of oneself, and in harmony with the society.

The next to mention under evil is atonement among the Akan religion. How do Akan make peace and reconciliation with the gods after desecrating the gods? The concept of making peace and reconciliation with the gods is central in the African Traditional Religions. Among the Akan, it is called *afodeɛ*, literally, "guilt offering." The word stems from two Akan compound words namely *ɛfo*, meaning "guilt" and *adeɛ*, meaning "thing." Therefore, *afodeɛ* is what is offered after being found guilty by the gods. Magesa has noted that "[t]he fundamental meaning of sacrifices and offerings lies in their efficacy to restore wholeness. If wrong-doing causes a dangerous separation of the various elements of the universe, sacrifices and offerings aim to reestablish unity and restore balance" (Magesa 1997: 203). The sacrifices can be personal or collective. Akan see this expiation as *mmusu yi*, or "removal of blasphemy." The slaughtering of a ram or presentation of certain foods or items as prescribed by the traditional priest is necessary to appease the gods.

8.9. Destiny (*Nkrabea*)

The notion of destiny is nothing exclusive to the Akan. It is fundamental in most of the world societies. To the Akan, each person is born with a destiny to fulfill. This destiny was fixed before the individual's entrance into the world. The concept is fashioned in two Akan words *nkrabea* and *hyɛbrɛ or hyɛbea*. *Nkrabea* owes its name to the *ɔkra*, signifying it as the bearer of a person's destiny (Gyekye 1987: 85). *Nkra* means "message" and bea means "manner" that is, to bid farewell or take leave (Gyekye 1987: 104, 112). The notion will, therefore, be understood as the manner that the *ɔkra* received its fate from God because Akan metaphysics postulate the fact that the *ɔkra* had preexistence with God. This interpretation leads Gyekye to affirm the general understanding of *nkrabea* as "manner of," indicating the way an individual's temporality is fixed in the world. The message the *ɔkra* receives from God determines the totality of the various temporal events and occurrences in the course of the person's whole life in the natural world (Gyekye 1987: 104, 112).

The other term *hyɛbrɛ or Ohyɛbrɛ* is better translated as "appointed time," whereby *hyɛ* means "appointed or fixed" and *brɛ* means "time or moment."[126] This description is expressed in the lyrics of Ghana's famous high-life musician Nana Kwame Ampadu (1945–2021) in one of his songs, "*Asiane bi yɛ nkrabea*" (Some accidents are destiny).[127] Nana Ampadu begins with this statement: "*Asiane bi yɛ nkrabea; nkrabea mu nsɛm wo yɛ ho hwee a ɛnyɛ yie, ɔhyɛbrɛ bɛn ni*" literally means, "An accident may be destiny; matters of destiny are unalterable, what kind of predestination (*ɔhyeberɛ*) is that?" Nana Ampadu uses the two words in a single statement to express different thoughts. *Hyɛbrɛ*, therefore, becomes a descriptive variant of *nkrabea*, even though both represent the same thing.

The Akan thought of *nkrabea* and *hyɛbrɛ* should be understood as the various preordained events in an individual's life which are unalterable and defines the meaning of one's whole life.[128] It is worth quoting Gyekye's definition of destiny here:

---

126 Definition by George P. Hagan as cited by (Gyekye 1987:109).

127 Nana Kwame Ampadu was one of the pioneer Akan musicians of the traditional Ghana highlife music. His musical career began in the mid 60's. He remains the most prolific songwriter of all time in Ghana and in the diaspora with more than seven hundred songs on albums. In 1973, he was crowned as "Nwontofohene" [King of Musicians] by the Arts Council of Ghana. Highlife is a musical genre which originated from Ghana and later on spread to the Western Anglophone African countries such as Liberia, Sierra Leon, Nigeria and Gambia. The lyrics of Highlife music are based on the traditional values and philosophy of the culture.

128 Gyekye contends that both terms are interchangeable and represent the same concept of destiny. He discusses the works of Eva Mayerowitz, J. B. Danquah, and Bishop Sarpong, to show that there is no dichotomy between the two. His interlocutors attempted to draw a subtle line between the two, which in the end, according to Gyekye's analysis, are not congruent with Akan linguistics. See (Gyekye 1987: 109-112).

> Patterns of individual lives, habitual or persistent traits of persons, fortunes and misfortunes, successes and failures, the traumas and enigmas of life; the ways in which propensities, inclinations, capacities, and talents show themselves in individuals; the observed uniqueness of the individual – all these suggest to the Akan that there is and should be some basis or reason for this individuality. That basis is destiny (Gyekye 1987: 106).

Thus, destiny is not defined by some particular events. It involves every aspect of the individual's total life in the world.

8.10. Death and Reincarnation

Whereas science may be limited by what happens in the death of an individual, the Akan traditional thanatology provides answers to some difficult questions often asked about what happens in and after death. Akan people accept death as part of life. Such an idea is found in the Akan proverbs *Owuo atwedeɛ ɔbaako nforõ* (One person does not climb death's ladder) and *Owuo da amansan kɔn mu* (Death is everyone's yoke). These proverbs bring to mind the idea of death as a movement from one point to the other, and as a natural condition. To the Akan, death is ontologically a separation. It is the separation of the *ɔkra* and the *nipadua* that results in death (Gyekye 1987: 86). Because the life of the individual has both material and immaterial dimensions, life and death are determined by the unity or disembodiment of these elements. For example, Gyekye noted that the body (*nipadua*) suffers death whiles the *ɔkra* survives it (Gyekye 1987: 88, 98). The destruction of the body leads to the separation of the person from the living. This separation seems to be only the physical disappearance of the individual since the dead lives always with the living according to Akan tradition. The *ɔkra*, travels to *Asamando* (the spirit world of the dead) as an apotheosized being called ancestor. In rare cases where the individual's destiny was altered by evil spirits or accidents, the *ɔkra* returns to life to fulfill its divine destiny (Aye-Addo 2013: 44, 45). The Akan understanding of death makes life both cyclical and linear based on the circumstance of death and dying.

9. All Human Beings Are the Children of God

> *"A human person is a person whatever his age or social status. Personhood may reach its full realization in community, but it is not acquired or yet to be achieved as one goes along in society. What a person acquires are status, habits, and personality or character traits... One is a person because of what he is, not because of what he has acquired"* – Kwame Gyekye (2010: 109).

9.1. Introduction

Sunsum is spiritual energy, and it is ontological to all existence and the very essence emanating directly from God's *Sunsum* (Clark 2012: 79, 80). In the Akan traditional anthropology, humanity bears this immaterial component. *Sunsum*, which is a volatile substance, or dynamic quasi-spiritual element that forms part of the very substance of a human being, is the operational force for human morality. *Sunsum* is responsible for *suban* (character), genius, temper, and quality (Asante & Abarry 1996: 453). Both *ɔkra* and *sunsum* come from the Supreme Being. Whereas *ɔkra* is the life-force of the person, *sunsum* is the activating principle of life as discussed earlier.

Sunsum is very operational in dynamic interactions between self and others. It is considered as the *dramatis persona* that operates in persons' dreams. Appiah has noted that *sunsum* can leave one's body temporally in life and especially during nightly dreams which is "thought to be the perceptions of a person's *sunsum* on its nightly peregrinations" (Appiah 1992: 157). As an illustration, an Akan reading Zechariah 3 will come to think of the figure of the high priest Joshua as *sunsum* standing before the heavenly jury in the vision.

Sunsum is very receptive and permeative. Since it sometimes appears as a being, it can be manipulated by spirit forces for either good or evil course. William Abraham writes: "A man's *sunsum* is also the spirit of a man which may be attacked by witchcraft. *Sunsum* as the basis of character is said to be strong or wicked or good. And when a person is a witch or wizard, it is through the power of the *sunsum*" (Abraham 1996: 453). Such definitions explain the ecstatic experience (*akōm*) of the traditional priest (*ōkomfo*). It is the *sunsum* that becomes frenzied by the *abosom* for the priest to manifest unconscious gestures to make prophesies. Gyekye confirms this when he writes: "It is the sunsum with which the Akan diviner (*ōkomfo*), believed to possess extrasensory abilities, communicates. It tells the diviner what it really wants without the person knowing or being aware of what he or she wants: Thus, sunsum may be unconscious" (Gyekye 1987: 102). In its general sense, *sunsum* is the connecting point between humanity and the spirit world. Again, without the *sunsum*, the unity of the body and the *ɔkra* will leave the person without any transcendental rationality.

The Akan concept of human beings as "*Nyame mma",* meaning "children of God", designates human beings as numinous—composed of divine presence and power to function according to the ways of God. This radical *ontological filiation* is a substantial paradigm that is parallel to the relationship between a child and his father in Akan worldviews.

In the Akan tradition, a child bears the image of the father.[129] When a person is confronted with an interrogatory question such as "whose child are you?", that person is expected to mention the father's name first.[130] The name of the father and his lineage will convey everything about the child. When speaking about this concept, Wiredu noted: "The biological input from the father is responsible for the degree of *personal presence* that each individual develops at the appropriate stage" (Wiredu 1992: 196, 197).[131] The "biological input" or "personal presence" (or what I will call paternal imprints of the father) is the *ntorɔ* which is instrumental in the formation of the child's degree of charisma according to Wiredu.

Naturally, from this background, an Akan child is interwoven by the image of the father. The individual becomes *receptive* and *permeative* of

---

129 In the traditional sense, a child bears the image of both father and mother according to the Akan proverb "Sɛ abɔfra nsɛ oni a, na ɔsɛ ɔse." Literally meaning: "If a child does not look like (affinity) the mother, he looks like the father."

130 It should not be confused with the question *wo firi efie bēn mu?* Meaning "Which family do you belong to?" Such question brings out a sense of belongingness which is the Akan concept of kinship of the matrilineal system. One's bloodline is the mother's lineage which forms the family unit of the child.

131 Italics are mine.

the paternal imprints that fashion his charisma. On the basis of such an ontological physiology, it can be said that *choretikos* has taken place. The child is capable to contain the father's image, and the father's image permeates through his child because the child has become capable. It is within this sophisticated bonding that a child receives paternal descent or membership of the father's *ntorɔ*.[132] Wiredu wrote that "Through the charisma principle one is a member of a grouping on the father's side which, although largely ceremonial, is nevertheless the framework of a lot of goodwill" (Wiredu 1992: 197).

At this point, one can argue with certitude that in the Akan physiological concept, the child bears the image of the parent. The image transposes itself in different facades of the child's life, and alongside with other spiritual and social mechanisms, the individual acquires an identity that is substantial, relational and functional, which is far removed from abstraction. But in the strictest sense, the individual needs to stay within this communal affiliation in order to actualize his or her humanness.

9.2. The Social Definition of Personhood

Having understood the existential component of the bond between the father and child, and the theistic anthropological concept of the Akan that "All men are children of God," the understanding of personhood begins to take shape in this study. The continuum between God and humanity is an ontological image: "as far as theology is concerned, to be person is to have the image of God and thus to exist according to the way in which God exists" (Owino Kombo 2007: 129). From this perspective, and the understanding of the personality of God as social, human beings in the image of God designates the term *person* to be social. As a result, the social idea of personhood is vital to reconsidering and delving into the intricacies of Akan theological anthropology, which holds that all human beings share a common identity under the auspices of God's parenting. If humanity can achieve a congenial inter-human social experience and a good relationship

132 It is within the father's descent that the child maintains his fatherhood. He bears the father's *ntorɔ*, heritage, etc. At the death of the father, the senior brother among the father's family becomes the father of the child.

with the surrounding world, this concept of being in the image of God should affect each person's consciousness.

9.3. Human Beings in the Image of God

From the philosophies of the church fathers, Owino Kombo understood that substance or nature refers to *what* of something or simply *what is*. Therefore, *what is a man* or *what is a person* should be recognized of as a "being in an absolute sense" (Owino Kombo 2007: 128). What a *person* is should have a substance that is common to all human beings and that which is metaphysically[133] axiomatic. Without such a ground, man would be designated as an autonomous *matter* permeating itself as a self-existing being without any dependency. Such an existence is flawed and axiomatically an error. This is because a human being "is subject to limitations of space and time" (Owino Kombo 2007: 128). A person's life needs substantial dependencies.

Consequently, to be a person, as Owino Kombo situated it after the philosophical and theological lineage of the church fathers' concept of the *Imago Dei*, "is only an image of God." This essential component regarded as residing in man "has to do with how to exist in the way that God exists" (Owino Kombo 2007: 128).[134] It is this *Imago Dei*, which according to theologians such as Jürgen Moltmann says it "dwells in the depths of every soul", making humanity capable of acquiring an inherent divine identity and dignity, and also that which makes the interconnection, and the religious experience possible (Moltmann 1992: 249). Moltmann explains further somewhere about this relationship that "Likeness to God means God's relationship to human beings first of all, and only then, and as a consequence of that, the human being's relationship to God" (Moltmann

133 Joseph Francis Hartel asserted that the notion of the image "is a metaphysical relation between existents". He further explained how humanity is bond to God for existence. That is, the relationship between God and His creatures means "a relation between one very essence of one being and the very essence of another being." This kind of bond to Hartel, becomes the source of life to creation since one needs to depend on God for life. So, the notion of the image even though a reflection in part is also, in reality —an essence of God permeating through His creatures. Hartel believes that such a relation is both logical and real. See (Hartel 1993: 10-11).

134 See a more detailed discussion of *Imago Dei* from (Middleton 2005).

1985: 220). Both Owino Kombo and Moltmann agree and thus confirm the effect of that relationship as a result of the personality of God. Owino Kombo concludes: "This is possible because the Divine Persons are, in the first place, not isolated individuals, but persons in relationship with one another" (Owino Kombo 2007: 130). We can reiterate the fact that it is the image of God in human beings which is instrumental towards any interrelation experience with God. To the Akan, this is the *sunsum* of God at work in humanity.

9.4. Human Transcendence

What could be the basis for human transcendence among the Akan? The Akan's understanding of human transcendence is contrary to the Western understanding of transcendence. The Akan conception of human transcendence or self-transcendence is much complicated. It is both metaphysical and natural experience. It has the premises of *a priori* and *posterior*. The first aspect to emphasize is the activating principle of the *sunsum*. In order for humanity to exercise some capacities or power to reason, there should be an activating essence. This activating principle has always been a part of the biological formation of a human being. Gyekye has already pointed out to this intrinsic property in natural objects as the basis of all activity and possession of power (Gyekye 1987: 75). As Akan scholars have attributed experience and personality to the activity of the *sunsum*, one's cosmic experience, and transcendence has an *a priori*: there is a metaphysical force which acts to extemporize, in tandem with the *adwene* (mind), a person's cosmic experience. Hence, the varying experiences of *sunsum* in personality formation. There are some persons known to be possessing "heavy *sunsum*", meaning that they are highly charismatic. Others are also considered as having "light *sunsum*", alluding to cowardice and weakling (Gyekye 1987: 90, 96). Human transcendence is however affected by the operational forces of the *sunsum*. The individual's charisma, which is inherited from the father as *ntorɔ,* also influences one's way of perception and understanding of the world around oneself.

Again, human transcendence comes as a reflection of the image of God in humanity, which has been identified as made possible by the instrumentality of the *sunsum* that facilitates an individual's sociability. God is transcendent; He is beyond everything. Akan people do not identify God with His creation, as seen in the previous chapter. Nonetheless, the operational forces of His *sunsum* makes the Akan see God as immanent at the same time in the form of human social experience. Communal experience makes individuals achieve a high level of self-actualization. The community can be considered good only through good relationships. Musopole has already pointed out the importance of human relationality to the health of the community as a principal feature of African societies (Musopole 1994: 179). The African understanding of transcendence is therefore not a movement of individualism. It is rather an evolution of the community towards perfection. It is the health of the community that each person tries to protect from one's individuality. Therefore, among Africans, it is imperative to be reconciled into the community. Reconciliation into the larger community launches the community into achieving health and wealth. The Akan maxim, "A human being needs help" sets out to demonstrate a communal solidarity where solitary life is overridden (Gyekye 1996: 24, 25). The community finally becomes a means to achieve human transcendence. Individualism is a major threat to African communities since it is a fall away from the communal transcendence.

9.5. Human Rights: All Human Beings Are Equal

How does one apply the Akan theological anthropology to human rights? The *sunsum* or image of God explains the human rights concept from different dynamics. The Akan maxim, "All human beings are children of God; no one is a child of the earth", vastly applies in explaining the theory and concepts of human rights. The maxim plays an important role in drawing a line of equality and justice of all human rights within the society. Regardless of class status, each person has the right to live, and to be treated with dignity. Gyekye thus writes: "A concept of human dignity can be linked with – or derived from – the concept of intrinsic value. Also implicit in the maxim is the equality of the moral worth of all human beings – of all the children of God" (Gyekye 1996: 150, 151). The idea is that God's image in humanity distinguishes a human being from other creatures; therefore, any human being in the world deserves equal treatment as God views all human beings as children. Given that man has deep insight and creativity, human beings have the ability to transform their surrounding by integrating various skill sets they have acquired. The ability endowed to human beings by God to understand the right from wrong ensures that human beings can freely understand each other and treat each other in the right manner as expected.

The concept of human rights for all human beings is directly related to the concept of all human beings being children of God in that it reminds human beings of the power in the value they each individually hold. In accordance with the human rights, each value should be upheld in the society and never limited, so as to ensure there exists inherent entitlement of everyone. With his ability to occupy the highest stand in creation with unique Godlike characteristics compared to other creatures, each human being has unique potential and is equal. Every human being is capable of fulfilling whatever that person desires in expressing the central purpose that God made the individual to function. Nothing is so important than the integration of an individual's right to live and to exercise one's creativity such as arts and music in the communal fraternity. Human rights, among the Akan, as Gyekye notes, is "not only in an individualistic but also in a communal context" (Gyekye 1996: 151). As stated previously, Africans' transcendence is a movement of community. Therefore, an individual's human right should "enhance cultural development and insure the material and political success of the community" (Gyekye 1996: 151). The world requires a common moral language that can respect everyone's desires, undertakings, and accomplishments since no one is a child of the earth according to the Akan proverb. The concept of human rights is enforced so as to encourage the *sunsum* bestowed in each person in the society and protect them.

The ability of human beings to be creative is in respect to the image of God and likeness, where God himself was creative in nature, and had the ability to create each in his image, and the entire universe. On the other hand, human beings are endowed with the ability to be creative by perusing their desires, this should be respected and never infringed by others. The human rights of acquiring the education that in turn gives human beings the ability to become creative in various fields is essential and should never be limited, irrespective of the ethnic community or social background. The ability in every human being to make things and modify various creations means that we are all made in the image of a Creative God.

The emphasis of a universal family should influence all political bureaucracy. The rights given to political authorities to rule should see to protect the right of all persons. Politics should not be disassociated from the virtues of the larger community. The higher political institutions should seek to protect and promote the legacy of human rights for all. The exercise of power to intimidate members of the society contravene the rights of people to live freely and to exercise their God-given freedom. Whereas individuals are morally obligated to respect authority, that moral submission is not a submission of a person's rights to that authority. Human rights belong to the individual, and thus the person exercises and functions within that capacity. Gyekye notes: "Human rights, then, are simple special or fundamental human values, generally or ultimately of a moral nature" (Gyekye 1996: 152). In the same way, political authority should be morally sound to be responsible for a just leadership, and to render accountability to the community.

9.6. Summary

In this chapter, I have discussed the theological anthropology of the Akan *sunsum*. It became apparent from the discussion that Akan worldviews of a human being has a direct ontological connection with God, i.e., human beings are children of God made in the perfect image of God. Because of this defined ontology, human beings exist to function within a universal family since all are created into God's parentage to share relationship and to function according to the way God exists. This conception is far removed from mythology. It is based on a rational ontology. Human beings are made up or have both immaterial, material, and social aspects namely *ɔkra*, *mogya* (blood line or clan), *ntorɔ* (fatherhood), and a dynamic spiritual force called *sunsum*. The *sunsum* acts as a unifying force, transposing itself in so many dynamic interactions in the individual's whole life and relationship with the things around him. By the grace of the *sunsum*, the person comes to bear the image of God and to function in society. Each human being possesses a unique spiritual potential that requires to be embraced in our respective society. This *sunsum* is in respect to God's image of communication and spirit and should be respected and protected by human rights. Human beings become transcendent through self-realization, communal fraternity, and the ability to intelligently improve the environment, and freely interact with each other. These processes are very essential to the foundation of the Akan theological anthropology.

The information provided by the Akan traditional religion about God and human beings has been the subject for the formulation of Akan theological anthropology. The Akan anthropology has a theistic connection that brings the immanence of the transcendent God into the history of human beings. The 'kra of God in the human being translates human experiences into relationships and functionality according to the way that God exists. All these find expressions on the following aspects:

9.6.1. Substance (Ontology)

Having discussed the various rudimentary elements in Akan anthropology, it should be clear at this point that the conceptual thought of the Akan on human beings as children of God is inherently a designation of human beings as containing the image of God as a child bears the image of his father. Even though the term 'image of God' (*imago Dei)* does not appear in the Akan traditional experience, the Akan people saw this interconnectivity between human beings and God, and all other things, as the work of the *'kra,* which is the divine vital force residing in each human being. The meaning of this conception is not an abstract but the very definition of the human being and the being of human among the Akan. In such definitions, one comes to understand the fundamental conception of the Akan theological anthropology as, first, having a *substance*. The *'kra* is the divine element that unites human beings to God, and as a bearer of destiny, it transposes itself in various dynamic activities for the wellbeing of human beings. Other elements like the *sunsum* and *ntorɔ* are responsible for personality formation and instrumental in the social experience.

9.6.2. Relational Ontology

In the social experience, Wiredu noted that "a person is social not only because he or she lives in a community, which is the only context in which full development, or indeed any sort of human development is possible, but also because, by his original constitution, a human being is part of a social whole" (Wiredu 1992: 196). Humanity has an ontological relationship with

God, which is rather an *ontological filiation* where God becomes the Ancestor, and humanity His progeny. However, to the Akan, there is a more social significance of such a conception than just relational ontology to God. Personhood is "being" in a relationship. It is a social experience with the community because all human beings are children of God. The Akan concepts of the *ntorɔ* and *mogya* explain this concept of relationality in the human experience. Thus, the interpersonal relationship of the individual within the social setup can be viewed as *a relational ontology*.

9.6.3. Functionality Ontology

Are human beings capable of functioning according to the ways of God? Yes, the human being is created to function according to the way God exists. The social identity makes the human being participative in the promotion of the wellbeing and wealth of society. The social ontology demands the contribution of the individual. In a continent that continues to suffer many socio-economic, religious and political challenges, it calls for the combined efforts of its citizens to address these challenges by exploring how the various institutions can affect the progress of the community through the promotion of human rights, human progress, and free access to government and information. The functional ontology calls for a confrontation of injustice, despotism, corruption, and leadership incompetence. A theological anthropology in this respect should be seen as a liberation theology that seeks to bring out the "Godliness" in humanity.

10. General Conclusion

Where does the gospel find relevance in Akan theological anthropology? While the Akan cultural traditions offer valuable insights into numerous theological issues, it would be surprising if God's plan to save humanity through Jesus Christ held no importance for the Akan people. As community is central to Akan culture, the divine intervention of the Triune God, representing the ultimate community, creates an ideal kingdom where the human family reaches its fulfillment. Moltmann rightly expresses the effect of this reunion with the Triune God: "All three determinations of the history of God's kingdom point towards the eschatological kingdom of glory in which people will finally, wholly and completely be gathered into the eternal life of the triune God" (Moltmann 1981: 213). In talking about friendship with God, Moltmann again writes: "By virtue of Friendship with God in the Spirit, we have the chance to influence God and to participate in his rule… God makes men and women his friends by inclining affectionately towards them and by listening to them… Friendship is the concrete concept of freedom" (Moltmann 1981: 221). The greatest relationship is a human being's experience with God, which without the gospel still wallows in obscurity. The gospel, therefore, must not be seen as alien to the Akan's religious experience of God. It must be seen as God coming to humanity, in a communal relationship. Akan concept of community, therefore, finds its perfect fulfillment in the gospel.

In the new kingdom of God's fellowship with humanity, Jesus becomes the immanence of God. He is immanent because He is Immanuel, "God with us" (Isa. 7:14; Matt. 1:23). The gospel, however, in the person of Jesus Christ who is "the image of the invisible God" (Col. 1:15), also gives humanity an image of Christ when people come to accept God's gift of salvation. To borrow the words of Musopole, "Jesus represents the almightiness of God" (Musopole 1994: 169). He stands as the human par excellence for the entire human race. The salvation provided through Jesus Christ becomes a return to God. Those who receive Him become one with God in God's redemptive plan, which redeems humanity from the clutches of evil and establishes justice on earth. The sacrificial death of Jesus Christ becomes a mediation towards a rebirth and renewal of self. Musopole rightly writes: "Jesus becomes one with us in order to perfect both persons and cultures" (Musopole 1994: 169). He again becomes the ultimate *Sunsum* who reconciles and unifies the world to God.

The gospel triumph in Africa is also a fulfillment of the *praeparatio evangelica* of the African traditional religions, as noted earlier in this study. The Akan people's practice of *afɔdeɛ* (guilt sacrifice), which is the expiation of evil, and a peaceful reconciliation with the deities, finds its consummation on the Cross. The idea of guilt offerings or sacrifices in certain parts of Africa is to restore peace with God and one another. Magesa says: "The fundamental meaning of sacrifices and offerings lies in their efficacy to restore wholeness. If wrong-doing causes a dangerous separation of the various elements of the universe, sacrifices and offerings aim to reestablish unity and restore balance" (Magesa 1997: 203). The death and resurrection of Jesus Christ fulfill this practice, and it inaugurates a new history and dispensation for a new life, and eschatological hope for all humankind.

To this end, Akan theological anthropology must see history as God's history. The history of man must begin with God and ends with Him. History must be seen as cyclical instead of linear, i.e., a return to God. This historicity is theological, other than scientific because it is God's history. The history begins with God, the supreme ancestor of all human beings, and the one who engendered all humanity into one family. His intervention into the history of humanity through various means and finally through Jesus Christ is to save human beings unto Himself. It is by Jesus Christ that history finds its purpose and hope. This concept is the sum of the Akan maxim "All human beings are the children of God, none is the child of the earth." Through this statement, one can assess the ontological realities that underline Akan anthropology. First, the human being has a numinous substance (ontology) and not only natural. Second, the human being does not live in isolation but has a relational ontology. And third, the human being has a functional ontology to live according to the ways of God. I, therefore, deem it appropriate and fundamental that the Akan theological anthropology should be communicated on the premise of these three ontological dimensions.

Overall, African theological anthropology does not seek to import God into the experiences of Africans, as some might assume. Rather, the revelation of God has long been an integral aspect of the lives and experiences of many indigenous African communities. God is self-evident, Creator, and

Sustainer of life. Many Akan festivities, art, and music possess a theophoric nature. The human experience is intrinsically both divine and anthropological. This understanding is exemplified by the Akan people of West Africa, who, for centuries, have recognized the presence of God in the history of humanity and the world at large.

GLOSSARY OF AKAN TWI TERMS

Abosom (pl)	Pantheon gods
Abrewa	Old lady (Nana)
Abusua	Clan
Adinkra	Symbols
Adwene	Mind
Akɔmfa	Mediumship
Asamando	Hades
Ɛboɔ	Stone
Fante	Fante tribe
Honhom	Breath/wind/spirit
Honhom Kronkron	Holy Spirit
Hyɛbea/hyɛbrɛ	Appointed time
Mogya	Blood
Nana	Eminent one
Nananom (pl)	Elders/Ancestors
Nkrabea	Destiny
Nsamanfo (pl)	Ghosts/Ancestors
Nsɛm	Words
Ntorɔ	Semen/ Paternal spirit
Odomankoma	God (Creator)
Onipa ('Nipa)	Human being
Onyame ('Nyame)	God (generic)
Onyame sunsum	God's power/Spirit
Onyankopɔn	God
Ɔbosom	Pantheon deity
Okomfoɔ (Akomfoɔ)	Traditional priest
Ɔkra	Life principle/ Soul
Ɔkrateasefo	Living soul
Saman	Ghost
Samanadzie	Ancestral world
Sankofa	Go back to take
Sãsã	Revengeful spirit
Suban	Character
Suman	Charm

Sunsum	Personality, Spirit
Sunsum bɔne	Evil spirit
Sunsum Kronkron	Holy Spirit
Sunsum mu	Spiritual/Mystical
Sunsuma	Shadow
Tumi	Power/Authority
Twi	An Akan language
Wiase	World (under the sun)

BIBLIOGRAPHY

Abraham, William E. "Theory of Human Society," In: *African Intellectual Heritage: A Book of Sources*. Philadelphia: Temple University Press, 1996.

Achebe, Chinua. "Chi in Igbo Cosmology." In: *Morning Yet on Creation Day*. London and Ibadan, Nigeria: Heinemann Educational Books Ltd., 1975.

Anderson, Allan. "African Initiated Churches of the Spirit and Pneumatology." *Word and World*, 23: 2 (2003): 178-186.

———. *Zion and Pentecost: The Spirituality and Experience of Pentecostal and Zionist-Apostolic Churches in South Africa*. Pretoria: University of South Africa Press, 2000, 241-242.

———. "Stretching the Definitions? Pneumatology and 'Syncretism' in African Pentecostalism." *Journal of Pentecostal Theology* 10/1 (October 2001), 98-119.

———. *Moya: The Holy Spirit in an African Context*. Pretoria: University of South Africa Press, 1991.

Antonio, E P. E. P. *Inculturation and Postcolonial Discourse in African Theology*. New York: Peter Lang, 2006.

Appiah-Kubi, K. "Jesus Christ: Some Christological aspects from African perspectives." In: Mbiti, J. S. (ed) 1977. *African and Asian Contributions to Contemporary Theology*, 51- 65. Bossey: World Council of Churches, 1977.

Appiah, Kwame A., and Allen R. Grossman. *In My Father's House: Africa in the Philosophy of Culture*. New York: Oxford University Press, 1992.

Appiah, Kwame A., and Co. *Libération ou adaptation? La théologie Africaine s'interroge*. Paris: Ed. L'Harmattan, 1979.

Asante, Molefi K. *An Afrocentric Manifesto: Toward an African Renaissance*. Cambridge Eng: Polity Press, 2007.

Aye-Addo, S. Charles. *Akan Christology: An Analysis of the Christologies of John Samuel Pobee and Kwame Bediako in Conversation with the Theology of Karl Barth*. Eugene, Or: Pickwick Publications, 2013.

Baffoe Antwi, E. *Creation in the Image of God: Human Uniqueness from the Akan Religious Anthropology to the Renewal of Christian Anthropology (Doctoral dissertation)*. Duquesne University, 2016. Retrieved from https://dsc.duq.edu/etd/1509.

Barth, Karl, and Godsey, John D. *Karl Barth's Table Talk*. Richmond, Virginia: John Knox Press, 1963.

Bediako, Kwame. "The Roots of African Theology." *International Bulletin of Missionary Research.* 13 issue 2: Apr 1, 1989; pp. 58–65. https://doi.org/10.1177/239693938901300203

———. *Christianity in Africa: The Renewal of non-Western Religion*. Edinburgh and Maryknoll, NY: Edinburgh University Press, 1995.

———. *Theology and Identity: The Impact of Culture Upon Christian Thought in the Second Century and in Modern Africa*. Oxford: Regnum Books, 1992.

Bevans, Stephen B. *Models of Contextual Theology*. Maryknoll, N.Y: Orbis Books, 1992.

Bill, George. *Until All Have Heard: The Centennial History of Church of God World Missions*. Cleveland, Tenn: Church of God World Missions, 2010.

Boesak, Allan. "La théologie de la libération en Afrique du Sud." In: Appiah, Kwame A, And Co. *Libération ou adaptation?: La Théologie Africaine S'interroge*. Paris: Ed. L'Harmattan, 1979.

———. *Pharaohs on Both Sides of the Blood-Red Waters: Prophetic Critique of Empire; Resistance, Justice, and the Power of the Hopeful Sizwe -- a Transatlantic Conversation*. Eugene, Oregon: Cascade Books, 2017.

Bourke, Joseph. "The Spirit of God in the Old Testament." *Life of the Spirit (1946-1964)*, vol. 13, no. 156, 1959, pp. 538–550. JSTOR, www.jstor.org/stable/43705403.

Brackney, William H. *The Spirit Among the Dissenters: Other Voices in Understanding the Spirit of God*. Eugene, Oregon: Cascade Books 2019.

Bujo, Bénézet. *African Theology in its Social Context*. Transl. from the German by John O'Donohue. Maryknoll, N.Y.: Orbis Books, 1992.

Busia, Abrefa K. "The Ashanti of the Gold Coast," In: *African Worlds: Studies in the Cosmological Ideas and Social Values of African Peoples*. London: Oxford University Press, 1954.

Byrne, Andrew. "Some Ins and Outs of Inculturation." *Annales Theologici 4* (1990), 109-149.

Chike, Chigor. "African Pneumatology in the British Context: A Contemporary Study." Ph.D. Thesis: The University of Birmingham, 2011.

Chitando, Ezra. "The (mis) Appropriation of African Traditional Religions in African Christian Theology," In: Antonio, Edward P. *Inculturation and Postcolonial Discourse in African Theology*. New York, NY [u.a.: Lang, 2006.

———. *Troubled But Not Destroyed*. Geneva: WCC Publ, 2009.

Christaller, Johann G. "A collection of 3,600 Tshi Proverbs in Use Among the Africans of the Gold Coast as Speaking the Asante and Fante Language, Collected, together with their Variations, and Alphabetically Arranged," Basel, 1879.

———. "A Dictionary of the Asante and Fante Language Called Tschi (Chwee, Twi) With a Grammatical Introduction and appendices on the Geography of the Gold Coast and Other Subjects," Basel, 2nd rev. ed., edited by J. Schweizer in 1893, published as "A Dictionary of the Asante and Fante Languages Called Tshi (Twi)," Basel, 1881.

———. *Dictionary of the Asante and Fante Language Called Tshi (Twi)*. Basel: Basel Evangelical Missionary Society, 1933.

Christaller, Johann G. Asante, David, Opoku, Theophilus. "*Anyamesem anase Kyerew Kronkron Apam-dedaw ne Apam-foforo nsem wo Twi kasa mu*" (The Holy Bible translated from the original tongues into the Twi language), Basel, 1871.

Christaller, J. G., Locher, C. W., Zimmermann, J. *A Dictionary, English, Tshi (Asante), Akra; Tshi (Chwee) Comprising as Dialects: Akan and Fante; Accra connected with Adangme; Gold Coast, West Africa*. Basel, 1874.

Christoph, Marx. "Ubu and Ubuntu: On the Dialectics of Apartheid and Nation Building." *Politikon*, 2002, 29:1, 49-69.

Clark-Soles, Jaime. "'I Will Raise [Whom?] Up on the Last Day': Anthropology as a Feature of Johannine Eschatology," in: Lozada, Francisco, and Tom Thatcher (Eds). *New Currents Through John: A Global Perspective*. Atlanta, GA: Society of Biblical Literature, 2006.

Clark, Jawanza E. *Indigenous Black Theology: Towards an African-Centered Theology of the African American Religious Experience*. New York: Palgrave Macmillan, 2012.

Connolly, Sean. *Apartheid in South Africa*. Austin: Steck-Vaughn Company, 2003.

Danquah, J B. *The Akan Doctrine of God: A Fragment of Gold Coast Ethics and Religion*. London: Cass, 1968.

Denteh, A. C. "Ntorɔ̄ and Nton." I.A.S. *Research Review*, vol. 3, No. 3, 1967, 91–96.

Dettwiler, Andreas. "The Holy Spirit in the Gospel of John from a Western Perspective," in: Dragutinović, Predrag, Niebuhr, Karl-Wilhelm, Wallace, James Buchanan, Karakolis, Christos (eds), *The Holy Spirit and the Church according to the New Testament, Sixth International East-West Symposium of New Testament Scholars, Belgrade, August 25 to 31, 2013, Wissenschaftliche Untersuchungen zum Neuen Testament. 1. Reihe (WUNT.1 354)*. Tübingen: Mohr Siebeck, 2016, pp. 149-171.

Dickson, Kwesi A., and S. G. Williamson. *Akan Religion and the Christian Faith; A Comparative Study of the Impact of Two Religions.* Accra: Ghana UP, 1965.

Dickson, Kwesi A., & Paul Ellingworth. *Biblical Revelation and African Beliefs*. New York: Orbis Books, 1969.

Dragutinović, Predrag. "The Holy Spirit and the Church in the Gospel of John. A Discourse Analysis of John 20:19-23," in: Dragutinović, Predrag, Niebuhr, Karl-Wilhelm, Wallace, James Buchanan, Karakolis, Christos (eds.). *The Holy Spirit and the Church according to the New Testament. Sixth International East-West Symposium of New Testament Scholars, Belgrade, August 25 to 31, 2013 (WUNT.1 354)*. Tübingen: Mohr Siebeck, 2016.

Ehrensperger, Kathy. *Paul at the Crossroads of Cultures: Theologizing in the Space-between*. London: Bloomsbury, 2013.

Engagement: *The Second AACC Assembly, 'Abidjan 1969.'* Nairobi: AACC, 1969.

Englund, Harri. *A Democracy of Chameleons: Politics and Culture in the New Malawi*. Uppsala, Sweden: Nordiska Afrikainstitutet, 2002.

Ephirim-Donkor, Anthony. *African Personality and Spirituality: The Role of Abosom and Human Essence*. Lanham, MD: The Rowman & Littlefield Publishing, 2016.

———. *African Religion Defined: A Systematic Study of Ancestor Worship Among the Akan*. Lanham, MD: University Press of America, 2010.

Ferdinando, Keith. "Christian Identity in The African Context: Reflections on Kwame Bediako's Theology and Identity." *Journal of the Evangelical Theological Society*, vol., 50:1, March 2007.

Ferguson, Sinclair B. *The Holy Spirit: Contours of Christian Theology*. Illinois: Inter-varsity Press, 1996.

Flint, John E. *Cecil Rhodes*. Boston: Little Brown, 1974.

Fotopoulos, John. "The Holy Spirit in Paul from an Orthodox Perspective," in Predrag Dragutinović, Karl-Wilhelm Niebuhr, James Buchanan Wallace, Christos Karakolis, eds., *The Holy Spirit and the Church according to the New Testament, Sixth International East-West Symposium of New Testament Scholars, Belgrade, August 25 to 31, 2013 (WUNT.1 354)*. (Tübingen,Germany: Mohr Siebeck, 2016).

George, Andrew (Trans.). *The Epic of Gilgamesh*. Penguin Classics, 2003.

Gibellini, Rosino. *Paths of African Theology*. Maryknoll, N.Y: Orbis Books, 1994.

———. *The Liberation Theology Debate* [transl. from the Italian by John Bowden]. London: SCM Press, 1987.

Gyekye, Kwame, & Wiredu, Kwasi. *Person and Community: Ghanaian Philosophical Studies, vol. I*. Washington, D.C: Council for Research in Values and Philosophy, 2010.

Gyekye, Kwame. "African Ethics," *The Stanford Encyclopedia of Philosophy (Fall 2011 Edition)*, Edward N. Zalta (ed.), https://plato.stanford.edu/archives/fall2011/entries/african-ethics/. Last visited March 29, 2023.

———. *African Cultural Values: An Introduction*. Philadelphia, PA: Sankofa Pub. Co, 1996.

———. *An Essay on African Philosophical Thought: The Akan Conceptual Scheme*. Cambridge: Cambridge University Press, 1987.

Hagan, George, P. "Modern Technology, Traditional Mysticism and Ethics in Akan Culture," In Lauer, Helen (Ed). *Ghana: Changing Values, Changing Technologies: Ghanaian Philosophical Studies, II.*

Washington, DC: Council for Research in Values and Philosophy, 1999.

Hartel, Joseph F. *Femina Ut Imago Dei in the Integral Feminism of St. Thomas Aquinas*. Roma: Editrice Pontificia Università Gregoriana, 1993.

Hauser-Renner, Heinz. "Examining Text Sediments–Commending a Pioneer Historian as an 'African Herodotus': On the Making of the New Annotated Edition of C.C. Reindorf's History of the Gold Coast and Asante. *History in Africa*, vol. 35, 2008, pp. 231–299.

Hesselgrave, David J. & Rommen, Edward. *Contextualization: Meanings, Methods, and Models*. Grand Rapids, Mich: Baker Book House, 1989.

Hildebrandt, Wilfred. *Old Testament Theology of the Spirit of God*. Eugene, Ore: Wipf and Stock Pub, 2019.

Idowu, E. Bolaji. *African Traditional Religion: A Definition.* Maryknoll, N.Y: Orbis Books, 1973.

Ilesanmi, Simeon O. "Inculturation and Liberation: Christian Social Ethics and the African Theology Project." *The Annual of the Society of Christian Ethics*, vol. 15, 1995, pp. 49– 73.

Karakolis, Christos. "The Holy Spirit in Luke-Acts: Personal Entity or Impersonal Power? A Synchronic Approach," in: Dragutinović, Predrag, Niebuhr, Karl-Wilhelm, Wallace, James Buchanan, Karakolis, Christos, *The Holy Spirit and the Church according to the New Testament, Sixth International East-West Symposium of New Testament Scholars, Belgrade, August 25 to 31, 2013, Wissenschaftliche Untersuchungen zum Neuen Testament. 1. Reihe (WUNT.1 354)*. Tübingen: Mohr Siebeck, 2016, pp. 87-109.

Kärkkäinen, Veli-Matti, Kim Kirsteen, & Yong A. *Interdisciplinary and Religio-Cultural Discourses on a Spirit-Filled World: Loosing the Spirits*. NY: Palgrave Macmillan, 2013.

Kato, Byang H. *Theological Pitfalls in Africa*. Kisumu, Kenya: Evangel Pub. House, 1975.

Knispel, Martin & Kwakye, Nana Opare. *Pioneers of the Faith: Biographical Studies from Ghanaian Church History*. Accra: Akuapem Presbytery Press, 2006.

Krüger, D. W. (ed). *South African Parties and Policies 1910-1960*. London: Bowes & Bowes, 1960. http://www.politicsweb.co.za/news-and

-analysis/apartheid-the-nps-1947-manifesto. Last visited March 19, 2023.

Kubat, Rodoljub S. "The Spirit in the Wisdom of Solomon and its Old Testament Background," in: Dragutinović, Predrag, Niebuhr, Karl-Wilhelm, Wallace, James Buchanan, Karakolis, Christos, *The Holy Spirit and the Church according to the New Testament, Sixth International East-West Symposium of New Testament Scholars, Belgrade, August 25 to 31, 2013, Wissenschaftliche Untersuchungen zum Neuen Testament. 1. Reihe (WUNT.1 354)*. Tübingen: Mohr Siebeck, 2016, pp. 287-308.

Lapping, Brian. *Apartheid: A History.* New York: George Braziller Inc., 1987.

Newbigin, Lesslie. *Foolishness to the Greeks: The Gospel and Western Culture*. Grand Rapids, Michigan: W.B. Eerdmans Pub. Co, 1986.

———. *The Gospel in a Pluralist Society*. Grand Rapids: Eerdmans, 1989.

Louw, Johannes P. & Nida, Eugene A. (eds). *Greek-English Lexicon of the New Testament based on semantic domains, 2 vols.* New York: United Bible Societies, 1989.

Magesa, Laurenti. *African Religion: The Moral Traditions of Abundant Life*. Orbis, Maryknoll 1997.

Maimela, Simon Sekomane. *What is the Human Being?* University of Pretoria, Pretoria, 1994.

Marguerat, Daniel. "The Work of the Holy Spirit in Luke-Acts: A Western Perspective," in: Dragutinović, Predrag, Niebuhr, Karl-Wilhelm, Wallace, James Buchanan, Karakolis, Christos, *The Holy Spirit and the Church according to the New Testament, Sixth International East-West Symposium of New Testament Scholars, Belgrade, August 25 to 31, 2013, Wissenschaftliche Untersuchungen zum Neuen Testament. 1. Reihe (WUNT.1 354)*. Tübingen: Mohr Siebeck, 2016, pp. 111-128.

Marshall, Molly. *Joining the Dance: A Theology of the Spirit*. Valley Forge PA: Judson Press, 2003.

Martey, Emmanuel. *African Theology: Inculturation and Liberation.* Maryknoll, NY: Orbis Books, 1993.

Mbiti, John. *African Religions and Philosophy*. London: Heinemann Educational Books, Ltd., 1969.

———. "The Biblical Basis for Present Trends in African Theology," In: *African Theology en Route: Papers from the Pan-African Conference of Third World Theologians*, December 17–23, 1977, Accra, Ghana, ed. Kofi Appiah-Kubi and Sergio Torres (Maryknoll, N.Y.: Orbis, 1979).

Meisel, Jacqueline Drobis. *South Africa At The Crossroads*. Brookfield, Connecticut: The Millbrook Press, 1994.

Meyer, Birgit. *Sensational Movies: Video, Vision, and Christianity in Ghana*. Berkeley: University of California Press, 2015.

Meyerowitz, Eva L. R., "Concepts of the Soul among the Akan of the Gold Coast." *Journal of the International African Institute*, Vol. 21, No. 1 (Jan., 1951), pp. 24 –31.

Middleton, J. R. *The Liberating Image: The Imago Dei in Genesis 1*. Grand Rapids, MI: Brazos Press, 2005.

Míguez, Bonino J. *Christians and Marxists: The Mutual Challenge to Revolution*. Grand Rapids, Mich: Eerdmans, 1976.

Minkus, Heleine K. "The Concept of Spirit in Akwapim Akan Philosophy." *Africa: Journal of the International African Institute*, Vol. 50, No. 2 (1980), pp. 182–192.

Miranda, José P. *Marx and the Bible: A Critique of the Philosophy of Oppression.* Eugene, Ore: Wipf & Stock, 2004.

Moltmann, Jürgen. *God in Creation: An Ecological Doctrine of Creation*. London: S. C. M. Press, 1985.

———. *The Spirit of Life: A Universal Affirmation*. Minneapolis: Fortress Press, 1992.

———. *The Trinity and the Kingdom: The Doctrine of God*. San Francisco: Harper & Row, 1981.

Mulago, Vincent. "Vital participation: The Cohesive Principle of the Bantu community." In: Dickson, K. A. & Ellington, P. (eds.). *Biblical Revelation and African Beliefs*. London: Lutterworth Press, 1969.

Müller, Louise. "The Reality of Spirits: A Historiography of the Akan Concept of Mind." *Quest: An African Journal of Philosophy*, XXII (1–2), 2008, pp. 163–185.

———. *Religion and Chieftaincy in Ghana: An Explanation of the Persistence of a Traditional Political Institution in West Africa.* Zürich: Lit Verlag, 2013.

Musopole, Augustine C. *Being Human in Africa: Toward an African Christian Anthropology*. New York: P. Lang, 1994.

Muzorewa, Gwinyai H. *The Origin and Development of African Theology*. Orbis Books: Maryknoll, NY., 1985.

Nadar, Sarojini. "Feminist Theologies in Africa." In: Kifon, Bongmba Elias (Ed). *The Wiley-Blackwell Companion to African Religions*. MA: USA. Blackwell Publishing, 2012, pp. 269-278.

Nalwamba, K.M.B. & Buitendag, J. "Vital Force As a Triangulated Concept of Nature and s(S)pirit." HTS Teologiese Studies/ Theological Studies 73(3), 4506: 2017, pp. 1-10.

Neville, A. Helen, Brendesha M. Tynes, and Shawn O. Utsey (Eds). *Handbook of African American Psychology*. Thousand Oaks, Calif: SAGE, 2009.

Ngong, David. *The Holy Spirit and Salvation in African Christian Theol ogy: Imagining a more hopeful future for Africa*. Oxford: Peter Lang, 2010.

Nkrumah, Kwame. *Neo-colonialism: The Last Stage of Imperialism*. London: Panaf, 1970.

Nyameti, Charles. "Contemporary African Christologies: Assessment and Practical Suggestions." In *Paths of African Theology*, edited by Rosino Gibellini, 62–77. Maryknoll, NY: Orbis Books, 1994.

———. *African Theology: Its Nature, Problems and Methods*. Kampala, Uganda: Gaba Publications, Pastoral Institute of Eastern Africa, 1976.

Oduyoye, Amba M. *Hearing and Knowing: Theological Reflections on Christianity in Africa*. Maryknoll, N.Y.: Orbis Books, 1986.

———. *Introducing African Women's Theology*. Sheffield: Sheffield Academic Press, 2001.

Okafor, Stephen O. "'Bantu Philosophy:' Placide Tempels Revisited." *Journal of Religion in Africa*, vol. 13, no. 2, 1982, pp. 83–100.

Okrah, K. Asafo-Agyei. *Nyansapo (the Wisdom Knot): Toward an African Philosophy of Education*. New York: Routledge, 2003.

Opoku, Kofi A. *Traditional Religion: Interviews with Priests, Priestesses, and Other Shrine Officials*. Accra, Ghana: Institute of African Studies, University of Ghana, 1968.

Owino Kombo, James Henry. *The Doctrine of God in African Christian Thought: The Holy Trinity Theological Hermeneutics and the African Intellectual Culture*. Leiden: Brill, 2007.

Owusu Agyarko, Robert. "'Sunsum' the Spirit of Life: Pneumatology in the [Akan] West African Context." Paper presented at the International Conference on Pneumatology and Contextual Theology, Geneva, March 2014.

———. "God of Life: Rethinking the Akan Christian Concept of God in the Light of the Ecological Crisis." *The Ecumenical Review,* Vol. 65, March 2013, pp. 51–66.

———. "The Sunsum of Onyame: Akan Perspectives on an Ecological Pneumatology." Journal of Reformed Theology, Vol. 6: 3, (2012), pp. 251-261.

———. *God's Unique Priest (Nyamesofopreko): Christology in the Akan Context (Doctoral dissertation)*. University of the Western Cape, South Africa, 2009.

Owusu-Gyamfi, Clifford. *What Is This Thing Called "Sunsum"?* Zurich: LIT Verlag, 2023.

P'Bitek, Okot. *African Religions in Western Scholarship*. Kampala: East African Literature Bureau, 1970.

Palombo, Matthew. "The Emergence of Islamic Liberation Theology in South Africa." *Journal of Religion in Africa*, 44, 2014, 28-61.

Phiri, Isabel. "Southern Africa," in: Parrat J. (Ed.), An introduction to Third World Theologies. Cambridge: Cambridge University Press 2004.

Platvoet, Johannes G. *Comparing Religions: A Limitative Approach: An Analysis of Akan, Para-Creole and Ifo-Sananda Rites and Prayers*. The Hague: Mouton, 1982.

Pobee John S. *Toward an African Theology*. Nashville: Abingdon, 1979.

Rattray, R S. *Ashanti Law and Constitution*. Oxford: Clarendon, 1929.

———. *Ashanti proverbs: (the primitive ethics of a savage people)*. Oxford: The Clarendon Press, 1916.

———. *Ashanti*. Oxford: Clarendon Press, 1923.

———. *Religion and Art in Ashanti*. Oxford: Clarendon Press, 1927.

Sakupapa, Teddy. "Spirit and Ecology in the Context of African Theology." *Scriptura: Journal for Biblical, Theological and Contextual Hermeneutics*, 111 (2012): 422-430.

Sanneh, Lamin. *Translating the Message: The Missionary Impact on Culture*. Maryknoll, NY: Orbis Books, 1991.

Sekyere, P. A. "Traditional Akan Ethics and Humaist Ethics: A comparative Study." *Advances in Social Sciences Research Journal,* 2016, 3(6), 110-120.

Shillington, Kevin. *History of Africa*. New York: St. Martin's Press, 1989.

Tedlock, Dennis (Ed. and trans.). *Popol Vuh: The Definitive Edition of the Mayan Book of the Dawn of Life and the Glories of Gods and Kings* (revised edition). Touchstone Books, 1996.

Tempels, Placide. *Bantu Philosophy* (Editions Réclame). Paris: Présence Africaine, 1959.

Thayer, J. H. *A Greek-English Lexicon of the New Testament: Being Grimm's Wilke's Clavis Novi Testamenti*. New York: Harper & Brothers, 1889.

Tutu, Desmond. "La théologie de la libération en Afrique." In: Appiah, Kwame A, and Co. *Libération ou adaptation?: La théologie Africaine s'interroge*. Paris: Ed. L'Harmattan, 1979.

Uzukwu, E. Elochukwu. *God, Spirit, and Human Wholeness: Appropriating Faith and Culture in West African Style*. Eugene, OR: Pickwick Publications, 2012.

Vahakangas, Mika. *In Search of Foundations for African Catholicism: Charles Nyamiti's Theological Methodology.* Leiden: Brill, 1999.

Van Eck, Ernest. "The Word is Life: African Theology as Biblical and Contextual Theology." *HTS Teologiese Studies / Theological Studies*, vol. 62, No. 2, 2006.

Van Jaarsveld, F. A. *The Afrikaner's Interpretation of South African History*. Cape Town: Simondium Publishers, 1964.

Vanhove, Martine. *From Polysemy to Semantic Change: Towards a Typology of Lexical Semantic Associations*. Amsterdam: John Benjamins Publishing Co., 2008.

Wachege, N. Patrick. "Charles Nyamiti: Vibrant Pioneer of Inculturated African Theology,"in: B. Buyo and J.I. Muya (eds). *African Theology: The Contribution of the Pioneers (vol 2)*. Nairobi: Paulines Publishers, 2006.

Washington, Joseph R. Jr. *Black Religion: The Negro and Christianity in the United States*. Lanham, MD: University Press of America, 1984.

Wilks, Ivor. "The Forest and the Twis," *Journal des Africanistes*, 75-1, 2005, 19-75.

Wiredu, Kwasi. "The Moral Foundations of an African Culture," in *Person and Community: Ghanaian Philosophical Studies*, vol. 1. Washington, D.C: Council for Research in Values and Philosophy, 1992.

———. "Toward Decolonizing African Philosophy and Religion." *African Studies Quarterly*, vol.1, Issue 4, 1998, pp. 17–46.

Wolff, Hans W. *Anthropology of the Old Testament*. Mifflintown, PA: Sigler Press, 1974.

Wood, Leon J. *The Holy Spirit in the Old Testament*. Eugene, Ore: Wipf and Stock Pub, 1998.

Wyllie, Robert W. "Pioneers of Ghanaian Pentecostalism: Peter Anim and James McKeown." *Journal of Religion in Africa*, vol. 6, no. 2, 1974, pp. 109–122.

Zizioulas, John D. "The Pneumatological Dimension of the Church: The Synthesis of Christology and Pneumatology is Necessary for a Proper Understanding of the Church," in *The One and the Many: Studies on God, Man, the Church, and the World Today* (ed. G. Edwards; Alhambra, 2010), 75-90.

Zumstein, Jean. *l'Evangile selon saint Jean (13-21)*, CNT IVb, Genève 2007.

Filmography

Owuo Sunsum (The Spirit of Death) I,II,III&IV. Dir. Theophilus Amoabeng. United Pictures, 2013. Film.

Sunsum mu awarea (Spiritual Marriage) I&II. Dir. Asare Bediako. Power Based Studio/Trinity Computers, 2012. Film.

Sunsum Mu Ndwuma (Spiritual works). Dir. Theophilus Amoabeng. United Pictures, 2011. Film.

Sunsum Mu Nsɛm (Spiritual matters). Dir. Frank Gyimah. Globalense Ventures & Above All Films, 2012. Film.

Sunsum Mu Oyɛfoɔ (Spiritual enemy) I, II, III& IV. Dir. Isaiah Kofi Appiah. Country Man Movie Production, 2013. Film.

Websites

"Nana Kwaku Bonsam collects his juju from fake pastor." https://www.youtube.com/watch?v=iI_lFCutgLo. Last visited on March 22, 2020.

2010 Population & Housing Census, Summary Report of Final Results. Ghana Statistical Service, May 2012. http://www.web-deploy.statsghana.gov.gh/nada/index.php/catalog/51. Last visited March 22, 2020.

Encyclopedia Britannica. Encyclopedia Britannica, Inc. Dec. 12, 2016. https://www.britannica.com/topic/apartheid. Last visited Mar. 22, 2020.

Mbiti, John, "The Role of Women in African Traditional Religion." http://www.africanamerica.org/topic/the-role-of-women-in-african-traditional-religion-by-john-mbiti. Last visited Mar. 22, 2020.

Pew Research Center. "The Future of World Religions: Population Growth Projections, 2010-2050. "http://www.pewforum.org/2015/04/02/sub-saharan-africa/163-3/. Last visited March 22, 2020.

South African History Online, http://www.sahistory.org.za/topic/segrega tionist-legislation-timeline-1920-1929. Last visited Sept. 5, 2017.

Music

Honhom Kronkron (Holy Spirit) by Advent Voices, of SDA Church. https://www.youtube.com/watch?v=qi8jKd5MxIk. Last visited May 7, 2020.

Honhom Kronkron (Holy Spirit) by Evangelist Diana Asamoah. https://www.youtube.com/watch?v=lP2Vmm2rCeQ. Last visited May 7, 2020.

Honhom Kronkron (Holy Spirit) by Osuani Okatakyie Afrifa. https://www.youtube.com/watch?v=2S4zd1PeYWU. Last visited May 7, 2020.

Honhom Kronkron A Wote Me Mu (Thou Holy Spirit who dwells in me) by Yaw Sarpong & the Asomafo. https://youtu.be/2gL3400S8o4. Last visited May 7, 2020.

Honhom Kronkron (Holy Spirit) by Eld. Emmanuel Kwasi Mireku, Church of Pentecoste, Koforidua.

https://www.youtube.com/watch?v=hQn3hD8Mw7A. Last visited May 7, 2020.

Nyame Sunsum Siane Bra (Descend Spirit of God), A popular Akan recreational song.

Sunsum Kronkron Bra (Come Holy Spirit) by Eld. Emmanuel Kwasi Mireku, Church of Pentecoste, Koforidua.

Afrikanische Theologie / African Theology / Théologie Africaine

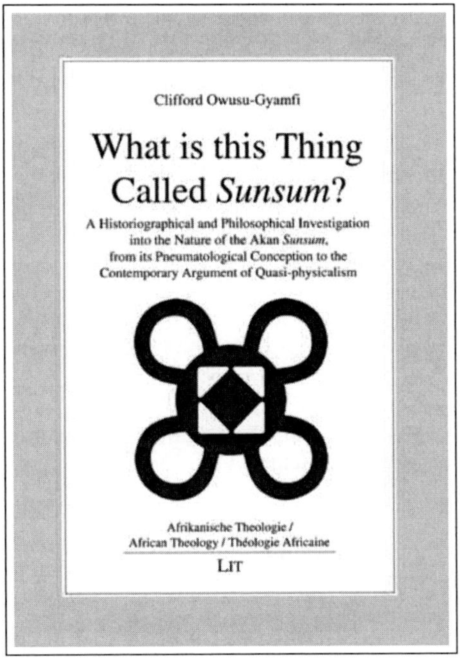

Clifford Owusu-Gyamfi
What is this Thing Called *Sunsum*?
A Historiographical and Philosophical Investigation into the Nature of the Akan "Sunsum", from its Pneumatological Conception to the Contemporary Argument of Quasi-physicalism
In recent decades, African scholarship has stressed the importance of regional oral traditions in academic learning. With this broad knowledge base in African studies, significant categories of socio-religious learning have been closely studied. This volume focuses on the notion of "spirit" as understood by the Akan people of West Africa.
vol. 10, 2023, 202 pp., 29,90 €, pb., ISBN-CH 978-3-643-80334-4

LIT Verlag Berlin – Münster – Wien – Zürich – London
Auslieferung Deutschland / Österreich / Schweiz: siehe Impressumsseite

Emmanuel Njoku
Youth Development in Nigeria
A Means to Poverty Alleviation and the Promotion of Peace, Justice, and Security. A Study in the Light of the Principles of the Catholic Social Teaching
Youth development is as a core aspect of human and national progress in Nigeria. The study suggests the development of young people as the means of poverty reduction. It indicates that amidst cultural, ethnic, and religious diversities, and in the light of threats to human life and property, the development of the youth is the way to promoting peace and unity, justice, and security.
The book argues on a two-fold contribution: While the Nigerian Church is to intensify efforts in the active participation of lay Christians in politics, the State is to tackle critical areas to ensure a decent standard of living for all.
vol. 9, 2020, 606 pp., 69,90 €, pb., ISBN-CH 978-3-643-91341-8

Henry Chukwudi Okeke
Igbo-Religion und Christentum – ein unversöhnlicher Gegensatz?
Die Spiritualtität des Igbo-Volkes als Beispiel von Religion in einer globalen Welt. Mit einem Geleitwort von Prof. Dr. Detlev Dormeyer
Bd. 8, 2019, 184 S., 24,90 €, br., ISBN 978-3-643-14528-4

Anthony Kofi Sackey
The Beginnings of Mission on the Gold Coast (present-day Ghana)
With special Emphasis on Basel and Catholic Missions
vol. 7, 2018, 352 pp., 34,90 €, pb., ISBN-CH 978-3-643-91048-6

Angelo Chidi Unegbu
The Institution of the Seminary and the Training of Catholic Priests in South-Eastern Nigeria (1885 – 1970)
A historical evaluation
vol. 6, 2018, 400 pp., 59,90 €, hc., ISBN-CH 978-3-643-91043-1

Claude Adouma Bonsou
Fruchtbarkeit in der Ehe
Überlegungen zur Bevölkerungsentwicklung und Empfängnisregelung in Schwarzafrika aus theologisch-ethischer Sicht
Bd. 4, 2016, 282 S., 34,90 €, br., ISBN 978-3-643-13331-1

John Chidubem Nwaogaidu
Jesus Christ – Truly God and Truly Man
Towards a Systematic Dialogue between Christology in Africa and Pope Benedict XVI's Christological Conception
vol. 3, 2016, 268 pp., 34,90 €, pb., ISBN-CH 978-3-643-90732-5

Benjamin Nzenekwesi Eze
Challenges of Health Care Workers Vis-a-vis Evangelical Mission of Jesus Christ in Igboland, Nigeria
vol. 2, 2014, 440 pp., 44,90 €, pb., ISBN-CH 978-3-643-90399-0

LIT Verlag Berlin – Münster – Wien – Zürich – London
Auslieferung Deutschland / Österreich / Schweiz: siehe Impressumsseite